DELIVER US
FROM EVIL

DELIVER US FROM EVIL

A NEW YORK CITY COP
INVESTIGATES
THE SUPERNATURAL

RALPH SARCHIE & LISA COLLIER COOL

🦁 ST. MARTIN'S GRIFFIN 🦋 NEW YORK

www.stmartins.com

Design by Molly Murphy

Prayers of Exorcism are excerpted with permission from the third edition of the *Catholic Laypersons' Exorcism Prayer Manuel* by Joseph Forrester, copyright © 1999.

The Library of Congress Cataloging-in-Publication Data is available upon request.

ISBN 978-1-250-05949-9 (trade paperback)
ISBN 978-1-250-05857-7 (mass market paperback)
ISBN 978-1-4668-6694-2 (e-book)

St. Martin's Griffin books may be purchased for educational, business, or promotional use. For information on bulk purchases, please contact Macmillan Corporate and Premium Sales Department at 1-800-221-7945, extension 5442, or write specialmarkets@macmillan.com.

Originally published in the United States in 2001 under the title *Beware the Night* by St. Martin's Paperbacks

First St. Martin's Griffin Edition: June 2014

D   14   13   12   11   10   9

To my beautiful girls, Christina Marie and Daniella Ann, your love and support in my life has enabled me to carry on. To my grandson, Jacob Michael, God keeps blessing me and I love you, little man.

My whole world revolves around all of you, and I feel that God has blessed me. I will love you all forever.

Ralph Sarchie

To John, Alison, Georgia, and Rosalie, you lift my spirit with your love and laughter.

Lisa Collier Cool

A special dedication to the late Father Malachi Martin, one of God's great warriors.

CONTENTS

	Foreword	ix
	Preface	xi
1.	The Halloween Horror	1
2.	Nightmare's End	21
3.	Cops and Soul Robbers	43
4.	The House by the Graveyard	65
5.	The Incubus Attack	92
6.	The Satanic Stalker	111
7.	Caught by the Occult	131
8.	The Werewolf	160
9.	Dabblers in the Damned	181
10.	Busting the Devil	202
11.	The September Curse	222
12.	Real-Life Ghost Stories	238
13.	A Deadly Sin	257
14.	Possessed Over the Phone	287
	Afterword	313
	Appendix I: Prayers of Exorcism	321
	Appendix II: The Rosary	345
	Appendix III: Act of Consecration to the Virgin Mary	353

FOREWORD

No one can claim to be a Christian, much less Catholic, who doubts or denies the Devil. Christ came to redeem mankind from the dominions of Satan and his apostate legions of fallen angels. "Now is the judgment of the world; now shall the prince of this world be cast out. And I, if I be lifted up from the earth [on the cross] will draw all things to myself" (John 12:31–32). The instances recounted in the Gospel of Jesus casting out devils from possessed persons demonstrate the reality of these unseen spirits. In the words of the Church's traditional prayer to St. Michael the Archangel, they "wander the world seeking the ruin of souls."

Today more than ever! Along with the ever-expanding abyss of immorality engulfing the world is a deluge of preternatural demonic infestation. The Devil's hand in immorality is on the ordinary level—Satan is the standard-bearer of sinners—but the demonic infestation involves his invasion of mind and body. When I was ordained some forty years ago, diabolical obsession and possession of people was almost unheard of—something the average priest, even though ordained an exorcist, would hardly encounter in his lifetime; something confined to the theology textbooks. But today, for those who have eyes to see, it is almost commonplace.

Exorcism exposes the Devil behind the veil of all too many, if not most, "psychiatric" cases. He talks to you, he defies you, he threatens you. He torments his victim in front of you and can test every fiber of those restraining him. Not in every case—in some he plays deaf and dumb—but in enough to show the pattern.

Whence this deluge? It stems from the spread—nay the plague—of the occult. In nine out of ten cases, the victim of demonic oppression has had connection, directly or indirectly, with witchcraft, open or disguised. This connection ranges from the possession of superstitious artifacts, such as Ouija boards, to "harmless" charms and outright satanic rituals. In between the two extremes are Charismatic and New Age movements. Satanism itself has been accepted as a religion, and there is even a "Bible" of Satan. Those who seek knowledge and power outside the order instituted by God seek it from His enemy and stand, for their correction, to be handed over to His power and suffer the consequences.

Ralph Sarchie, author of this book, is well qualified to write on the demonic. For years he has been investigating cases of it, and he, with others, has stood by me in exorcisms. Without assistants to restrain those who may become violent, it is perilous, as I have indicated, to exorcise anyone who is possessed. No subject, I daresay, could be of more practical, if not urgent, interest. May this book serve the humanitarian purpose for which it has been undertaken.

Bishop Robert F. McKenna, O.P.
Our Lady of the Rosary Chapel
Monroe, Connecticut

PREFACE

I never set out to write a book about the supernatural. I am a
New York City police sergeant, and cops write about police
work, not demons, ghosts, and exorcism. But I live in two
worlds: one of cop life, down and dirty in the streets with
very real blood and guts, and one plagued by a different sort
of crime, perpetuated by forces that are evil beyond imagination. These worlds seem very far apart for most. People ask
me, "How can you see all that gritty reality as a cop for sixteen years and then believe in the spirit world?" But I have
found that most cops do believe in spirits, and, most important of all, the vast majority believe in God and are religious
people. That makes me happy because what cops see every
day can have a corrosive effect on spirituality. I have experienced that effect firsthand.

It is because of my profession that I can distinguish between the two worlds and know that the preternatural and
supernatural exist. To live in the world of crime and justice
helps me to deal with the reality of pure evil when it strikes
real people with real terror. As Joe Forrester, my partner in
spiritual investigations, so eloquently says, two different types
of evil exist: primary evil, which comes from the Devil, and

secondary evil, which is the evil that people do. Although all evil stems from the Devil, I am not always quick to blame the Devil for the nasty deeds that one human being can inflict on another. I know the difference between human and inhuman evil when I see it.

I had no idea what I was letting myself in for when, a decade ago, I started in "the Work," investigating haunted houses and cases of demonic possession. Like police work, it takes its toll on you, but I have no regrets. Due to the Work my faith has grown, and my love for Jesus Christ is just as real as the love I have for my wife and children. When you read this book, keep one thing in mind: The book is not about some cop or the Devil, it is about God. When you read about a situation that seems hopeless for the people involved, always remember that with God all things are possible. Although some of the people I write about continue to experience their troubles, one thing has changed for them: God has now entered their lives, and He makes it bearable for them to live with their spiritual problems.

Before I go on to acknowledge the many people whom I have become friends with due to the Work, friends I hold dear in my own way, I want to say that I have always handled my investigations in an honest, straightforward, and professional manner. Everything in this book taken from my cases is exactly as it was told to me by eyewitnesses or from what I observed personally. These events are documented in my notes, and in the video- and audio-tapes I've made of my investigations. My experiences are not embellished in any way; I have changed some names and certain identifying details to protect the privacy of families or individuals who sought my help.

To my daughters, Christina and Daniella, I have no words

to express my love for you both, and I thank God every day for the special blessings that you are. You are my pride and my joy, and I will love you both for eternity.

My mother, Lillian, has always been a source of joy and inspiration for me—keep smiling, Mom. My father, Ralph Sr., has taught me more than he will ever realize: Dad, your guidance has enabled me to reach this point in my life. To my sister Lisa, although you are scared witless about the Work, you have unfailingly given me your support, and your kindness is heartfelt. To my godson, Joseph, my nieces Stephanie and Jessica, and my nephew, Vincent, may the good Lord watch over you and smile on you all your days. To all my brothers and sisters in the New York City Police Department, you do a fantastic job serving the people of this city.

To Bishop McKenna, without your love for God and humanity, many would suffer. You have given me and countless others the opportunity to carry on. To Sister Mary Philomena, I owe you special gratitude for so graciously leading me to the Blessed Virgin Mary and teaching me that the rosary is a devotion that I should not be without. To all the Sisters at Our Lady of the Rosary Chapel, thank you for all your kindness and prayers. Monsignor Richard M., you gave generously of yourself, and your friendship is greatly valued. Father Mike S., Father Mike T., Father Frank P., and Father John F., I rejoice in your friendship and your prayers. Brother Andrew, I have no words to honor you enough for all that you have done for me, both in the Work and in my personal life. Without you I don't know how things would have turned out for me, but you know better than anybody.

Without these people, the Work would have been next to impossible. I thank each and every one of them for giving of themselves and being dedicated to the service that they provided to the children of God. Phil W., Rose W., Chris W., Tony B., Antonio and Vicki B., Kathy D., Fred K., Dennis M., Millie M., Marie P. (may you rest in peace), Scott S., John Z., Joe Z., Dean L., Steve I., David A., and Matt M.–although I have lost contact with some of you, you will forever be in my memory and prayers.

Lisa Collier Cool, thanks for putting up with me on this journey. I could not have a better writer working on this book with me. Jimmy Vines, this was all your idea, and I thank you for having faith in me. Doug Montero, your interest got the ball rolling and for that I am grateful. Joe Veltre and Joe Cleemann, your editorial wisdom has been a tremendous help in guiding this book to publication.

And last, but not least, to my special friend and partner Joe Forrester: From the very beginning, you have taught me the most in the Work, and your everlasting friendship is cherished. You are a man I have entrusted with my life on so many occasions without hesitation. Thank you for all your guidance and your help in writing this book. With the grace of God our friendship will last throughout the ages, in this life and the next.

I would like to leave you, the reader, with one thing. You can tell me that you don't believe a damn word that I say about my cases and the demonic. If you're skeptical, that's okay—but if just one person tells me that he believes in God after reading these stories, I will walk away from this project smiling. I know if you are that person, you've won half the battle.

God bless you all,
Ralph Sarchie
Bethpage, New York

1

THE HALLOWEEN HORROR

I hate Halloween. It wasn't always this way: When I was a child, I liked to dress up and collect candy from the neighbors; and when I was a little older, I was one of those guys who would go out with eggs and shaving cream, ready for a night of nasty fun. After I became a cop, patrolling dangerous public housing projects, I saw another side of this holiday: Every pervert and nutjob in New York thinks it's suddenly open season on kids. At the Forty-sixth Precinct in the South Bronx, where I work as a sergeant, the 911 calls start pouring in. We race from one crime scene to the next, our sirens screaming, locking up the animals who prey on children as fast as we can. But awful as the crimes of man can be—and in my sixteen years on the police force, I've seen more blood and gore than you could ever imagine—they're not the only evil that intensifies on October 31.

Halloween has a malevolent history: According to two-thousand-year-old legends, it's the night when spirits of the dead roam the world, intent on playing terrifying tricks. To appease ghosts, our ancestors used to leave food offerings outside their homes and sacrifice animals. Early Europeans feared that these marauding spirits had a much darker motive: They

were hunting for live bodies to inhabit. To prevent possession, it became the custom to wear a mask or disguise on the
Day of the Dead, as this holiday is known in some countries.
The ancient dread of this date is rooted in more than just folklore or superstition, I discovered after I entered what I now
call "the Work"–investigating haunted houses and demonic
possession. Almost invariably, I get a sudden surge of cases
around the end of October, either on Halloween itself or the
day before, which, appropriately enough, is called Devil's or
Mischief Night.

One of my most harrowing supernatural investigations
began on Halloween, 1991. My partner in the Work, Joe Forrester, was putting out candy for trick-or-treaters when he got
a call about a haunted house. The caller was Father Hayes, the
exorcist for a Catholic diocese in a nearby state. He wanted us
to investigate a report of demonic activity in Westchester
County, a wealthy county just north of New York City. While
this priest had discerned some signs of a diabolical presence
when he spoke to the family over the phone, he didn't give Joe
any specifics about the problems they were having. Since my
partner and I knew Father Hayes from other investigations,
we trusted that he wouldn't send us out on a case unless it
had merit.

Like me, Joe comes from a law enforcement background, but
he works on the other side of the fence, as a polygraph examiner for the Legal Aid Society. Although he looks like a middle-
aged monk, with his round, untroubled face and his fringe of
brown hair around a balding head, he's actually an extremely
adept demonologist. Not only is he a walking encyclopedia of
the occult—definitely the man to call for a quick rundown on
Nigerian crocodile cults or Brazilian black magic rituals—but

as a decorated Vietnam vet, Joe has more than enough guts to face down supernatural terror. Combine that with the built-in bullshit meter he's developed from years of administering lie detector tests to con men and crooks of every other description and to the wrongly accused, and you have an ace investigator.

When Joe and I handle cases as demonologists in our off-duty hours, we don't charge a cent for our services. Helping people who have spiritual problems isn't a career for us—it's a calling. As devout Catholics, we take Jesus Christ's biblical injunction to "cast out demons in My name" literally.

Before going out on a case, I put aside my gun and police badge and arm myself with holy water and a relic of the True Cross.

Don't get me wrong. I'm not a religious fanatic and I'm anything but holy, as any of the guys who work with me at the Four-Six Precinct can tell you. I am a cop, and I would rather kick down doors and arrest ten armed robbers with my bare hands than take on the demonic. Plain and simple, the Devil frightens me much more than anything I'd ever seen on street patrol—and in all my years on the force, I've seen just about every horror one person can inflict on another: I've responded to countless shootings and stabbings; I've put the cuffs on people who commit rape or murder as if these crimes meant nothing at all.

I've had to tell people that their loved ones have died in car crashes or have been the victim of every terrible crime you could imagine. I've seen the broken bodies of little kids hurt in senseless accidents because their parents were too busy getting high to watch them. I've arrested drug dealers who turn their fellow human beings into the living dead with their poison—and a mother who sold her ten-year-old daughter for sex, all for a vial of crack. Recently I was called to a house where I found a woman stoned out her mind on drugs. That wouldn't be particularly unusual in the places I patrol, except that she was stumbling around with a newborn baby dragging between her legs—still attached to its umbilical cord—and she didn't even know she'd given birth. It turned out that this was her tenth kid: Child Protective Services had already taken all the others because of her crack addiction.

This has been my reality night after night. Dealing with the tragedy and devastation that crime causes has helped prepare me for the Work, to a certain degree. It's certainly taught me to recognize evil when I see it. When cops I work with find out that I help with exorcisms and investigate demonic activity, a lot of them ask, "What gives an aggressive and sometimes nasty guy like you the right to do this pious stuff?" I tell them, "Don't you see the beauty of God using a sinner like me to fight evil?" The truth is that I like to help people. When I joined the police force I took an oath to get bad guys off the street, and I have made over three hundred arrests to that end. As a committed Christian, I have a different mission: to bust the Devil and his demons.

I've never investigated cases officially for the Roman Catholic Church, but I have worked on official church cases for individual priests. Much of my work is with Bishop Robert McKenna, a Traditionalist Catholic priest and exorcist who has never shied away from doing battle with Satan and his forces of darkness. (Traditionalist churches use the Pre–Vatican II Latin mass.) From assisting him with nearly two dozen exorcisms over the past ten years, I've developed the utmost respect for this saintly man of God. If he ever needed me to walk into the depths of Hell with him, I'd go without a second thought.

Most major religions have ceremonies to expel evil spirits. The Roman Ritual of Exorcism dates back almost four hundred years. Years ago Catholic priests were given the minor order of Exorcist, and with the permission of their diocesan bishops were ready to undertake the tasks associated with that order. The problem today is that many priests, clergy of other faiths, and even bishops of the Catholic Church don't believe in the Devil, even though Jesus Himself performed exorcisms. When a priest friend of mine spoke of Satan during one of his sermons, he actually said to the congregation, "The Devil does exist. Sorry, folks." My wife said I looked as if I were about to jump out of my pew. If it were me, I'd make no apologies for telling people the Devil is real because I've seen his satanic fiends at work.

Most of the people who call Joe and me for help don't believe in the Devil either—until they are tormented and terrorized by bizarre, otherwise inexplicable events. Since neither of us has ever sought publicity for our involvement in the Work, our cases come to us through word of mouth. We both believe that if God wants people to get help, He'll see to it that they get it, either from us or from someone else. Asking for the help of a demonologist isn't the first impulse of the families who contact us: It's usually a last resort, after they have exhausted every logical explanation for the horrifying phenomena they're experiencing and may even have begun questioning their sanity. By the time they dial my number or Joe's, they're at their wit's end and have nowhere else to go. Or they may have turned to one of the many priests we know and been referred to us that way, as happened in our Halloween case.

After the call from Father Hayes, Joe and I arranged to visit the Villanova family on November 2, All Souls' Day on the

Catholic calendar, where priests recite the Office of the Dead and the faithful pray that the suffering of souls in Purgatory will be eased. Because we had no idea of what we would be up against, we made some dangerous mistakes. First, since we'd only been asked to videotape an interview for the exorcist to evaluate—and were told that the parish priest would join us afterward—Joe and I went to the house alone, without our usual team of investigators. Not expecting to perform any religious rituals ourselves, we packed a minimal supply of holy water and other sacramentals. In retrospect, this was a lot like patrolling a high-crime area with a gun loaded with only one bullet. Fortunately, as it turned out, I also armed myself with my most potent relic, a splinter of the True Cross.

As we parked outside Dominick Villanova's modest two-family house in Yonkers, I noticed a Catholic chapel down the street. Ed Warren, a well-known demonologist I've worked with, always says that the Devil likes to operate in the shadow of a church, and I've found that he's right. It's amazing how many of my cases take place within sight of a house of worship. Don't get me wrong: Having a church close by doesn't automatically make you a target for the demonic. Lots of people live near religious centers and *never* have a problem. But if something else, like a curse or satanic rituals, happens to draw an evil power your way, having a holy place nearby can *heighten* the spirit's hatred and fury.

Although I have a firm rule against getting emotionally involved with the people I help, I nearly lost it as soon as Dominick answered the door with his five-year-old son at his side. The first thing I noticed was how frightened the little guy looked. He had that blank, bewildered stare kids get right after they scream themselves awake from a nightmare—except this child had no soothing reality to wake up to and no escape from fear could be found in his mother or father's arms. Looking at his skinny body and unexpectedly big feet, I thought, *This kid should be out kicking a soccer ball around, not feeling scared out his mind in his own home!*

His father also wore a shell-shocked expression. He was a tall, bald man of about forty-five and wore thick glasses. With his slumped shoulders and air of defeat, he reminded me of a dazed prizefighter stumbling around the ring, waiting for the next blow to land. Seeing how confused and upset he was, I immediately sympathized. As a man, I could only guess at how utterly impotent he must have felt having to stand by and watch his family being assaulted by some nameless horror.

He led us to a living room that looked like a refugee camp. Not only was it packed with sad, somber people who all appeared ill and exhausted, but along each wall were haphazard piles of clothing and rolled-up bedding. *Was the entire family sleeping in here?* I'd seen that in other cases, where people became so unnerved by supernatural events that they ceased to exist as individuals and refused to go anywhere in their house alone, even to the bathroom. A home is supposed to be a safe haven where you relax at the end of the day, a place of peace and comfort, but that clearly wasn't true in any room of this house. And as I was soon to discover, the basement held a special kind of fear.

"Sorry about the mess," Dominick said. Struggling for the right words to explain the inexplicable, he added, "There's been a lot of, uh, trouble here."

Knowing how important it is to establish rapport and get people to confide in us when we go into their homes as complete strangers, Joe took control of the interview in a friendly but businesslike manner instead of letting the father ramble on. From his long experience as a polygraph examiner, he's become very skillful at reading people, defusing volatile emotions, and getting to the truth. "Mr. Villanova, I'm Joe Forrester and this is my partner, Ralph Sarchie. As you know, we're here at Father Hayes's request to investigate the problems you're having. You have agreed to have us here, and know we don't charge anything for our services."

"Call me Dominick," the father replied, sounding steadier, then introduced us to his wife, Gabby, a striking woman in her early forties. She had thick black hair with streaks of pure white on each side of her face and such strongly defined features that she resembled a figurehead engraved on a coin. Although overweight, she had a flamboyant style: Her dress was a vivid red, printed with colorful birds, and several large, silver bracelets jangled on each of her wrists. In younger, happier days, she was probably the life of the party, but right now, despite the exuberance of her clothing, she seemed very nervous, lighting cigarette after cigarette with trembling hands. Before asking this couple, their four children, and three friends who were gathered here to relate their stories, we gave each of them a St. Benedict medal to wear around their neck. This saint performed many miracles and had great power against demons.

After I put a medal on DJ (Dominick Junior), the little boy, something very peculiar happened. Just seconds later, the medal tumbled to the ground, even though the string it was on hadn't broken. I carefully checked the string and replaced the medal—only to find it on the floor a second time, and then a third. *This was one bold demon to fling around a saint's medal that had been personally blessed by the Bishop right in front of our eyes!* Most evil spirits are cowardly and hide from holy water, religious medals, and relics. Only the most powerful satanic forces, the true devils, can manipulate sacred objects.

During the interview, we gradually discovered just how dangerous this devil really was. Initially, it attacked with stealth, appearing in Gabby and Dominick's bedroom one autumn evening in its own hellishly inspired Halloween disguise. "My room got very cold, but it wasn't a cold night," Gabby said, gesturing so emphatically that her bracelets clanked. "In the corner of the room I saw white smoke, and out of this smoke came a woman. I could see her from the waist up. I was staring and screamed for my friend, who came running in with my husband. 'Do you see her?' I asked, and they said no, they didn't. She said her name was Virginia Taylor. That's all I remember."

Dominick, however, remembered a little more. "For about three minutes, my wife was in a trance and Virginia spoke through her. 'No harm, no fear,' she said—in other words, we shouldn't be scared. 'I just want your help,' she said, but she didn't say *why* she wanted help. I shook my wife awake, and the last thing she said before she came to herself was 'help, parents.'"

Despite "Virginia's" reassuring remark, Joe and I already recognized her for what she was—a demon operating under an alias. But there was one mistake in this masquerade that revealed the supposed human spirit was literally blowing smoke: It took the form of a woman only from the waist up. That's typical of the demonic; they always give themselves away with some abnormality of appearance when they try to manifest themselves as human beings.

Also characteristic of an infernal force was the demon's divide-and-conquer strategy. By showing itself to only one person, it sowed the seeds of panic, confusion, and self-doubt.

Is this really happening—or am I just imagining it? victims in such cases will ask themselves. Often they are reluctant to tell their friends or family what's happening to them, fearing that people will think they've lost their mind. Instead, they withdraw into themselves, feeling more and more alone in their bizarre ordeal. This, of course, is the goal of the demonic, since self-doubt and emotional turmoil eat away at their prey's will, paving the way for possession.

So far, this is all standard operating procedure for the demonic—but there was an unusual twist in this case. Rather than wear at Gabby's nerves with the unsettling ploys of *infestation*—the first stage of diabolical activity in most cases, marked by such unnerving events as midnight knockings, peculiar phone calls, or tormented animal cries—the satanic spirit was hell-bent on full-blown oppression from the start. *Oppression* is the second stage of diabolical activity, and involves terrifying mental and physical attacks on the victim. The way it behaved in Gabby's bedroom reminded me a little of police calls I've responded to where people are actually held prisoner in their own home, because they invited someone to stay with them for a short time, then had their guest take over their house.

This "guest" was quite charming at first. The next day, according to Gabby, the spirit returned in broad daylight, while she was down in the basement. "My attention was directed to a large mirror we have hanging there, and in it I saw Virginia," she reported. "Again she said, 'Parents, help,' then told me she'd been in finishing school abroad and had followed her parents here. In quaint, old-fashioned speech, she said, 'What manner of place is this?' Upon looking around the room and at me, she asked, 'What manner of dress is this?' I answered that this is how we dress in the 1990s, but she insisted that the year was 1901. I felt no fear of her, and we had a lengthy conversation."

Joe and I were impressed by how cleverly the spirit slowly unfolded its intricate tale, like a spider spinning a web to catch unwary prey. Ever so smoothly it was drawing Gabby in, plying this suburban housewife with girl talk about fashions and finishing school—a sly tactic to suggest that this was a ghost of great refinement. I also noticed the subtle bid for a mother's sympathy: The so-called ghost had somehow lost her parents and wanted to be reunited with them.

Gabby was enthralled and couldn't wait to hear the next installment of the spirit's intriguing soap opera. Yet her intuition was already warning her about Virginia's true nature. "The third time she came to me was also in the basement. I felt her presence and said, 'If you wish to speak, do *not* enter me. I'll relate whatever you say.' She paid no attention and immediately entered me. When she came into me, her voice was stuttering, and she kept saying 'Parents, help.' "

Although Gabby didn't fully grasp what was happening to her—and her suspicions were blunted by the spirit's lies about "no harm, no fear"—on some level she knew her mind and body were under siege. Instinctively she resisted having the spirit invade her body—but not forcefully enough. A demon has no respect for human pleas, requests, or even orders for it to depart unless the command is made in the name of Jesus Christ.

Despite her misgivings about the bullying spirit that had forced itself on her against her wishes, she found its voice so seductive that she couldn't stop listening. Apparently sensing that it was time to turn up the drama, the alleged ghost returned with theatrical flair when Gabby was talking to another resident of the house, Ruth. This middle-aged woman and her twenty-five-year-old son, Carl, had recently moved in, after Carl became engaged to the Villanovas' oldest daughter, Luciana. As the two women sat in the future bride's bedroom, chatting about the upcoming marriage, the spirit offered a tearjerking tale of woe.

This time she didn't bother with smoke or mirrors or any physical manifestation. Instead, the spirit seized control of the housewife's mind and communicated telepathically, while Gabby answered out loud. "Virginia was crying hysterically, and I kept asking what was the matter. She told me she'd been murdered on her wedding day! Her fiancé was falsely accused of the murder—and was so grief-stricken that he committed suicide in prison. Only after his death did they find out that they had the wrong man. I asked who *had* murdered her. Her reply was 'Must not say.' "

The human con artists I've arrested weren't half as good bullshitters as that, which is probably why they're in jail now. I remember one guy who had the gall to impersonate a police officer in an effort to swindle a woman out of thousands of dollars, only to have the scam go sour when the woman suddenly changed her mind just as she was about to hand over the cash. Then this perp's luck got even worse when he decided to punch her in the mouth and grab the loot—just as I was driving by on my way to work. After a little persuasion from my 9-millimeter semi-automatic, he stopped the assault, surrendered the cash, and let me snap the cuffs on his wrists. I only wish busting the demonic was that simple.

Incredibly, however, Gabby didn't question the astonishing coincidences between the spirit's story and her own life. I often marvel at how adept evil powers are at exploiting people's good natures. You'd think people would be a lot more skeptical about the claims of a supernatural being that shows up in a puff of smoke as they're planning their daughter's wedding and announces that, lo and behold, it just so happens to be the ghost of a murdered bride-to-be! But the demonic have an uncanny knowledge of human psychology—as well as of real events—and therefore know exactly which emotional buttons to press to win people's hearts and minds.

Clearly, a cover story that revolved around a wedding gone wrong was the right strategy here: As the mothers of a future bride and groom, Gabby and Ruth actually wept over this tragic tale. Ruth was particularly touched by the supposed suicide of the wrongfully accused fiancé. One of her relatives had also been arrested and briefly jailed for a crime he didn't commit. Soon almost everyone in the house was completely captivated by the fascinating ghost story and dying to know more. Only Dominick saw a sinister side to these events. A pragmatic man who worked in an accounting firm, he felt that a lot of what he was hearing simply didn't add up to the truth. "Even though my wife didn't seem scared, I was. I didn't like what was going on at all! Virginia was coming to my wife more and more, and I felt the ghost was starting to, well, *possess* her, if that's the right word."

He looked at us with the timid expression of a schoolboy who suspects that he has just given a ridiculously wrong answer and is about to be laughed at by the whole class.

"Tell us what you mean by 'possessed,'" Joe replied in a deliberately neutral tone. Since both of us have a law enforcement background, we've been trained not to lead witnesses or suggest explanations during the fact-finding stage of our investigation.

"Well, this spirit would actually go *into* my wife and try to talk though her lips," he explained. "Often she'd stammer—which *isn't* the way Gabby normally talks—or we couldn't understand her words at all. During these trances, or whatever you want to call them, she'd get stiff as a board. She'd be completely out of it, but when I'd put the light on or shout her name, Virginia would usually leave. Sometimes I had to shake her or even smack her to wake her up. The ghost said 'no harm, no fear,' but when I saw my wife like that—stiff, stuttering, and not knowing what was going on—I felt it *was* doing harm, and there was plenty to fear."

Here was further proof of oppression, an intense terror campaign by the demonic that paves the way for their ultimate goal: possession. Although transient possession was already taking place, Gabby's will wasn't broken down enough for full possession. Not suspecting what terrible danger she was in, Gabby and her large, extended family ignored Dominick's doubts. Predictably, that provoked arguments and hostility between husband and wife, just as the demon intended. Night after night, the bookkeeper would come home from work to find the house a mess, or no dinner on the table because his wife and Ruth were off at the library trying to solve intriguing mysteries the ghost had described. Joe and I could also feel the tension between the couple during our visit and noticed that they'd often interrupt each other or dispute petty details about how certain events unfolded.

The two mothers, however, relished the opportunity to escape the humdrum world of housework and play detective. Virginia eagerly egged them on, claiming that her parents, Nathaniel and Sarah Taylor, had mysteriously disappeared shortly after her fiancé's suicide. "I fear they may have been murdered," she tearfully lamented. "If only I knew their fate, perhaps I could rest easy, at last." Almost every day the ghost offered new clues to help the women trace her purported parents: They came to the United States around the turn of the century, from an unspecified European country, and moved in with their cousins, the Clarkes, while Virginia stayed behind to graduate from finishing school.

To pique their curiosity and heighten the sympathy factor, Virginia tearfully volunteered new details that any mother could relate to. It seemed that the Clarkes were also touched by family tragedy: Their only son was stillborn. Unable to have any more children, they adopted a son, Oliver, who later fell in love with Virginia and asked her to marry him.

A bit impatient with this intricate satanic scam, Joe cut to the chase. "So, did this story check out?"

Not exactly, Gabby replied. "We went through old newspapers, phone books, and public records. There was nothing about Virginia or her parents, just some stuff about the family she lived with. Apparently, the Clarkes were landowners around here at one time, but we didn't see anything about them having a son named Oliver."

Although diabolic forces have knowledge of the past and can view the lives of departed humans as if they were watching a videotape, these lying spirits will mix just enough fact with their disingenuous fictions to keep their victims hooked. All Gabby and Ruth had proven was that someone with the very common name of Clarke had once lived in Westchester. No doubt if they'd spent even more time at the library, they would have found some Taylors too.

The utter lack of any newspaper coverage of a dramatic story that definitely would have made headlines—a bride murdered on her wedding day and the arrest of the groom—didn't lessen the family's faith in Virginia, who soon asked them to tackle another mystery. "She wanted us to find the grave of her fiancé," Gabby said. "After his suicide, there was a big cover-up and no one knew where he was buried. Virginia—"

Dominick broke in. "She had my wife in tears. Gabby felt very bad that she'd failed to find out anything about the parents, and now the ghost was weeping and carrying on about her dead boyfriend's unknown grave."

Once again the spirit supplied a clue: The body was probably buried in Sleepy Hollow Cemetery. Since the next day was a school holiday, Gabby, Ruth, and their five kids drove over to the beautiful old graveyard in North Tarrytown that holds the final resting place of Washington Irving and the friends he used as characters in *The Legend of Sleepy Hollow*. After trudging through the modern and historic tombstones for several hours without finding the grave, the two exhausted families decided to give up and go home.

Just before they reached the church by the graveyard, Gabby suddenly went into a trance. "Something was pulling me up the walkway and back into the graveyard. I was yanked over to one of the headstones, which said 'Catherine Clarke, 1859–1926.' Virginia got very excited and said we'd found Oliver's mother. There was a smaller stone next to it, but it was so worn that I couldn't make out the name. Was it Oliver's grave? Virginia didn't say."

I was getting pretty curious about this devil myself. The trip to the cemetery was a stroke of genius: Because the spirit had dragged their mother over to a tomb near a church, they made a leap of logic and concluded that this was a nice Christian ghost. They were totally unaware that they'd ventured into the Devil's favorite hunting ground!

Gabby stopped resisting the spirit and actually gave it permission to enter her, so it could reveal more. "My oldest daughter went to the historic society and got old maps of Westchester. I spread them out on the table, got a pen, and asked Virginia to show me where she'd lived. My hand began to shake from side to side and was pushed to a certain area. It drew a letter we thought was either an 'M' or a 'W.'"

It all fit the demonic M.O. Not only do they do everything that's opposite of holy, but at times they'll write backward, so you have to read the words with a mirror, or upside down. Their writing is often crooked, as if a right-handed person were using her left hand. Strange writings, sometimes using obscenities, profanities about God, or phrases from obscure languages are also a hallmark of oppression. In this case, the demon's deliberately ambiguous scrawl was a symbolic way of blowing more smoke and increasing Gabby's confusion.

The housewife, who clearly was *still* enthralled with Virginia, eagerly offered to show Joe the marked-up map so he could try to divine whatever hidden meaning it held. My partner shook his head: He wasn't there to decode demonic messages or give the evil power in this house *any* unnecessary recognition.

It was time to clue these people in. "Gabby, let's get one thing straight. We're not going to call this spirit 'Virginia' anymore, because it doesn't *deserve* a human name. This isn't a human spirit or ghost—it's a demon." After Joe explained the nature of these spirits, he began to debunk the demon's tale. "This wedding story is a lot of crap to snare you through empathy and make a psychic connection with your lives. From now on, when we talk about anything this spirit provoked, we'll say 'The demon did it.'"

Dominick's meek, bewildered expression changed to a sly, triumphant look that shouted "See, I told you so!"

Gabby didn't need much convincing either. Instead, she described what the demon did on Halloween, right after Dominick called a priest, Father Williams, for help. "Virginia—I mean the demon—told me she wasn't evil." Once the parish priest was brought in, the demon knew it was only a matter of time before it was exposed for what it truly was. Therefore, it accelerated its plans for possession.

On that same day the spirit tried to lure Gabby to its lair, the basement. She added, "She said she wouldn't hurt me. I didn't want to go there, then she said, 'I've dealt with Father Hayes before—and this time I'll win the battle!'" Even Gabby had to admit that it was more than a little strange for the spirit to claim it didn't want to hurt anyone—and had only the most benign intentions—then announce that it was all set to kick ass against a man of God. But what was odder still was *which* priest the spirit named—not the one Dominick had contacted, but an out-of-state exorcist the family didn't even know had been called.

In its stuttering voice, the spirit delivered one final ultimatum: "H-h-holy ones must *not* come!"

I should have been warned, but I wasn't. Seeing that Joe didn't need my help in conducting the interview, I decided to do the same thing I do in every case: Walk around the house and form my impression of the place. I can tell a lot about a family just by looking around. I check for signs of the occult, what religious articles are present, how the home is kept, what kind of books the people read, evidence of drug use, and any signs that might indicate there's something wrong with their lifestyle. If I see anything that bothers me, I ask them about it later in the interview.

With my tour of the house, I can sometimes pick up vibrations about the situation. I'm not psychic, so I can't rely on my intuitions 100 percent, but every human is born with some degree of a sixth sense, as a gift from God. My big mistake, in this case, was walking through the house alone. I started with the upstairs, where there was a recently vacated apartment the family had been renting out. As I walked into the apartment, a doorknob in one of the rooms started rattling. I've run across this kind of low-level bullshit from the demonic in other homes, so I noted the location for further investigation.

The rooms inside were unnaturally dark. When I found the light switch, I saw why: Everything was painted a deep, vivid black. Even the windows were so thickly coated that no light from the outside could penetrate. I searched the place, but the former occupant had left absolutely nothing behind. I would have loved to get a look at *his* possessions, because I was ready to bet my next paycheck that this guy, whoever he was, sure as hell didn't spend his spare time praying the rosary! I made a mental note to ask the family about their ex-tenant.

In the first-floor apartment, where the family lived, I didn't find anything out of the ordinary in Gabby and Dominick's bedroom, or those of the three younger children. In the future bride's room, I saw an extremely bright ball of light whiz past me and vanish down the hall. I'd seen a blazing sphere like this once before, in an earlier case, so wasn't particularly alarmed. I returned to the living room to ask the Villanovas if any of them had ever experienced this strange phenomenon.

My question created a family uproar. "Yes, I've seen that light," Luciana exclaimed.

"So have I," added Gabby. "It's scary." One by one the other members of the household described various occasions where the ball of light had appeared to them.

Only Dominick was silent. He looked disappointed. Finally he interrupted the discussion of the light with a grumpy outburst. "*I've* never seen it! How come *you* can see these things, Mr. Sarchie, and I can't?" He actually sounded insulted that the evil spirit hadn't manifested itself to him.

"Don't feel bad," I said. "Just be thankful that you don't."

He gave a grudging nod of agreement, and I resumed

checking the house. The remaining rooms were normal enough, though the kitchen was rather messy and the sink was piled with dirty dishes, I headed downstairs. I didn't have any sense of evil when I first entered the basement, but when I got to a storage room with double doors, I could feel menace from eight feet away. The feeling was so overpowering that I stopped dead in my tracks, so afraid that I couldn't move. I've been a cop for a long time and have been scared plenty of times before, but I always have reacted aggressively—that's how I've trained myself. This was different: I couldn't take my eyes off those doors, my heart started racing one hundred miles a minute, and I couldn't catch my breath. Then the pain started in my head—it wasn't like a headache, but a piercing pain in my right temple that I've sometimes experienced on other cases or during exorcisms.

As the pain in my head got stronger, my stomach churned and I felt like I was going to vomit. There was no outward sign of anything that I could see—just a feeling of hellish terror and absolute evil. I was too frozen to move my lips or speak, so in my mind I commanded the demon to leave in the name of Jesus Christ. It released its hold on me just enough so I could reach the bottle of holy water in my pocket. I threw holy water at the doors and was able to back away to the stairs—not daring to take my eyes off those dreadful doors.

Once I reached the living room, where the family was waiting, the pain and the sick feeling disappeared. I took Joe aside and told him what had happened.

"Ralph, I think you should take a look at this," he said, handing a note the "ghost" had dictated to Gabby the night before.

One sentence immediately leapt out: "Harm will come to those below. Beware the night!"

2

NIGHTMARE'S END

While I was under attack in the basement, Joe had uncovered an alarming new twist to the case. About two weeks after the spirit began playing its smoke-and-mirror games, Gabby's oldest daughter, Luciana, was subjected to a series of stunningly cruel preternatural assaults. Although the young bride-to-be was definitely the beauty of the family, with her long wavy black hair, pale olive skin, and dark flashing eyes, she had a sullen, almost hostile expression on her face. Everything about her radiated such an intense misery that it surrounded her like a thick, black cloud. You got the feeling that if you said the wrong thing, she'd lash out with thunder and lightning.

Joe's polite request that Luciana put on her St. Benedict medal, instead of leaving it on the table in front of her, immediately set off sparks. "I had a medallion of the Blessed Mother on a chain around my neck and this morning it was gone," she announced angrily, glaring around the room as if she suspected one of her relatives of stealing it while she slept. "It was real gold too!"

"Don't worry about it," my partner soothed. "The demon could have made your medallion disappear, to stir up trouble and turn you against the other members of your family. These spirits *want* to get you people at each other's throats. Why don't you put the other medal on?"

"The string's too long," Luciana complained. She handed the medal to Carl, who was hovering in the background, looking both protective and wary of his fierce fiancée. Although he was only about twenty-five, his hairline was already receding, making his broad forehead and large, hawklike nose even more prominent. He was dressed entirely in black and wore a gold earring on his left ear. Reaching in the pocket of his rather tight jeans, he took out a Swiss Army knife and carefully trimmed the offending string.

"What are you doing? Now it's too short!"

As Luciana looked on peevishly, Carl cut more string from the ball we'd brought. "Is this okay?"

She grabbed the necklace and pulled it over her hair, taking care not to snag it on her thick ponytail. "I guess so," she reluctantly allowed. Suddenly embarrassed by her display of bad temper, she added, "I'm sorry to be such a bitch, but I only got a half hour of sleep last night."

"Forget it," advised Joe. "I know you're very upset and scared. Let's bring Ralph up to speed about the problems you've been having."

No longer animated by anger, she slumped back in her chair, as if she were carrying a very heavy weight on her thin shoulders. "Several weeks ago, around 2:00 A.M., I was reading in my room. I had a glass of water by my bed, and when I got up to turn on the hall light for my sister, who was out at a party, the glass flew at me and just missed my head."

This was the first attack on her person—and her screams brought the whole family running. Afraid to sleep alone, she spent the next night in her sister's room. In the middle of the night, the bunk bed the two girls were sharing began shaking violently, actually jumping up and down off the floor. Again the family was jolted from sleep by screams, but as soon as they turned on the light, the shaking instantly ceased.

This is characteristic of infestation; scary things happen in the dark and stop when the light goes on. It's a typical demonic head game, where the goal is to create fear and bewilderment, as the victims ask themselves "Was the bed really shaking, or was it just a nightmare? Did we *both* imagine it?" Although the evil spirit operated covertly at first, it became more brazen each day. Infestation quickly progressed to outright oppression: No longer did the evil force flee at the flick of a light switch—in fact, it even began attacking during broad daylight.

Each time the demon picked on the same person: Luciana. "I get scratched every day," she told us. "Usually I get wide red marks up and down my arms that go away very fast, sometimes in minutes. One night, around two in the morning, I felt a very painful burning on my skin and woke up with a pentagram scratched into my stomach. Another time my arm started burning and stinging like it was on fire. When I looked in the mirror, I saw the number of the Beast—666— written on my arm in huge red welts."

Why the bride-to-be became the focal person is rather puzzling: Her two teenaged sisters both said she was the strong one, their beautiful, high-spirited, and rather willful leader. Yet, in the Work, I've found there's no predictable pattern that explains why one family member is singled out for diabolical abuse, except that people are attacked through weaknesses the demonic are quick to exploit. Very often the focal person is a child, since these bullying spirits love to pick on kids. It's a cruel but effective tactic: While the evil spirit was clearly out to get the mother, what better way to break down a parent's will—and reduce her resistance to possession—than by brutalizing her child?

Although the dark power could have accomplished the same thing by going after any of Gabby's four children, I had a theory why Luciana bore the brunt of the abuse. Since the force of doom was posing as a pitiful ghost of a woman who was murdered on her wedding day, it may have reasoned, with perverse logic, that a mother would be most empathetic with its alleged anguish if her daughter, a genuine bride-to-be, was also suffering.

If so, the plan worked: Gabby immediately asked "Virginia" what other spirits were in the house. Naturally, the demon had an answer: "She said there were two poltergeists in the house," Gabby reported. "One was good, and the other poltergeist was very nasty and dangerous."

Joe winced. We both hate this term, which has become popular with parapsychologists, at least the ones who believe in spirits—and some don't. They explain away cases of infestation, oppression, or actual possession as the work of "poltergeists," a German term for "noisy or mischievous spirits." (Others claim they are the result of natural phenomena like electromagnetic energy or underground springs—anything but the demonic.) That makes diabolical powers sound like a bunch of pranksters who are just out for some spooky fun. It's like saying rapists and muggers are simply socially challenged party animals, not a very real menace to society.

I don't care if you don't believe in the Devil—I just pray you and your family never feel his wrath and undying hatred yourself. What I do object to is parapsychologists who "investigate" hauntings from the scientific point of view, going in with their cameras and gaussmeters instead of holy water and relics. They take their readings, snap some pretty pictures of spirit energy, and go on their merry way, while the family is left in a nightmare. How the demonic must delight at this! What better spin to put on their mission to destroy humanity than to claim it's just the harmless mischief of so-called poltergeists?

My partner didn't let this go by. "The game here is good cop/bad cop, or good poltergeist/bad poltergeist—except that there's no such thing as a 'good poltergeist' because this is just a euphemism some people use for the demonic. Make no mistake about it: The only spirits in your home are *evil* spirits, bad guys."

After scaring Gabby with its ominous pronouncement about the nasty poltergeist, the demon moved into phase two of the con game—volunteering to "help" the family with the very problem it had inflicted on them. This reminded me of human criminals who surreptitiously break a store's front window, then show up a few hours later to offer the unsuspecting shopkeeper their overpriced repair services.

The malignant force didn't stop there. That same day it sent yet another "ghost" to vouch for its kindly intentions. "I saw my father, who died a couple of years ago, standing in front of me," Gabby explained. "He called Virginia 'the lady' and said she was a good person. He came to me four or five times, and we had long conversations. One night DJ saw him too and spent a good hour talking to him."

"Was there anything unusual about his appearance?" Joe asked.

"To me, he *was* my father," Gabby insisted. "He talked about things from my childhood that only he and I knew about. You saw him, DJ—how did he look to you?"

The little boy hesitated, then decided to be truthful. "Don't get mad, Mom, but I don't remember Grandpa that good from when he was, you know, alive. When I was sitting on the couch with him, his face was all wrinkled up and he looked really old. He had a brown suit on and was wearing jewelry. He talked in my ear, kind of loud, and said my mom should listen to 'the nice lady.'"

DJ squirmed around, refusing to look his mother in the eye. "One time he talked to me at school, and I got in trouble with the teacher for not listening." He paused again, then blurted out angrily, "I didn't really like Grandpa that much. It was very cold when he was around, and I felt funny inside."

Although neither DJ nor his mother noticed any oddities about the apparition, I was certain this was another satanic impostor, trying to add to "Virginia's" credibility with its little plugs for her supposed goodness. Its uncanny knowledge of Gabby's childhood proved nothing, as the entire population of Hell has access to the events of human lives and can quote them when it serves the demonic purpose. Clearly this innocent child detected something disturbing about the spirit, even if he didn't have the words to explain exactly what it was. There's always some sign of the diabolic presence, even if it's not as obvious as a pair of cloven hooves.

Although the demonic can masquerade as anyone, even a saint, there's always some telltale sign—something wrong or out of place—if you know how to look for it. The Devil came to one of St. Francis of Assisi's followers in several guises, trying to destroy his faith. All of them failed, until Satan took the form of a crucifix. Pretending to be the Son of God, he told the pious man that his prayers and penances were pointless, as both he and St. Francis were already marked for damnation. The brother was deceived and lost his devotion to his spiritual leader until the saint reminded him the words of Jesus would never plunge a person into sorrow and despair but fill him with love and joy.

St. Francis then told the brother how to unmask the enemy of his soul. The next time he saw the false crucifix, he should command the figure of Christ to "open Thy mouth." Since the Devil can't speak through Jesus' lips, he was instantly exposed for the foul liar he really was, and departed in such fury that huge stones rolled down a nearby mountain, striking each other with terrible force and igniting a blazing inferno. The brother begged God to forgive him for listening to the Devil. The real Son of God then appeared to him and said, "Thou did well, my son, to believe in St. Francis; for he who made you so unhappy was the Devil." So sweet were these words that the brother became enraptured by God and never again doubted his salvation.

In a similar way, I advise people to ask spirits who pose as departed relatives, pitiful ghosts, saints, or even Christ Himself to say "I love God." That's something the demonic will never do, so the satanic power is sure to be exposed. Or you can simply order the spirit to leave in Jesus' name—this command has power over the forces of darkness but no effect on human spirits. It's also important to remember the lesson St. Francis taught: Holy spirits make you happy, while demonic ones bring misery, conflict, terror, and hatred to your life.

That was certainly true here: After the grandfather's ghost appeared, the attacks on Luciana intensified from one assault a day to many, at completely unpredictable intervals. The future bride never knew when she'd be punched, kicked, flung on the floor, dragged out of bed, bitten, or yanked around by her hair. Her life became a living hell, as she was brutalized in every imaginable way. Earlier in the interview we'd seen how raw her nerves were, and now we knew why. Because she was attacked night after night, in order that the demon could feed on her fear and gain power over her mother, she was angry, exhausted, and on the edge of complete despair.

Put yourself in that house for a minute, and try to imagine what it was like for this young woman and her family. It's late at night, and you're in your own comfortable bed. But you know there's something evil in your home with you and lie awake, scared witless, just waiting for something to happen: Will you be attacked—or will a loved one be? Then you hear your daughter screaming. Your legs can't carry you fast enough, your heart is racing, and you can't breathe. That's exactly the horror this family endured, twenty-four hours a day, for nearly three hellish months.

So they stopped sleeping in their separate bedrooms and huddled together in the living room, in sleeping bags and makeshift beds. Even then rest was fitful and unrefreshing. Midnight screams punctured what little sleep they got, as the foul force clawed its bloody mark on Luciana and terrorized the other family members. Their possessions were flung around like trash: The future bride's cherished collection of clown dolls was repeatedly found on the floor, and her books kept flying off their shelves, sometimes striking nearby walls so violently that they left dents in the plaster. Stranger still, Gabby found that the silk flowers she kept on her dresser had mysteriously left their vase—and arranged themselves on her bed in the shape of a cross.

Heavy furniture began to move on its own, shaking up and down as if from an earthquake or levitating off the floor. Large chairs—or on one occasion, Luciana's bed—started flying around, smashing into walls, and knocking the family's pictures to the floor in a hail of glass. The demonic also used other terrorist tactics: One of the most unnerving was the way the TV or stereo would suddenly blare to life in the middle of the night, at full blast. Horrible moans and growls were heard in the basement, and on some mornings, creepy messages would be found on the bathroom mirror, Ruth said. "Several times we found the word 'help' written backwards on the glass."

Too scared to be alone, even when using the toilet or standing naked in the shower, they took to visiting the bathroom in groups. There was some safety in numbers, Ruth explained. After she was twice menaced by flying objects—a box of tissues that struck her in the face when she was in the basement by herself and a can of peas that levitated off a kitchen shelf and just missed the back of her head—she asked her future daughter-in-law to stand guard as she took a shower. "I was drying myself off when Luciana shouted 'Watch out!' I ducked and a heavy soap dish came flying over the shower door and smashed into the wall behind me. If she hadn't warned me, I'd have definitely gotten clobbered! Whatever this thing is, it has a lot of power!"

Ruth also noticed that the infernal force had a peculiar effect on her body. "When it's around, I'm one of the first people to get cold and start shivering uncontrollably. If something is starting to happen to Luciana, I feel like needles are poking my thighs, and my leg muscles go crazy. Several times this happened when she was in another room, and I didn't have any way of knowing she was getting scratched or bitten. The time she was pulled from her bed by her hair, just before the attack, I saw a white bullet—or a white ball—streak by."

There was only one pattern to the violence, the bride-to-be added. "When stuff happens to my mother, I usually get hit." Seemingly worn out by the effort of getting these words out, she sagged wearily back in her chair. I could see what a toll this waking nightmare was taking on her: The circles under her eyes were as dark as bruises, and she spoke haltingly, like an old person with a chronic illness. Her fiancé gave her a comforting squeeze, only to have his hand brushed away as if it were an annoying insect.

Although he seemed a bit stung by the rejection, Carl didn't remark on it. Instead, to give us a better idea of Luciana's suffering, he showed us a handwritten diary of the attacks he'd started keeping right after Dominick called the exorcist, hoping a written record would help with our investigation.

Here's how his tormented fiancée and her family spent Halloween night:

6:20 P.M. *Luciana slapped twice in face.*
8:03 P.M. *Ashtray flew across bedroom.*
11:28 P.M. *L. scratched on stomach, in the shape of "N."*
11:31 P.M. *L. pushed into wall.*
11:39 P.M. *Circle scratched on L.'s face.*
11:46 P.M. *L.'s head slammed against the table.*
11:48 P.M. *L. dragged off chair.*
11:52 P.M. *Heard growling.*
11:56 P.M. *Chair moves across dining room.*
12:05 A.M. *L. knocked into Ruth.*
2:14 A.M. *L. yanked out of bed.*
2:16 A.M. *L. punched in stomach.*
2:17 A.M. *L. pushed off chair again.*
2:18 A.M. *Flash of light, rotten egg smell.*
3:15 A.M. *L. hit on head with a shoe.*
3:56 A.M. *L.'s fingers pinched.*

Sitting up from the near stupor she'd fallen into as we were reading this, Luciana said that yesterday had been even worse. "I got really scared. The mattress I was sleeping on was lifted a foot or two in the air, and I was thrown to the floor. I saw something horrible, sitting there laughing at me. I'd seen it once before: a white creature that was hairy all over, with no eyes, just awful black eye sockets that stared and stared at me. I tried to kick it away from me—and it gave me the finger! Then it vanished!"

The monster, now invisible, laughed again—a horrible snicker that raised every hair on Luciana's body in dread. "Then something forced my legs open. I was trying to scream 'Help!' but no words came out of my mouth. It was like a nightmare. My father, Carl, and Ruth all tried to push my legs together, but they couldn't. Then it let go." Knowing how incredibly bizarre this sounded, she turned to her boyfriend in tears. "Carl—you saw it too! Right before it disappeared."

We'd gotten there just in time. This sickeningly perverse fiend was planning an incubus attack, the rape of a human female by a demon! This young woman had no idea of what a grotesque violation she'd so narrowly escaped! Had we not arrived when we did, there's no doubt in my mind that she eventually would have been molested in an unspeakably vile manner.

Carl confirmed everything she had said, then added that there had been other Halloween horrors. Turning to the next page in his diary, he described how he and his fiancée had gone out for cigarettes around 4:00 A.M., since Gabby had run out. No one in the house could sleep, because the attacks were going on twenty-four hours a day, seven days a week. That's the M.O. of the demonic—when sleep is virtually nonexistent, the victims are constantly on edge, making it easy for the evil spirit to stir up discord between the exhausted family members. These strategies also help break down the will which enables possession to take place.

While he was in the store and Luciana was waiting in the car, a rubber ball hanging from his rearview mirror spontaneously burst into flame. Luciana tried to put the fire out, then beeped the horn frantically until Carl came running out, threw the burning ball on the ground, and stamped it out with his feet.

Back at house, he settled uneasily down to sleep. Just as he was finally drifting off, Carl had the chilling feeling that someone—or something—was lurking nearby. "I tried to ignore it, because I was really tired and needed rest. My body got paralyzed and I couldn't move at all. I heard Luciana scream 'What's it doing to you, Carl?' It released me, and I nodded off again. It came back later that night, and the second time was much worse. I felt something crawling on my right leg, then it 'entered' me. I was shaking all over, especially my hands, trying to fight it off."

He actually felt an alien presence inside his body. I've heard several descriptions from people about what this feels like. Some victims say it becomes difficult to breathe, as if someone were pressing a hot rag over their face, while others feel heavy pressure on their chests, paralysis of their entire body, or electricity coursing through them. Some people have a combination of these sensations. The one thing all of their descriptions have in common is the utter fear the demonic presence evokes, which is what these evil spirits thrive on.

As Carl described the attack, I realized he'd experienced the very thing the ancient Druids dreaded on Halloween: becoming possessed by one of the ravenous spirits that roam Earth, looking for human bodies to inhabit. "For a second, it slipped out of me and I relaxed," he said. Too soon, as it turned out: "It came back in and lifted my whole body off the bed. The next thing I knew, I was talking in different languages—and fighting with everything I had. I passed out and don't remember anything else, except that it was gone when I woke up."

Shaken to his very soul, he asked Gabby to see what light "Virginia" could shed on this ghastly invasion. Predictably, the diabolic force had an ominous answer: There were now five demons in the house, it warned the mother. "She said they wouldn't leave unless blood was drawn! Supposedly, they'd gotten rid of the 'good poltergeist' and now they wanted the 'girl child'—my daughter Luciana!"

Even my normally impassive partner was shocked. With uncharacteristic anger, he thundered, "Nobody's going to get Luciana, so there's no problem there!"

But where were all these evil spirits coming from? As we conducted the interview, we kept hearing doorknobs rattling in empty rooms. Each time the entire, exhausted family seemed to come alive, offering further proof that this wasn't a case of mass hysteria, as skeptics might argue, but a house where no one escaped demonic attack—not even the family dog, who jumped at the eerie noises, whining and barking.

Joe asked if anyone present had played with a Ouija board. The two teenaged sisters both confessed that they had experimented with this practice at a party, asking silly questions about whether certain boys liked them. "The board answered us 'yes' or 'no' but didn't say anything else interesting, so we put it away," explained the middle sister, a slender brunette named Monica. "That was the only time, I swear!"

With a stern look, my partner explained that that was once too often. "There's no guarantees when you cross into the psychic dimension. I don't blame you for not knowing this, but when you play with a Ouija board, you open a door—and could meet pure evil on the other side."

When Luciana heard this, she flew into a rage at her sisters. "How could you play with that! *You* did this to us!"

I can hear some of you out there saying "Hey, I used a Ouija board and nothing happened." Consider yourself lucky, then. It's like playing Russian roulette. When you put the gun to your head, if you don't hear a loud noise, you made it. Same thing with the board: The more times you pull the trigger, the more likely that on the next shot, your entire world will go black. I've had one case where a young mother played with a Ouija board at a party, with horrifying—and tragic—results.

She quickly became hooked on the practice, buying her own board and consulting it daily. One morning a spirit "guide" showed up, saying it was the ghost of a seventeen-year-old boy who had committed suicide. This spook concocted an elaborate fairy tale about an unmarked grave it wanted her to find— and managed to so preoccupy the woman's time with wild goose chases that she began neglecting her husband and little kids. This, of course, caused demonically induced disputes between husband and wife, but the mother was interested only in the board, and the spirit that seemed to understand her better than her husband did.

Then things took a terrible turn. One night the mother had the worst nightmare of her life, dreaming that she was being chased by a large man with a hatchet, who was going to kill her. The vision was so vivid that she woke up crying hysterically, drenched in sweat. Now, all of us have dreams like that once in a while, but not every night, as this unfortunate woman did. The real nightmare began after the dreams stopped. While awake, she began hearing a voice. It made perverse, sexual remarks, then said something far more chilling: It commanded her to take a knife and stab her children. Petrified, she told her husband, then checked herself into a mental hospital out of fear that she would hurt her family.

After thorough physical and psychological tests found no diagnosable disorder, she was released—and contacted Bishop McKenna for an exorcism. During the ritual, nothing happened until the bishop touched a relic to her head and said, "Devil, if you are in her, I adjure you in the name of Jesus Christ Our Lord to reveal yourself."

The demon spoke in the mother's normal voice, saying "I am the spirit of a person." Already it had betrayed itself, since human spirits aren't subject to exorcism.

The bishop ignored this and asked, "Why did you enter her?"

The response was extremely revealing. "Because she offered herself through a Ouija board." I can still remember how this woman sat through the ritual still as a statue, with only her eyes moving in a strange circular motion. It's a very sad story, because the ritual ultimately failed. We never saw the young mother again and can only pray that she hasn't given up fighting the demon that enslaved her though a Ouija board.

In the Westchester case, however, Joe and I felt that these foolish children were probably not to blame—and assured them that we didn't hold them responsible for the troubles that had befallen their family. Although their Ouija board use may have brought the demon, we didn't want to burden them with guilt, especially since we had another suspect. As the interview continued, we learned that the mysterious extenant had a dark side that went well beyond his taste in wall colors. Although the Villanovas weren't able to give us a lot of detail about him, they'd recently found out that Mr. Paint-It-Black had a criminal record and was rumored to be into a lot of strange stuff, including the occult. Admittedly, the evidence against him was circumstantial, but we both felt it was he who had invited the powerful demon—or demons—into this home.

Just as we were wrapping up the questions, Luciana let out a horrible shriek. The demon had brazenly attacked her, right in front of us! A curved red gash now ran down her smooth cheek, like a taunting calling card from the Devil. While we were videotaping the mark, she screamed again. The unseen force had just pulled her hair, hard enough to jerk her head to the side.

That settled it: Even though an exorcist was involved, the evil in this house was so strong that we decided to attempt our own ritual in the house that very night. Although we weren't as well prepared as we'd like to have been, we didn't get into the Work to walk away from people in trouble. To leave a family alone in this situation would be a crime.

Soon after we began the Pope Leo XIII prayer, a minor form of exorcism we use in the Work, all the dogs in the neighborhood—including the Villanovas' pet, who had been following us around from room to room, with his St. Benedict medal jingling on his collar—became extremely agitated. Joe and I had never heard such deafening barking and howling in our lives, and asked the family if this had ever happened before. The answer was no, so we knew that at that very moment, demons were fleeing the house.

The most powerful spirit, however, wouldn't be banished so easily. It knew it was close to a full possession, so it chose to stay and fight, while the lesser forces ran from our relics and holy water. While we were in the basement, near the doors I'd backed away from earlier that night, it brazenly attacked again.

Carl came racing down the stairs. "Come quick! Something's happening to Gabby!"

In the living room, we found the mother trembling uncontrollably, as if she were having a seizure. The demon was trying to possess her—right then and there. In a breathless, gasping voice, she told us she could feel it entering her body. Then she went completely rigid. Her mouth opened stiffly, like a marionette's jaw, and she stammered, "H-h-holy ones, begone! H-h-harm will come to all!"

We couldn't believe our eyes—we'd seen possessed people before, but never had a diabolic power invaded someone while we were standing there with holy water in hand, conducting an exorcism. We knew we were in the presence of one of Hell's more dangerous devils.

We weren't about to be chased off by some demon, no matter how terrible its powers might be, so we came on strong, our guns blazing. Holding up our two relics of the True Cross, Joe's and mine, we touched the precious slivers to Gabby's head and used the most potent weapon of all—the name of Jesus Christ—to command the evil force to depart and leave this woman in peace. Powerful as this spirit was, it couldn't withstand the ultimate torment, and grudgingly released its grasp on Gabby. She slowly returned to her senses, as if waking up from a dream, and had no memory of what had occurred.

There was still dreadful danger in this room, so we checked that everyone was still wearing a St. Benedict medal, and then anointed each person with blessed oil. Now that the family was secure, we resumed the ritual, reading the Pope Leo XIII prayer numerous times throughout the house until we were practically hoarse. All that wasn't enough to bring the case to a close: We knew that we'd managed to weaken this demon and halt its attempts at possession, but to get rid of it entirely, we'd either need a full team of investigators or an ordained clergyman, trained as an exorcist.

We were still reluctant to leave the family, knowing that phenomena would still take place, though to a lesser degree. But we took comfort in knowing that they now had the means to fight back. We'd exposed the demonic charade and put an end to any communication with the foul spirit. We'd also given the family weapons: holy water, blessed salt, and, most of all, the name of Jesus Christ on their lips.

We continued our prayers until Father Williams, the parish priest, arrived. After we brought him up to speed on our investigation, he agreed that the family would now come under his guidance, until Father Hayes was able to perform an exorcism. As we packed up our equipment, the look on the little boy's face was like a kick in the gut to me. "Daddy," he cried. "Don't let these people leave!"

We hated to go but were sure the family was in good hands. Unfortunately, we were wrong. Several months later we got a call from the Villanovas: They were still under supernatural siege. To his credit, the local priest had followed through with what he promised, but due to health problems, the exorcist wasn't able to come after all.

Joe and I had learned a lesson or two from our first visit, and after intense spiritual preparation, we returned on a Saturday afternoon with three investigators and enough supplies to exorcise an entire city block. Sadly, Dominick was now in terrible financial straits: Because of the problems his family was having, he'd missed too many days of work and had lost his job as a bookkeeper. Unless he found new employment soon, the bank would foreclose on his house. Hearing this news fired us up with even more determination to expel the demon and allow this good man to get on with his life.

First, we sent the women and children to a nearby church with Chris, one of our investigators, for their protection, then got a quick update on the situation from Dominick. After our first exorcism, the spirit left the family alone a day or two: a normal M.O. for the demonic, who love psychological warfare. Just as the Villanovas thought they were safe, the attacks resumed. Shoes, books, and jars began flying around again but rarely hit anyone. Doors inexplicably slammed, and the imprint of a face appeared on the dining room ceiling.

While the violence toward Luciana had dwindled—she still suffered an occasional scratch—the demon had now taken to venting its wrath on religious articles. Holy water we'd left on our last visit mysteriously turned brown in its bottle, and the figure of Jesus Christ was torn off one of the children's rosaries. After two priests blessed the house, the imprint of an animal skull appeared on the basement mirror. In one of the stranger manifestations I've heard of, a pale, disembodied arm grabbed at the bride-to-be when she was sitting on the living room love seat; and a featureless black shape was seen drifting down the stairs.

You may be wondering why Father Williams, the parish priest, didn't conduct an exorcism himself. Unfortunately, he wasn't able to get his bishop's permission to do this—a requirement in the Catholic Church before a priest can perform the ritual. However, he did his utmost to help and support the family, not just with spiritual guidance, but by spending an entire night in their house, along with another priest. I admire both priests' guts for this: It couldn't have been easy for them to spend so much time in a demonically oppressed home. In fact, during their stay, they actually witnessed a terrifying phenomenon, when a bedroom bureau began jumping around right in front of them.

For two hours, we fought the Devil room by room. Armed with blessed incense, holy water, blessed salt, and the most potent weapon of all, our relics of the True Cross, we stationed investigators on each floor to hold simultaneous rituals, thus attacking the demon from above and below. We worked in pairs, so one person could focus on conducting the ritual, while the other was alert for any sign of demonic activity. And more important still, the backup investigator kept a close watch on his partner—to make sure that the person doing the exorcism wasn't being attacked himself. External phenomena don't need to be taking place: The attack also can be psychological, like the stark terror that seized me in the basement of this house on our previous visit. If an investigator has any psychic abilities, he or she could be assailed through those powers. Since an attack could come at any time, to either partner, everyone must be constantly on guard.

We began by opening every closet, cabinet, and drawer in the room we were exorcising, leaving no dark, enclosed space for the demonic to hide. Because they are spirit and have no physical bodies, malignant beings can conceal themselves anywhere. Next, we lit blessed incense, which helps dispel negative vibrations and repel evil spirits, since they are tormented by anything holy or blessed. As always, we started the ritual with the St. Michael prayer, one of two prayers that were divinely revealed to Pope Leo XIII. While celebrating mass in 1884, the Holy Father was suddenly seized by such a profound rapture that he fell to the floor as if dead. When he woke, he told his cardinals of a terrible vision he'd had, in which the Devil taunted Jesus by saying that, given enough time and power, he could destroy mankind. Our Savior gave

Satan permission to test humanity over the decades to come. No sooner did the Pontiff finish relating this prophecy than he asked for pen and paper and wrote prayers to help defeat Satan.

Pope Leo XIII directed that the first of these prayers, officially titled "Prayer to St. Michael the Archangel," be added to the official Catholic mass. It calls upon the archangel to "be our defense against the wickedness and snares of the Devil" and "by the power of God thrust into hell Satan and the other evil spirits who prowl about the world seeking the ruin of souls." This prayer was said at the end of mass until 1968, when it was eliminated as part of the changes of Vatican II. It continues to be recited in Traditionalist Catholic churches, and Pope John Paul II urged it be restored to the modern Catholic mass, feeling that the grave evils of this world mean that we need St. Michael's intervention more than ever before.

Pope Leo XIII's second prayer, "Exorcism Against Satan and the Rebellious Angels," which we call the Pope Leo XIII prayer for short, is extremely powerful against the demonic. The Holy Father exhorted priests to say this prayer as often as possible to curb the Devil's power and prevent him from doing harm. He gave the faithful permission to say it in their own name, as they would any approved prayer, "whenever action of the Devil is suspected, causing malice in men, violent temptations, and even storms and various calamities." That's exactly what we did in the Villanovas' home, moving from room to room as we prayed. We sprinkled all four corners of each room and the interior of every closet with holy water to consecrate the area, then repeated the process with blessed salt, which has the same effect, except that it has the virtue of lasting longer.

As we performed the ritual, we burned so much blessed incense that the place looked like it was on fire. Ironically, this case, which had begun with a figure who rose from a cloud of smoke, was ended in the swirling, sweet-smelling fumes of holy incense and the sound of fervent prayers, which made the house so hostile to the demonic that "the lady" was forced to disappear, this time for good. A feeling of peace pervaded the home, signaling that we'd succeeded in evicting the spirit. When the women and children returned from the church with Chris, they rejoiced that their ordeal was over.

The family's gratitude was humbling because we knew it wasn't us who should be thanked, but God, whose Son gave us authority over evil in His name, and all praise should be given to Him. We led the Villanovas in a prayer of thanksgiving to Him who is above all.

3

COPS AND SOUL ROBBERS

Even in my wildest boyhood fantasies, I never imagined I'd grow up to be a cop—or a demonologist. Actually, I considered both occupations pretty scary, though I loved to read about them. One of my earliest memories was going into the Queens Center Mall and seeing the book *The Exorcist*. I talked my mother into buying it for me and couldn't wait to get home and start reading it. I found the story extremely frightening. When the movie came out, I begged my parents to take me. Because of all the hype about it being the scariest film ever made, they debated if I was too young to see it but relented after quite a bit of pleading from me. They knew how much I loved horror movies.

Standing in line outside the Utopia Movie Theater on Union Turnpike, in Queens, I was filled with a mix of excitement and apprehension. I was the only kid my age in line, and that added to my fear. Throughout the film, I was riveted to my seat, but what sticks out in my mind and terrified me the most was when the eyes rolled back in the girl's head and only the whites were showing. I'm sure that most people's vision of what demonology is all about came from that movie: Mine certainly did—until I participated in real exorcisms, years later, and learned that only in the imagination of Hollywood screenwriters do people's heads spin around. And although I've heard of people levitating during the ritual, I have yet to see it happen myself. All that revolting green vomit was more Hollywood hype, but I know of cases where possessed people have vomited stranger things than that—such as worms or nails—during an exorcism.

That night, after seeing the movie I lay in bed with the lights turned out, scared shitless being all by myself, and remember my father calling to see if I was all right. When he heard the sound of my voice, he knew I wasn't, and told me to come and sleep with him. What a relief! I particularly appreciated that kindness from my father because he was a strict disciplinarian with a quick temper—a trait I've inherited myself, and struggle to control. My dad and I also have the same name, so my mother, Lillian, called him "big Ralph" and me "little Ralph," even after I reached my full size of five foot ten and 200 pounds.

My mom was an easygoing woman who always had a smile on her face and liked to laugh and joke around. That made her popular as a beautician, and customers flocked to our kitchen in Flushing, Queens, every Saturday to get haircuts. I would eat my oatmeal surrounded by the cloying smell of hair spray, which I hated, and wish she'd get some other job.

Although we lived in a mostly Jewish neighborhood, my parents were Catholics. I wasn't a particularly devout kid myself, even though I was an altar boy. I trembled throughout the first mass I served, terrified I'd somehow screw up and embarrass my mom and dad. Over the years my parents never pushed me to go to mass, saying they didn't want to pressure me into religion, but thought I should make up my own mind. I got a good feeling from the old-fashioned church we attended, and sometimes went there at lunchtime to sit in a pew and enjoy the silence and warm protection I felt there. That church was a refuge during turbulent times in my youth—and I got quite angry when I went back there a few years ago and saw its beauty had been destroyed by an ugly, misguided renovation.

While my dad didn't push God on me, his fondest dream was that I would become a professional baseball player. By the time I was three, he was putting a bat in my hand and teaching me how to hit. I quickly came to share this passion, and devoted every spare second to the game. I attended Queen of Peace Parochial School and played baseball for the Catholic Youth Organization every April. The rest of the time I played in pickup games after school; in the summer, I was out on the field with my bat from sunup to sundown, just for the fun of it.

As I got a little older, I got involved with a street gang, the Falcon Boys. Compared to the gangs I see now as a cop, ours was almost laughably tame. We never shot or stabbed anybody—and didn't even carry weapons. Sometimes we'd get drunk and have fistfights with another local gang or get into some minor mischief around the neighborhood. I was afraid to take it any further than that, because my dad took me aside one day and said, "If the cops ever bring you home, I'll break both your legs!" Being the kind of guy he was, I saw no reason to doubt him. His guidance was more powerful than any peer pressure, so even though my friends and I were a bunch of obnoxious little punks, I never got in any real trouble. In fact, thanks to my father's warning, I was scared witless every time I saw a policeman!

Although I wasn't much of a student—and certainly was no intellectual—I was an avid reader. When I was thirteen, I found a bookstore where I could get used books for a quarter apiece, and I eagerly devoured everything I could get my hands on about police work and the occult. When I heard the owner of the store telling another customer that he was going to the police academy, I thought he was incredibly lucky to be a cop chasing bad guys, just as I'd seen in the movies. At night I'd sit in front of the TV and watch cop shows, but every Saturday night it was *Creature Feature* and *Thriller Theater* for me. While I couldn't get enough of these shows, they frightened my little sister Lisa, who always left the room when they were on. Though my young mind didn't understand everything I was reading and seeing, I knew that some of the horror stories must be true.

My favorite books were about a pair of real-life psychic researchers named Ed and Lorraine Warren, who have been investigating the supernatural since the late 1940s. This couple, founders of the New England Society for Psychic Research in Connecticut, became internationally famous in 1972, when they were asked to investigate bizarre phenomena at West Point, the U.S. Military Academy. An Army major there complained that a general's residence on the property appeared to be haunted: His family often found that someone—or something—had rifled through their belongings or stolen valuable objects, yet no intruder could be found. A wet spot on a kitchen cutting board refused to dry, no matter what was done about the dampness; and an invisible force kept tearing the sheets off one of the beds.

Using her psychic ability, Lorraine inspected the building and detected several spirits. In one bedroom, she clairvoyantly felt the presence of President John F. Kennedy, to the amazement of onlookers who knew that he had slept there. In another room, her mind's eye saw a bossy female ghost that she identified as the culprit in these mysterious happenings. She learned later that General MacArthur's mother, well known for her extremely dictatorial personality, had ruled as lady of the house between the general's marriages.

She also got a mental picture of someone else, a very angry African American man in a nineteenth-century Army uniform, strangely bare of military braid and emblems. This struck the major and his aides as improbable, since they knew of no black man at West Point during that era. The general, however, did some digging and discovered that an African American soldier was tried for murder at West Point around the turn of the century. Although he was acquitted, Lorraine felt sure that his anger and guilt over the trial was what made his ghost linger at West Point.

That was exciting stuff to me, but I was even more mesmerized by another of the Warrens' cases, which took place in a Long Island suburb. Around Christmas of 1975, a young couple, George and Kathy Lutz, and their three small children, moved into a house they'd just bought. This house had a lurid history, since the oldest son of the previous owner had gotten up one night, grabbed his .35-caliber rifle, and slaughtered his mother, father, two brothers, and two sisters in their sleep. Within a month of moving in, the Lutzes fled their new home in abject terror, describing a savage supernatural assault that later became infamous as *The Amityville Horror*.

Although I would have been content to while away my time playing baseball and reading these hair-raising but incredibly fascinating books, when I got to the third year of high school, my dad told me I should think about what to do with my life, should I not become a pro ballplayer. I said, "That's easy, I'll become a cop." My picture of what police work was all about came mainly from cop shows on TV: I imagined nonstop action as I saved lives, solved mysteries, and made one spectacular arrest after another. After my high school graduation, I enrolled in the John Jay College of Criminal Justice, mainly to play baseball for the college. If the major leagues somehow decided they could live without me, I'd at least be learning about law enforcement. And since I'm now wearing a badge, not a baseball mitt, it's not hard to guess how things ended up.

In 1984 my childhood interest in cop life turned into what I now call "the Job," when I entered the New York City Police Academy. I quickly discovered real-life police work wasn't anything like TV shows: It's hours of boredom, riding around in a patrol car looking for trouble—and responding to radio runs—with spurts of pure adrenaline and stress when you suddenly get a 10–13 call (officer needs assistance), flip on the sirens, and speed to the crime. On the way, your body gets pumped for action, so you're ready to charge through a blazing gun battle, if need be, and collar the perps. Half the time, however, the emergency is over when you get there, and it's back to cruising the streets while your racing heartbeat slowly drops to normal.

A year later, as a twenty-three-year-old housing cop, I was overwhelmed by terror in broad daylight after reading *The Haunted*, a book about a family under diabolical seige. Here I was a police officer who'd faced down armed perps in public housing projects, and I was scared to death in my own bedroom imagining the living hell these people had endured. The book confirmed what I've known for years: These aren't just stories. Not only do ghosts exist, but there are spirits that are pure evil, which I now refer to as demons or the demonic. I remember thinking that I'd never want any of this to happen to me and had absolutely no desire to get involved with investigating this stuff.

Initially attracted by the action-filled aspects of police work, I began rethinking my life after being shot in the line of duty in 1986. I was off-duty at the time, looking out the window of my mother's apartment, when I saw a guy running down the street with a box under his arm. Call it a cop's instinct, but I knew something was wrong, so I strapped on my gun and went down to investigate. Then the guy started zigzagging down the street, the typical body language for a 10–30, police radio jargon for a robbery. I started running too, sure some poor soul—probably the nice store owner down the block who'd been a frequent target of bandits—had been relieved of his valuables.

With all the running I did during my baseball playing, I caught the guy pretty quickly. The box tumbled to the ground, and jewelry spilled out. That was enough probable cause for me, so I drew my gun and identified myself as a police officer. The guy seemed meek and was shaking all over, but he suddenly grabbed my gun and got a round off.

Although I took a pretty good hit in the arm, and blood was everywhere, I managed to slam the guy against a chain-link fence and tried to wrestle my gun away from him. I knew if I didn't, his next shot might be the last sound I ever heard. After a lot of screaming on his part, and bleeding on mine, I got my weapon back, but the guy got away. Somebody called 911, and more cops and an ambulance showed up in no time. I gave the anticrime unit (plainclothes cops) the best description I could of the perp—who was arrested two weeks later, and pled guilty to the attempted murder of a police officer— then let the paramedics put me on a stretcher.

With all that blood on the pavement, you'd think I'd had a major brush with death. Luckily, the wound turned out not to be that serious: The scar is now hidden under a tattoo reproducing a photo of my daughter Daniella's face, at age three. I also have a portrait of my other daughter, Christina, on the same arm. I love having pictures of my kids there because no matter how old they get, I'll always remember them as my little girls.

While I was at the hospital, the police chaplain came in case I needed the Last Rites. Talking to that priest made me feel guilty: I'd let my Catholic faith lapse after my days as an altar boy and rarely attended church or received communion anymore. In those days, religion just didn't seem that important or relevant to me. I was working in a violent, dangerous environment that seemed to have little to do with God. My first assignment, Operation Pressure Point, landed me in Manhattan's drug-infested Lower East Side to combat street crimes. There I saw "demons" in human flesh, predators who spent their days and nights robbing, raping, and killing their fellow citizens. Of course there were plenty of good people in this inner-city neighborhood too, but I rarely met them unless they'd been the victims of some ghastly crime.

People who are skeptical about religion often ask how I can believe in God at all. They see that the world around them is full of corruption and violence, and say, "What kind of God would allow evil to happen?" Even when my faith was at a low point, I never thought this way. What these people don't understand is free will. God doesn't interfere with people's decisions in life, because He doesn't want robots: He wants us to *choose* Him. But there's a stumbling block along the way—and that's the Devil. When people deny the existence of God, how can they possibly believe in His most potent adversary?

But if anything, all this horror shows just how real the Devil, and the evil he inspires, is. It wears away at even the most devout cop: Alcohol abuse, divorce, and suicide are common among my fellow officers—and on every police force in the world.

Although I felt good about helping get crooks off the streets—first in the Lower East Side, then in the slums of the South Bronx and Brownsville, Brooklyn (East New York), and now as a sergeant in the Bronx again, where I work the midnight-to-8:00 A.M. shift in the Forty-sixth Precinct—the savagery never stops. Although the Four-Six–"the Alamo," as this precinct is known by cops—is only 1.32 square miles in size, it's one of the busiest and most dangerous in the world. More than 118,000 people—nearly two-thirds of them Hispanic, one-third African American, with about 2 percent white and 1 percent Asian—live in this crowded inner-city area, which is also home to 1,950 violent parolees.

In a typical year, we investigate 32 murders—roughly one every eleven days—87 rapes, 682 violent assaults, 870 robberies, 1,022 burglaries, and 2,234 car crashes. Our cops also help 4,472 sick and injured people, respond to 76,789 radio runs (911 calls)—and make 10,353 felony arrests. Even in New York City, that volume of calls is incredible: When our seven sector cars turn out for patrol at midnight, at least 19 jobs usually await each one. As a sergeant, I have to respond to every serious call that comes over the radio. It's my job to decide whether to make the location a crime scene and whom to detain for questioning and whom to release. I decide whether we need detectives, helicopters to chase suspects, an evidence collection team, the accident investigation squad, the canine unit, or a whole array of other specialized resources.

To give an idea of what that's like, here are a few cases I handled this week: The first call came over the radio as a 10–53 (car accident). "One man down, likely," Central added, meaning that there was a victim who was likely to die. At the scene, we reconstructed what happened: After smashing into a parked taxicab at such high speed that one passenger was flung through a window and landed eighty-three feet away, the driver sped away, utterly indifferent to the fate of his friend. We arrested the callous son of a bitch later that night. Although the injured man was lying in pools of blood and brain fluid when we arrived, he was still alive when the ambulance came.

So was the assault victim in another case, who'd been stabbed in the heart during a dispute over twenty dollars.

Another night I got a call that's every parent's nightmare: A baby wasn't breathing. Even though we all knew it was too late when we saw the one-month-old boy, paramedics spent long, desperate, and ultimately futile minutes trying to breathe life back into him. What upset and infuriated me the most was that this little boy didn't have to die. He'd be cooing in his crib right now, if his parents had put him to bed on his back—the sleep position that lowers the risk of crib death by 50 percent—instead of his stomach.

The next day I caught a homicide where the victim had no face. His features had been totally obliterated with one blast of an assault rifle, except for an eyeball, which dangled from his head. What was left of his brain was still throbbing inside his shattered skull. I'd never seen anything like it—and neither had the paramedics. We found bits of brain and skull fragments splattered on a sidewalk twenty-five feet away.

Even the animals are violent where I work. Earlier this

month I got a call about a berserk pit bull. From the size of the crowd at the scene—and the screams I heard—I knew something really bad had happened. We pushed our way through the horrified spectators, some of them little kids, and found the dog growling furiously as it shook something small, limp, and bloody in its mouth. The victim was a tiny Chihuahua, still wearing its little pink leash, that the pit bull had attacked and killed right in front of the pet's shrieking owner. As a dog lover myself, I felt awful about the whole thing.

The constant brutality I saw after joining the police force had a corrosive effect—I felt myself becoming brutal too. After having been shot once, I was all too ready to get rough with a mugger who resisted arrest or a batterer who got in my face when I showed up at his door to stop him from beating his wife or kids to bloody pulps. I got angry too easily in these situations, and didn't like what I was starting to see in myself. I didn't want to become one of those sadistic cops you read about in the headlines after some awful act of brutality.

To relax on my days off—and to put the projects out of my mind—I liked to get together with friends for a few drinks at Kate Cassidy's, a neighborhood bar in Queens. On one of these nights, even though I was with a date, my eye was drawn to a dark-haired beauty sitting at a table in the back. Unfortunately, she had a date too, and I didn't get to talk to her. I couldn't get her out of my mind the next day, and asked my friends if they knew her name. No one did, but a few days later I was in Gantry's, another Queens bar, and saw another tall, gorgeous brunette. I spotted her immediately: I guess you could say it was love at first sight, or second sight, since I realized, as I subtly made my way over to her side of the bar to start a conversation, this was the same woman I was drawn to at the other bar. She'd just changed her hairdo.

Once we got to talking, I discovered I'd met my mirror image in female form, because twenty-one-year-old Jennifer Lanfranco was every bit as hot-tempered, outspoken, and stubborn as I am. That was exactly what I wanted in a woman—someone who would stand up to me as an equal, instead of meekly saying "Yes, Ralph" all the time. I was also delighted to learn that she was a film buff too and worked for a prop rental company that's said to have supplied the bed used in *The Exorcist*. When we got married, a year later, I suggested we buy the bed, but Jen vetoed the idea as bad luck. I didn't argue with her—our relationship was already stormy enough.

It was also in 1990—the same year I married Jen and we had our first child—that I felt the call to enter what I now call "the Work." Jen and I were at the mall, shopping for baby clothes for our new daughter Christina, when I spotted a bookstore. Well, I can't pass a bookstore without stopping in and seeing what's new. Knowing of my fascination with the occult, Jen pointed out a title she thought would interest me: *Satan's Harvest*. When I saw that the book was about demonic possession—and that Ed and Lorraine Warren had investigated the case—I grabbed it and headed to the cash register. At home, I couldn't put the book down, and read it cover to cover that very day.

Swept up by this book, which sharpened the spiritual hunger I'd been feeling, I called the Warrens. I don't know why I waited until this particular point in my life, after having read about these people for years without ever picking up the phone. Perhaps I wasn't ready to do God's work until I had the foundation of a wife and family to make me stronger.

Although I thought I'd lost my faith, it was just below the surface without my realizing it. The Work was just waiting for me to grab it—or maybe it grabbed me. I'm not really sure. But I knew I could no longer live without it.

Lorraine answered the phone, and I told her how much I admired her courage. She asked what type of job I had. When I told her that I was a cop in the South Bronx, she said, "And you admire *my* courage? I think I admire yours!" Extremely excited to be speaking to someone I'd been reading about all these years, I told her I'd like to get involved in the Work, and she gently inquired if I truly understood what that meant. "Lots of people think they'd like to do this work—until they actually try it," she warned. I felt I was more than up for it but wanted to take the classes she and her husband held at their house. We talked a long time, and I was impressed that such a well-known person was so nice and normal. I asked her to send me whatever literature they had about their work and gave her my address.

All of sudden, she sounded excited and said, "Hold on Ralph, this is strange." She got back on the phone and said one of her investigators was a man named Joe Forrester who also had a law enforcement background and lived in Queens. When she gave me the address, I just about fell off my sofa, because it was only two blocks away from my apartment—on the same block where my wife, Jen, had grown up. With all the millions of people in New York, what are the chances of two people calling the Warrens from practically the same block? Lorraine and I were both amazed and felt this was no coincidence, but God's destiny.

More enthusiastic than ever, I called Joe. We talked for quite a while, then he met me on the corner of his block. He was a large man—over six feet tall—and carried himself with military confidence. I learned later that he was a Vietnam War hero, who earned a Purple Heart when he was wounded in combat. We eyed each other cautiously, because Joe knew I was a cop with a gun—and could be some lunatic for all he knew—while I had my doubts about him, since he worked for Legal Aid as a polygraph examiner and might be a raving liberal.

I figured we wouldn't get along at all, because I'm out there busting crooks while he's helping to defend them. That made him the enemy in my book, until I learned that he's an extremely upfront guy who has no problem saying "This dirtbag is guilty" if that's what his tests show. He's the same way off the job: From so many years of evaluating people's truthfulness, he's developed a built-in bullshit meter that almost never fails to detect a liar. He also has very strong opinions about what's right and what's wrong and isn't shy about expressing them. If he likes you, he can be the kindest friend you'll ever have; and if not, watch out! Joe's not a man who forgets a grudge easily, but due to his strong Catholic faith, he will put it aside.

We made fast friends right there on the corner, though, and he later became my partner in the Work. He gave me some holy water, a crucifix, and a copy of Father Malachi Martin's brilliant book, *Hostage to the Devil*, the best I've ever read on the subject of demonic possession. Realizing what a devout Catholic he was, I was ashamed to admit that I rarely set foot in church—and hadn't yet had my three-month-old baby baptized! I promised myself—and Joe—that I'd have Christina christened as soon as possible, so she'd be protected from whatever evil I might encounter in my new vocation.

Not only does he have a powerful faith in God, which has inspired me to become a better Catholic too, but of all the people I've met since becoming involved in this work, Joe has taught me the most about the occult. Since we both have forceful personalities, however, we had some terrible arguments—and have sometimes stopped speaking to each other for a couple of months—but true friendship always pulled us back together. I blame a lot of this on our work: If there's one thing the demonic love to do, it's stir up discord.

When the Warrens came to New York to give a seminar, I went with Joe, Jen, and a priest friend of Joe's. Both in their sixties, the couple looked more like kindly grandparents than experts on the occult. Lorraine was thin, with lively eyes and brown hair swept up into a bun, while Ed was big with silvery hair, a quick wit, and down-to-earth manner. Their lecture was full of the stuff I'd read about—ghosts, demons, possessed people, and exorcisms—but they'd actually witnessed these phenomena, and had photos, videotapes, and recordings to prove it. Afterwards they invited us to their house in Connecticut for coffee, cake, and a tour of their occult museum.

Attached to Ed's office, this collection of strange and sinister objects from the Warrens' cases is plastered with warnings not to touch any of the diabolically charged items gathered there. This room was literally chilling, as it is always unnaturally cold, even in the summer. The reason, Ed explained, is that these objects draw the heat from the room and use it for negative energy. If you touch one of them, you'll mix your aura with evil and open yourself to problems with the demonic. It's to safeguard innocent people from diabolical assault that the Warrens keep this collection locked away in their home. It's also visible evidence of the reality of evil—and its devastating impact on people's lives. Should any of these objects be destroyed, Ed added, its cursed force might rebound back to the person who originally owned it, putting him or her in mortal jeopardy. Jen and I considered ourselves thoroughly warned and made sure to keep our hands safely at our sides.

Each object had a story: There were human skulls that have served as "chalices of ecstasy" for black magic blood-drinking ceremonies, crucifixes melted or shattered by evil forces, handwritten pacts with the Devil, Ouija boards, mysterious amulets, a coffin a possessed man used to sleep in every night, and rocks that fell from the sky and pounded a family's house like hail from Hell. Some of the items looked so innocent that they seemed strangely out of place in such a collection, such as a large Raggedy Ann doll seated in a wooden cabinet. Yet when you looked closer, the doll's hands were arranged around a simple wooden crucifix.

These same soft, mitten-shaped hands had once been animated by a demon—and made a bloody claw mark on a man's chest, then tried to strangle him. When the Warrens subdued the doll with holy water and brought it to their home, it sometimes moved from one room to another, with Ed's easy chair being its favorite resting spot. A few times the doll even brought a "friend" into the house—a black cat. No ordinary cat, this creature would prowl Ed's office looking around carefully, as if it were spying on him, then slowly vanish. Unlike the Cheshire Cat in *Alice's Adventures in Wonderland*, where the body dematerialized until nothing remained but its grin, this cat faded away headfirst, leaving its sharp claws for last.

Another deceptively harmless-looking toy was a plastic model of Godzilla. Having built such models as a kid, I wondered about its origin. It turned out that a possessed boy had built and played with it—a case the Warrens wrote about in their book *The Devil in Connecticut*. Although an inanimate object can't be possessed, it can be manipulated by the demonic or give off evil energy. That's just what happened to this toy: Although it wasn't motorized, it began to walk across the boy's room, and a voice spoke not from it but from somewhere around it. The following year I experienced the strange powers of this toy myself. One day as Ed and I were standing in the museum, discussing a case I was working on that had some parallels to that of the Connecticut boy, the model's head exploded right in front of my eyes. With a loud *pop*, the reptile's head was violently propelled right off the green plastic body. It shattered into two pieces that landed on the floor with a thump.

Whenever you discuss a particular case, you give recognition to the demonic spirit connected with that case. At times, that can cause the satanic force to be drawn to you and reveal itself through strange phenomena. That's exactly what happened the next day, when I had the first personal supernatural experience of my entire life. After I entered the Work, Joe had given me a St. Benedict medal—commemorating a saint who used the sign of the cross to perform many miracles and had tremendous power over the demonic. I have hundreds of these medals—which I get from the Benedictine Mission House in Nebraska, and use in all my cases—but this one was very special to me, because I wore it on my very first case and have never taken it off since. Among its many pious purposes are warding off dangers from the Devil, protecting people who are tormented by evil spirits, and providing relief to those afflicted by bodily ills or natural disasters. On the back are Latin words reading "Begone Satan! Suggest not to me thy vain things. The cup thou profferest me is evil; drink then thy poison."

As I was changing out of my uniform at EOT (end of tour) the next day, I felt for my medal as a matter of habit, but it was gone. The chain was still around my neck and there was no break in the soldered link that had held the medal. I couldn't understand how it could have gotten lost. The medal had been under my T-shirt, which was covered by a form-fitting bullet-proof vest. I checked inside my shirt and even the cuffs of my pants, in case it had worked its way down there. I hadn't been involved in any fights or chases: It was a very mellow day for the projects. I searched my patrol car but came up empty. At home, I reluctantly put on one of my other St. Benedict medals. Before going to bed, I prayed I'd find my favorite medal.

The next morning when I was in the bathroom getting ready for work, I heard what sounded like a gunshot. It was faint and off in the distance, but being a cop I thought I should note the time, in case a crime was being committed. Just at that moment something struck me in the neck and slid down my back. There on the floor was a St. Benedict medal. I grabbed my chain to see if the new medal had fallen off, but it was still there. When I realized it wasn't that medal, the hair on the back of my neck stood up and an ungodly chill ran through my body. I knew then that the demonic was involved: The sound of the gunshot was the evil force sending my medal back into this plane of existence. The spirit that took my medal and sent it back was a very powerful devil, because only the strongest demons can manipulate blessed objects. The medal has never left my neck since.

I was really shaken by what had happened. I went into the bedroom where Jen was sleeping and called her name. Even in sleep, she could sense the distress in my voice and leapt out of bed. I told her what had happened, and she couldn't come up with any natural explanation for it either. Although neither of us knew it at the time, this was just the start of harassment by the demonic that we've endured since I started in the Work.

Although nothing unsettling happened to Jen at the museum at that first visit, she pronounced it "creepy"—saying she was petrified to be around these things and never wanted to return there. I, however, was intrigued by what I'd heard and seen. Soon I became a regular at the Warrens' Monday night classes for psychic researchers and spent hours soaking up the lore of demonology. During these lectures Ed talked about the hundreds of cases he's handled over the years and the frightening, violent, and inhumanly cruel phenomena he'd witnessed firsthand. But the best times of all were when Ed and I would get together, just the two of us, and he'd tell me things that weren't in the books I'd read or relate some of the incredibly fascinating experiences he had in his long life.

I realized that investigating the demonic is a lot like police work: You've got to arm yourself, not with a gun and badge but with prayer, holy water, and a crucifix; you've got to examine the "crime scene" for clues, assess the credibility of the witnesses, interview terrified victims, keep meticulous case notes, and, finally, try to bust the perp—before he strikes again. This particular perp was more dangerous than any gangbanger, crackhead, or killer I'd ever meet on a slum street: the Devil himself. My work on the Job was ideal preparation for "the Work."

I also saw that I couldn't go up against Satan without improving my relationship with God. From the moment I first spoke with Lorraine, then met Joe on the street corner, my faith started to grow, and it continues to get stronger each day. It's true I found my faith through the Work, but it is my faith that *keeps* me in this work, not the other way around. It just goes to prove what I firmly believe: The Work is about dealing with the most negative force imaginable, but God never lets evil happen without something positive coming out of it. And faith is the ultimate positive: It is in every person—all you have to do is a little searching, and it has the power to change your life.

Through the Work, I became friendly with an extraordinary man of truly awesome faith, Father Malachi Martin. Along with literally writing the book on demonic possession, in his bestseller *Hostage to the Devil*, Father Martin was one of God's great warriors and had performed exorcisms all over the world long before I was born. Although he was a renowned Jesuit priest who spoke eight languages, had helped translate the Dead Sea Scrolls, and had been a close confidant to Cardinal Bea and Pope John XXIII in the 1960s, he always treated me like an equal. Like Bishop McKenna, he was so pious that he seemed to have no ego at all, just a profound reverence for God that overshadowed his own brilliance.

Yet, as I discovered the first time we met, over dinner at Sparks, a famous New York City steak house, this thin, scholarly Jesuit was a warm and worldly man, with a gift for putting people at ease. When I hesitated about ordering a drink, not sure if it would be proper to indulge in alcohol in the presence of such a holy man, he sensed my dilemma and said, in his thick Irish brogue, "Go ahead, Ralph, have a Jack Daniel's—on me." He slapped a five-dollar bill down on the table, and we spent the next two hours chatting away like old friends.

A couple of weeks later I drove him to Connecticut, where he was giving a lecture. For three hours I drove along the dark, winding road, drinking in this great man's remarkable knowledge about the Work. It was a great experience.

"Tell me, Ralph, what do *you* get out of an exorcism?" he asked. We'd just parked at my favorite rest stop on the Merritt Parkway, where they have the best coffee in the world, and got out to stretch our legs after the long drive from Manhattan.

I was a little confused by his question and replied, "I don't get anything out of it." He nodded his head, and I continued, "I am totally drained, physically, mentally, and spiritually."

"Good," he said. "That's exactly what you should be getting out of it."

More perplexed than ever, I asked what he meant.

"You don't ever come in such close proximity to evil without losing some of your humanity," he explained. "The demonic take a piece of that away, because of the hatred they have for you."

"Will I ever get it back?"

He had a big smile on his face, as he answered, "It's like money in the bank when you go to your final reward."

"Father, all I want is a peaceful life."

He studied me for a moment, then said, "Sorry, Ralph, but that is one thing you'll never have."

"Gee, Father, thanks a lot," I said.

"There's something important God wants you to do," he explained. "On what scale, I can't tell you, but when your time comes, you'll find out." His smile was gone, and I saw the sorrow deep inside this man.

Curious about his book, which describes five twentieth-century cases of possession, I asked if he was one of the exorcists in the book. He nodded yes. I longed to know which of these harrowing exorcisms he'd done, but there was such indescribable pain in his eyes that I couldn't ask.

No longer looking at me, but at something far away, he suddenly spoke in an achingly sad voice. "Ralph, I got my ass handed to me in Cairo."

We were silent for a while. I waited for him to say more, and when he didn't, I wondered what fearsome and mysterious peril he'd encountered there. In his book, Father Martin calls exorcism "grisly work . . . [with] the mordant traits of nightmare . . . a one-on-one confrontation, personal and bitter, with pure evil . . . a dreadful and irreparable pillage of [the priest's] deepest self." For the first time I realized that this white-haired old exorcist had risked much and lost even more, battling Satan and his forces of doom over the years. Yet through his painful sacrifices, he'd freed many suffering souls from the Devil's grip and piled up great riches in Heaven.

But this man's love for God was strong, and it was evident in the way he spoke of his experiences in life, the good and the bad. The lecture he gave later that night was a big success. Every person in the room, including me, was riveted and listening intently to what he related.

When this great man died in July of 1999, at the age of seventy-eight, I deeply mourned his loss but felt sure he was rejoicing to be with God at last. As he wrote in his book, the best epitaph for an exorcist is the loving words of Jesus Himself: "Greater love than this no man hath: that a man lay down his life for his friend." Piece by painful piece, exorcism by exorcism, Father Martin had done just that. I lift a glass to his memory.

4

THE HOUSE BY THE GRAVEYARD

As graveyards go, Machpelah is one of my favorites. Located in a sprawling 200-acre cluster of cemeteries not too far from my old apartment in Glendale, Queens, it holds the tomb of the legendary magician Harry Houdini, who died on Halloween in 1926. I've visited his grave many times: It has a massive, weathered marble headstone, surrounded by stone benches and a beautiful statue of a weeping woman. There I like to think of the fascinating secrets the master of illusions took to his grave—his amazing and never-duplicated escapes from straitjackets, shackles, and a sealed coffin that was lowered underwater for an hour until he burst free. During his lifetime, Houdini also predicted that he'd pull off the greatest escape of all—and come back from beyond the grave.

Each year on Halloween, devoted fans gather by his cemetery plot, which is guarded by two unfortunate police rookies. These officers have to stand there, freezing their butts off all night long, until dawn breaks and the disappointed crowd disperses. Although Houdini remains locked in his final resting place so far, I don't hold it against him. Actually, I greatly admire him for his lifelong crusade against spiritual charlatans, whom he gleefully exposed at every opportunity.

This cemetery has also figured in two of my occult cases. In the first one, I conducted an unofficial investigation—not as a policeman, but as a private citizen—after learning that several graves had been desecrated. This wasn't the usual cemetery crime, where teenaged punks topple tombstones or spray-paint hate graffiti in an ethnic section of the graveyard. Instead, corpses had been disinterred and stripped of their skulls. So brazen were these grave robbers that they had even backed a pickup truck into the cemetery, attached chains to its bumper, and used them to rip the doors off sealed mausoleums, all the better to get at the bones inside.

Given the likely occult overtones of these ghoulish acts, I did some digging of my own—and soon identified the perp, a Brooklyn Palo Mayombe priest. The Palo Mayombe religion, originally from Africa, spread to parts of Brazil, Cuba, and Suriname, and worships spirits of the dead. In Spanish, "palo" means "branch" or "tree" and "mayombe" means "black witch." In this cult, the priest is called a *ngangelero* (the first "n" is silent) or is frequently known as Tata Nkisi, and is as much feared as Christians fear the Devil. Ngangeleros deal with black magic and destruction, and their satanic practices are known as the left-handed path. In one of its more gruesome rituals, a human skull is put into a caldron called a *nganga*, along with dirt, knives, guns, the cadaver of a black dog, scorpions, herbs, and other objects believed to have mystical powers, then used to conjure up black magic. The spells of this particular priest were in such demand that he was able to pay his accomplices $2,000 a skull—and he may remain active, since he has never been arrested.

This type of magic, which is practiced secretly, sometimes surfaces in New York City police cases, most recently in August of 2000, when one of its practitioners died under bizarre circumstances. When Manhattan cops went to the dead woman's apartment, they found a ghastly collection of human remains, including the body of a perfectly formed newborn girl floating in a jar of formaldehyde. The baby's tiny feet had been inked for footprints, presumably at the hospital where she was born, and her umbilical cord still had its medical clamp. A ritual caldron contained the skull of another baby—coated with blood, decomposing flesh, and candle wax—while the floor of the apartment was strewn with human bones and cemetery dirt.

After learning that fellow cops had handled these gruesome occult objects to voucher them as evidence—without taking the proper religious precautions—I became so concerned that I decided to call the Three-Six precinct and offer my help. These men had mixed their auras with dangerous evil and could experience disturbing aftereffects: nightmares, unexplained weight loss or health problems, or even demonic manifestations in their homes.

But even though I'm a cop myself, how was I going to explain all this to someone on the phone? I knew I'd be running the risk of being ridiculed or thought a lunatic for my beliefs. Even knowing this, I felt I had to reach out to these men, who had no understanding of evil incarnate—but didn't have to believe in it to be affected by it.

When I spoke to the lieutenant at the Three-Six precinct, I could tell he was a real hard-ass. As soon as I said I was calling about the case and identified myself as Sergeant Sarchie of the Four-Six, he got sarcastic. "I didn't know you guys in the South Bronx could read," he jeered.

Well, I hadn't been a cop all these years without learning how to talk to guys like this, so I joked back, "I was just transferred here, so maybe the illiteracy hasn't rubbed off yet." I explained that I'd been involved in investigating the supernatural for many years and wanted to offer my help if any of the cops who'd been in the apartment experienced any problems afterward.

"Are you jerking me around?" he asked. "I've been getting prank calls about this case all day." *Great*, I thought, *this guy thinks I'm off my rocker!*

"I'm very serious," I emphasized. "I don't want cops to get hurt by something they don't understand."

There are guys on the New York City police force who have heard about what I do and think I'm nuts. I just tell them, "Think what you like, but if you're home and objects start flying around the room, the first call you'll make is to me!" Once these people get to know me, however, they realize I'm *not* a nut job, and start asking questions like "What is this stuff you do? How did you get into that Work?" Other cops will say "I believe in the Devil, but you're crazy to get involved with that shit. It's dangerous!"

Hearing the sincerity in my voice, the lieutenant changed his tone. I could tell he was starting to wonder, just a little bit, if there *was* some danger. He thanked me for calling and took down my number, saying he'd like to have it on hand, "just in case."

My other investigation took place in a beautiful two-family house right next to Machpelah cemetery. It had been vacant for some time before Angelo, the owner of an Italian delicatessen in my old neighborhood, rented the basement apartment. A couple of weeks later I ran into Angelo's dad, Sal, who told me in a low voice that his son was scared in his new home. "He thinks it's haunted," the old man whispered, looking around anxiously to make sure no gossipy neighbors had overheard this. I asked what had been going on. "I don't like to talk about that spirit stuff you're involved in," Sal said, quickly making the sign of the cross over himself. "But Angelo believes it might be something like that."

Yeah, right, I thought. *This guy moves into a house by the graveyard, and now he thinks he has a ghost. Sounds like he's been watching a few too many horror movies!* Still, I was curious, and told the old man that if Angelo continued having trouble, he should give me a call. No sooner did I get home than the phone was ringing. Sure enough, it was Angelo, sounding really spooked.

"Can you come right away?" Much as I wanted to help, I had to disappoint him, at least temporarily, because I never go off on a case without getting all the facts first, then praying on the matter. I did a quick interview over the phone to get a feel for the problem, if there was one.

Angelo said it had all begun very subtly: "The night I moved in, I was woken up by scratching noises. It sounded like it was coming from the ceiling over my bed. I figured it was mice, maybe even rats. I didn't think it was a big deal until I saw how my kitten, Snowball, was reacting. All the hair on her back and tail stood straight on end, and she started hissing," he explained. "Next, she began to move sideways, in an eerie-looking, unnatural dance. It was the damnedest thing I've ever seen. I've owned cats all my life, and none of them ever did anything like that before!"

He grabbed his baseball bat and went upstairs to check for rodents, but found nothing out of the ordinary. This went on for several nights, always at the same time: 3:00 A.M. When I heard that, the hairs on the back of my neck also began to prickle, since that's the "witching hour," a prime time for demonic activity. Not only do satanic powers often do things in threes, to show contempt for the Holy Trinity, but their terrorist strikes frequently occur at 3:00 A.M. This is another insult to God, whose son Jesus Christ died on the cross at 3:00 P.M. The demonic will do the opposite of anything holy, so they like to attack at exactly the opposite hour—with supernatural phenomena you might call miracles in reverse.

I was also intrigued by the kitten's behavior, since I've found that pets have a sixth sense for demonic activity, just as they do for impending earthquakes and other natural disasters. I've seen cases where diabolical phenomena will get all the dogs in the neighborhood howling. Evil spirits can also attack pets—animals are God's creatures—so I always make sure to put a St. Benedict medal around the neck of each pet in the house before an exorcism begins, to keep them safe from evil forces.

While Angelo's story sounded suspiciously satanic, I wasn't ready to call in the troops yet, and urged him to continue. In a gravelly baritone he added, "A few nights later I heard the scratching again. That wasn't all—this time I also heard footsteps, heavy steps like a man's. First they were in the driveway, crunching on the ice. Then I heard them coming closer and closer, until it sounded like somebody was right outside. Then they stopped right outside my window," which was level with the ground, since his apartment was in the basement. Again he grabbed his bat, ready to do battle with whatever was out there, but he found no one. His deep voice broke a little as he added, "There were *no* tracks in the fresh snow! Absolutely none!"

Perplexed, he went back inside—and heard the noise again. "That's when I really got nervous. Now the footsteps were *inside* the house, like somebody was walking upstairs. But those apartments were empty, and I was the only one living here!

The ghost—or whatever it was—paced slowly from the rear of the apartment overhead to the front of the house, then it started running back and forth."

"How many times?" I asked, although I was already pretty sure I knew the answer.

"Three times, faster and faster," he said. "My heart was really pounding, I'll tell you." Double-locking every door and window, the deli owner finally went back to sleep. The eerie events didn't end there—the next night he heard a loud tapping coming from the hallway in his own apartment. He lay in bed listening to the sound but didn't bother to get his Louisville Slugger, knowing that even if he did get up, he'd find nothing.

Understandably, he didn't get much rest that night—or the next, when he was treated to thunderous poundings that practically made him jump out of his skin. This time he had to see what was going on, so he got his bat, turned on all the lights, and searched every inch of his apartment. What did he find? Absolutely nothing, of course.

About a week after Angelo moved into his apartment, other tenants arrived. A single guy took the second-floor apartment, and a few days later a young couple with a four-year-old son and new baby set up house on the first floor. At the risk of being thought crazy, Angelo felt he just had to ask his new neighbors if they'd noticed anything at all odd about the house. *Yes,* they said, *there's something very wrong here!* And when he told them he'd called a spiritual investigator, all agreed they wanted our help—right away, if possible.

The streets were covered with black ice, and a winter storm warning was in effect when Joe and I parked by the graveyard and headed for the house, with a bitterly cold wind at our backs, to wait for the rest of our team. Originally it was just the two of us handling cases, but we now had other investigators working with us. A year or so earlier the Warrens had come to New York to give a seminar. As always when they spoke, there was a big turnout and several people expressed interest in learning more. So with Ed and Lorraine's blessing, the New York City chapter of the New England Society for Psychic Research was born, with Joe and me as founders.

We held classes once a month in the basement of my home in Glendale, much to the consternation of my wife, Jen. She grew to dread those nights because scary things sometimes happened. Lights in our apartment would go on and off on their own. We were constantly buying new light bulbs because they burned out so fast. One night she had the same eerie experience Angelo did: She'd heard heavy footsteps coming up the creaky basement stairs. Thinking it was me bringing my video equipment upstairs after the class, she opened the door—and found no one there.

Understandably, she was very upset. "I don't like what these classes are drawing here," she said after I'd finished teaching—and she didn't calm down until I'd blessed our entire apartment with prayer and holy water. It troubled me also to have my wife harassed this way, but I felt God had provided this group of people for a reason. Not only could Joe and I teach others about the Work, but we also learned from our students, since they brought faith and fresh ideas to our cases. There are no handbooks on demonology, so we developed our techniques through trial and error. The students came from all walks of life—Millie was a school crossing guard, Dennis had a 7-Up delivery route, David was a bodyguard, and Fred was a doorman. Antonio and Vicki were a married couple who'd met while they were in the Army and now worked for a Manhattan lawyer. They both dressed in military-style camouflage clothing. These people came from all faiths; belief in God was our common bond.

We never forced anyone to get more involved than he or she wanted to. Some members of our group just came to the classes; and others assisted on our cases. Those who preferred to remain students rather than investigators were still an important part of our team because they supported us with their prayers. Some contributed in other ways too: Kathy, who worked for the Catholic Church, was too shy to go out on cases, but turned out to have unexpected psychic talent. Before we left for the graveyard case, she gave me a warning. "Be very careful," she said. "Somebody's going to get hit."

I run my cases like a police operation and enforce strict discipline. First, each investigator is expected to be in a state of grace when he or she accompanies Joe and me on cases. For a Catholic, that means having gone to confession. While our church only suggests monthly confession, I didn't feel that was enough and made a rule that investigators also go to weekly confession, if possible, before going up against the demonic. People of other faiths were to perform whatever rituals their religion prescribes to be in the best possible relationship with God. I also instructed people to perform a "black fast" before cases, where they spent three days eating very little and praying a lot.

"Basically, your job is to watch each other's back and do exactly what Joe and I tell you," I instructed the three student investigators who had volunteered to help with this case. Phil and Chris were father and son—and had joined the group along with Phil's wife, Rose—but the two men didn't look at all alike. The dad, the computer professional in our group, was heavyset with dark hair, while his teenaged son was very thin and fair, like his mother. Both had similar temperaments, however: They were enthusiastic, outgoing guys who made friends very quickly. I was impressed with how close they were: There was none of the tension you'd expect between a father and his adolescent son. Chris was a very good kid any man would be proud of.

Phil and Chris had been on cases before, but it was the first time for Tommy, a cop I worked with in East New York. We shared a passion for the martial arts and became friendly while training together. He was a wiry little guy who could move with astonishing speed. Although I'd never been on patrol with him, since we worked on different shifts, I'd heard he was very quick-witted and knew how to handle himself on the street. Since any cop who works in the ghetto has to be aggressive, I cautioned him that he wasn't to mix it up with anybody. "We may be met with force on this case," I told him. "If that happens, take the person down if you have to, but don't hurt him."

The final member of our group, who arrived a few minutes later, was Brother Andrew, an extremely gifted psychic who belongs to the St. Paul Society, a religious order in Staten Island. A tall, thin man with flowing dirty blond hair and a scraggly mustache that makes him look like an Old Testament prophet, he sensed as soon as we walked into the house that there *was* a malevolent presence—and it was scared of us! That told me we were dealing with a low-level demon, since it was frightened before we even began our exorcism of the house.

There is a hierarchy in Hell, just as in Heaven, where there are nine orders of celestial spirits: seraphim are the most exalted, followed by cherubim, thrones, dominations, virtues, powers, principalities, archangels, and finally angels. From the Bible, we know that Lucifer was once supreme among the seraphim, but he committed the deadly sin of pride, by imagining himself the equal of the Almighty. In his arrogance and envy, he refused to give glory and thanks to God, and became God's adversary.

Like humans, the angels were given free will, so they could *choose* to love God. He created humans with a soul and directed the angels to care for us. Then God allowed His only son to become a man. Although the virtuous angels adored Jesus Christ, Lucifer said he would not worship a mere human. Many angels joined his rebellion, then a challenge rose from one of the lowest orders, as the Archangel Michael called each angel who "was like unto God" to join the metaphysical battle. As punishment, Lucifer and one-third of the angels were cast out of Heaven, forever banished from seeing the beatific face of God.

These fallen angels, now the demons that inhabit Hell, lost their supernatural graces but not their inhuman powers. It's been said that their leader, Lucifer, is represented by the scorpion and that Satan, the ruler of Hell, is represented by the snake. Father Martin went so far as to say that Lucifer and Satan were two distinct and separate beings. Not much is known about this subject, but since there is the Holy Trinity of the Father, the Son, and the Holy Ghost, why can't there be an *unholy* trinity as well? I can see a correlation between God, the Father, and Lucifer, father of lies, who tries to bring us into eternal damnation. The Son, Jesus, gave us salvation, while His antagonist, the Antichrist, will appear on Earth during the last days as a false messiah. And the Holy Ghost, who helps us understand God and become more holy, is opposed by Satan, the destroyer who seeks the ruin of souls by turning us away from God.

Since demons that serve this unholy trinity came from every heavenly order, their powers vary from great to small. The most powerful demons are referred to as "devils." They can manipulate blessed objects. Low-level demons cannot. But even the lowliest demon is much more powerful than us human beings and is filled with hatred and perversity. The only weapon we have against them is our faith and prayers. Despite knowing what we had in store for it, the evil spirit in this house wouldn't flee. The demonic are not so quick to give up what they've gained—they must be forced to leave—and that's just what we had in mind!

From what Angelo had described, I was reasonably sure we were dealing with the first stage of demonic activity: *infestation*, where the serpents of Hell worm their way into people's lives with small, malicious acts designed to create doubt and fear, an emotion dark forces draw energy from. The demonic will announce themselves in a subtle way. Your phone may ring three times, with unnaturally short or long rings. When you pick it up, you may be greeted by unearthly growling, strange noises, static, or no sound at all. Just then there will be three knocks at the door, but no one is there when you open it. Or you may hear far more disturbing sounds: someone whispering your name when you're alone in the house, heavy breathing in your ear, or a baby or animal crying in terrible torment, an unnatural crying that tears at your soul. You may feel someone tap you on the shoulder or have your hair pulled, and turn around to find an empty room.

Certain areas of your home may develop cold spots that won't go away no matter how much you turn up the heat or may have sudden, drastic changes of temperature, as if something has just sucked all the warmth from the room. You may hear footsteps walking around in empty parts of the house or the sound of heavy furniture being dragged across the floor. When you look to see the cause of the sound, nothing is out of place. Or you may be all snug in your bed, drifting off to sleep, when you hear a tapping or scratching noise coming from the walls or under the bed. Try as you might, you can't find the source of the noise. Suddenly you may get the unmistakable feeling of being watched, a sensation that makes your skin crawl. A certain room may become hostile to all who enter—even pets may refuse to go into the room, no matter how much they are coaxed. Lights may abruptly turn off, leaving you in darkness, only to blaze on in the middle of the night, jolting you from sleep. The TV or radio will turn itself on full blast—even when it's unplugged. Out of the corner of your eye, you see something move, maybe a black or smoky shape that disappears as soon as you turn your head to get a better look. Perhaps a shadow glides by your bedroom door, a shadow darker than night. Revolting smells that have no earthly origin fill the air.

Objects seem to develop a will of their own, moving around the house no matter how many times you put them back. Perhaps you put your key ring or wallet in the same place every day, but it's mysteriously disappeared when you want to go out. You look all over the house without finding the object, only to have it turn up days later in a place where you already looked. This can lead to arguments, accusations, and disharmony, which are just what the demonic thrive on. But there's also a more sinister plot working here. The phenomena are usually centered around one particular person—an individual chosen for possession, whom we call the "focal person." He or she will experience all or most of the eerie phenomena, but when these people tell the other family members, he or she will be ridiculed and not believed. Or the person may not say anything at all but may begin to question his or her own sanity and withdraw from the rest of the family. Isolation makes it harder for the focal person to fight back, and there follows a systematic breakdown of that person's will. Once the evil spirit has entrenched itself, it will progress to the next stage, *oppression*, where the rest of the family is also treated to the horrifying phenomena. These scare tactics have a simple, cruel purpose: to break down the victim's will, rendering the person less and less able to resist possession, the demonic's ultimate goal.

Before any of this can happen, however, there must be an invitation that opens the door, allowing a demon to slip into our world. This can happen by accident or by design. Many people make the big mistake of not taking occult practices very seriously. Several TV shows with supernatural themes— ranging from *Buffy the Vampire Slayer* to *Charmed*—depict witchcraft as glamorous. What really disturbs me is that these programs are geared toward kids, giving children the dangerous misconception that dabbling in the occult is harmless fun. Never do they warn viewers that casting spells can lead to an attack by the demonic, nor do they show the living hell some people go through because they thought it would be interesting to mess around with a Ouija board, tarot cards, séances, or witchcraft rituals. Sometimes nothing at all happens; other times, something you can't see sneaks through and starts raising unholy hell in your life.

There are also people who know the spirit world exists and try to manipulate it to do their bidding. Maybe they deliberately invite the demonic into their lives, hoping to gain wealth and power. These people are Satanists and worship Satan as a god who will bring them earthly delights. What they don't grasp—until it's too late—is that once you cross that line, you put yourself in debt to the Devil. Sooner or later, he is going to collect, possibly in this world, certainly in the next.

Along with dabblers and practitioners of the dark arts, there are also innocent bystanders who somehow get snared by the occult. Like tragic victims of a drive-by shooting, they are simply in the wrong place at the wrong time. They might buy their dream house or move into a nice little apartment, not suspecting the horror that awaits them. Although the demonic aren't necessarily bound to any particular place, they may linger on the scene if something bad happened there in the past: A homicide, domestic violence, child molestation, satanic rituals, and drug abuse are all draws for the forces of darkness, due to the intense negative emotion associated with these events. As my partner Joe puts it, such houses sit like Venus flytraps, waiting for their unwary prey.

While Angelo didn't know if any of these things happened at this particular house—or what its history was—he did mention something curious about the landlady. Several times after he'd moved in, she'd stop by to collect mail. Although he politely invited her in, she always insisted on standing out on the street while he went to get the letters. *How very odd*, I thought. *It seems that this woman is afraid to set foot in her own house! I bet she knows exactly what's waiting inside—and how it got there!* One possibility is that the building was once the home of a wicked person, whose human spirit lingers there. Since one of the laws of the spirit world is "like attracts like," a place haunted by an evil ghost (the spirit of a departed person) can become a magnet for demonic forces as well.

Whatever the explanation for their problems was, I felt the people I was meeting tonight definitely fell into the innocent victim category, especially after Jill, the new mother, began relating her story. She was a big, athletic redhead with a ruddy face, pale blue eyes, and a sharp, beaklike nose. Although her body was slightly softened from her recent pregnancy, she was bursting with health and vigor: I could picture her as the captain of the lacrosse team in high school. In sharp contrast to her Amazon-like build, she had an unexpectedly high, girlish voice.

Her living room was cluttered with colorful toys and baby equipment. For all the cheerfulness of the surroundings, I could see she was very upset. Like Angelo, she said a disturbing incident had happened to her family on the day they moved in—but they didn't take it seriously until later on. That night, she told us, "my four-year-old son came into the bedroom and told me he'd seen a woman in white standing at the foot of his bed. I said, 'Go back to bed, Timmy, it's just a dream.'"

Over the next two weeks, she was quick to dismiss other odd events—too quick, she now admitted. As they settled into their new home, she kept hearing Timmy talking to someone in his room. When she muted the TV to hear what he was saying, he'd quickly call out, "It's only make-believe, Mommy." Sometimes she'd go into his room and see him chatting away, engrossed in some game with his apparently imaginary friend. When she'd ask what he was doing, he'd immediately assure her it was just pretend.

What happened next sent chills down Jill's spine. It was one of those really beautiful winter days we sometimes have in New York—so nice, in fact, that she decided to let Timmy go out in the backyard to play and get some fresh air. The little boy was very excited and asked his mom to bring out his new toy car. Just big enough to hold a child, it was made of bright yellow and orange plastic, had doors that really opened, a driver's seat, and was operated by foot pedals. Timmy climbed in—and was still in the car an hour later, when Jill came to the door to call him in for lunch.

Obediently, Timmy drove the car over to the house and got out, making sure to close the plastic door. What Jill saw then made her doubt her sanity: The door to the toy car opened by itself, as if some invisible child had just gotten in. It drove around the yard, stopping at the exact spot Timmy had parked it. Again the door opened and closed all by itself, much to the delight of Timmy, who was jumping up and down, so thrilled he was squealing. His new friend had taken a joy ride in the toy car. Seeing his mother's jaw drop in terror and her wide-eyed astonishment, he calmly remarked, "It's only make-believe, Mommy."

Too shocked to speak, she beckoned her son to come inside. She couldn't believe what she'd just seen. Dread washed over her, as she struggled to calm herself. *There must be some logical explanation,* she thought, *but what?* Deep down, she knew there was none. As soon as her husband, Bruce, came home, she told him what she'd witnessed.

"It must be the wind," he said, knowing his wife was a practical soul, not given to imagination.

"But it wasn't windy," she insisted, getting upset all over again. "The air was completely calm, I tell you!"

"Still, there must be a reasonable explanation, honey. Maybe it was a vibration from a truck," Bruce suggested.

Close to hysterics, she shouted, "No, that wasn't it. How many times do I have to tell you: Timmy's toy car drove all by itself!"

"That's simply not possible," he insisted. But it *was* possible, because Timmy's new friend was older than mankind

and evil beyond comprehension. Their family had been chosen by a demon and had just entered the infestation stage of
diabolical activity.

Trying to push the unsettling episode out of her mind, Jill
busied herself the next day with unpacking. As she put Timmy's clothes into his bureau drawers, she suddenly smelled
the unmistakable scent of cologne. A man's cologne, but not
her husband's, the fragrance was so overpowering that it filled
the room, as if someone had sprayed it everywhere. Just then
a closet door was flung open with such force it banged into
the wall, leaving a dent. Everything she'd carefully arranged
in the closet came flying out. Scared and confused, Jill just
shoved the mess back into the closet and slammed the door
shut, unable to make any sense of what was happening to her
in this house.

As an investigator of the preternatural, I'd heard all this
before. I'm well beyond being shocked by what takes place in
these cases, but what Jill said next really made me sit up and
take notice. She explained that when she was living in her
previous apartment, several miles away, she'd suddenly gotten the urge to move to a new building. "I'm not sure *why* I
felt a need to look at this particular time, because everyone
was telling me it was the middle of winter, and I should wait
until spring. But I just had to move, and nobody was going to
talk me out of it."

Once she called a real estate agent, something strange
happened. "Timmy said to me, 'Mommy, don't take the place
on Fresh Pond Road, because there's no room for my baby sister.' I didn't know what he was talking about, since I hadn't
looked at any apartment on Fresh Pond Road, but two days
later, we did see a place on that street, decided it wasn't big

enough for the baby, and turned it down. I didn't connect this to what Timmy had said. Actually, I'd forgotten about it."

A few days later Timmy had another suggestion. "Mommy, take the apartment two blocks from Myrtle Avenue." Again Jill didn't pay much attention, since she hadn't seen an apartment off Myrtle Avenue.

"I just needed to move, and that was all I was concentrating on," the young mother emphasized. "A couple of days later I heard about this place. When I saw it, I told Timmy it was perfect. He was very happy, so I asked if he liked it too. 'Yes, Mommy! This is the place I was telling you about.' Although the apartment *was* two blocks from Myrtle Avenue, I thought it was a big coincidence, a little weird maybe, but I didn't think a thing about it until creepy stuff started to happen. Now I really believe I was *led* here!"

That feeling was correct. Jill and her family were led—or lured—to the demon's lair. Incredible as it sounds, satanic powers can draw someone to a particular place by influencing the person to make a decision he or she wouldn't ordinarily make. The peculiar thing, I immediately noticed, was that this apartment didn't have a room for the baby either, yet Jill had found it "perfect."

And how did this four-year-old know in advance what apartments they'd see? And was it really *he* who was so eager to live by the graveyard? I believe Timmy, for all his youth, was a very special kid, and the demonic had singled him out for his strong psychic abilities. While there's no special personality trait that defines who will be selected as the prey, generally this person has some weakness or point of vulnerability that can be exploited. I'm convinced that if we hadn't intervened when we did, Timmy ultimately would have become

possessed. It's extremely rare, but satanic spirits can—and do—
take over children.

I could feel my blood starting to boil. Looking at this little
red-haired boy, who was now scampering around the apartment without a care in the world, still certain it was "all make-
believe," and his adorable six-month-old sister, with her fuzzy
bald head and big blue eyes that followed every move I made,
I thought, *How dare the demonic pick on these innocent little kids?*
Although I try not to get emotionally involved in my supernatural cases, knowing that strong feelings make me more
vulnerable to demonic attacks and manipulation, I just can't
help it when I see a kid being mistreated.

It's the same way when I walk my police beat: I'm still
haunted by the time I was called to a tenement in East New
York and found a desperately ill one-month-old baby lying
still and blue on the kitchen table, because the creatures who
called themselves her parents were too damned lazy to call a
doctor when it would have done some good. The paramedics
and I did our best to revive the tiny girl, but she was pronounced dead on arrival at the hospital. The mother cried a
bit, but the dad just got up to leave. "Where the hell do you
think you're going?" I demanded.

"Home," he replied matter-of-factly. "I've got to get ready
for work." He had eight other children with various women
around the 'hood, so apparently losing this one didn't mean
much to him. One less mouth to feed, I suppose. It was all I
could do not to rip his head off, as he coldly turned his back
on his dead baby and walked off into the night.

Jill, however, looked extremely upset as she concluded her
story. "I have never felt the anger, the hostility, the *hate* I've
felt in the few short days I've been here," she said. "I don't
know what's come over me since I moved in—I'm frightened

of myself and feel like I might go on a rampage at any time. This just isn't me at all."

I got there too late to save that baby in East New York, but I'm right on time for these kids and Jill. "No," I told her. "It's not you but what's in this house that's making you feel this way." I could talk for hours about the demonic, but before I got another sentence out, the baby's loud wailing suddenly interrupted us. The wail stopped as abruptly as it started when Timmy suddenly slapped the baby. *I immediately thought of Kathy and her warning "Somebody's going to get hit!" Her prediction had come true!*

"Look at that!" her mother exclaimed. "Timmy's *never* done that before." I could tell she was wondering if the evil spirit was to blame, but to tell the truth, I wasn't quite sure. From what I'd seen so far, Timmy was a rambunctious boy who clearly hadn't experienced much discipline from either of his parents. Whether it was sibling rivalry or dark forces that provoked the slap, however, it was clearly time to begin the ritual. Since no one here was possessed—yet—we'd do an exorcism of the house rather than of the people living there.

Looking around the room, I noticed that someone was missing, the other single tenant. "Where's Bill?" I asked.

"I don't know," Jill replied. "I told him you'd be here at eight, but I haven't seen him all day."

I couldn't help but get annoyed. We'd agreed to take the case—and to come here in the middle of an ice storm at that—only because we'd been promised the cooperation of everyone in the house. To expel the demon, we needed access to every area of the house, so there would be nowhere for the fiend to hide. I'd also like to hear Bill's story, but that wasn't crucial to my investigation, since the sinister events had begun before he moved in. Obviously, he'd had no role in attracting this demon, but I was still curious to hear what he had to say.

While we waited for him, Brother Andrew conducted a psychic scan of the two apartments, walking from room to room with his long, thin arms outstretched to help him feel the spiritual vibrations. He detected two areas of intense chill—"psychic cold," we call it—one in the parents' bedroom and the other in the room the little boy shared with his sister. "Can you see it?" I asked him.

He was silent for a moment, as if listening to a sound I couldn't hear. "It's masking itself; it doesn't want us to see it. It's trying to hide."

"Definitely demonic?" Tommy queried, although we were all sure of the answer.

"Yes, it's inhuman. It's scared, but its hatred is stronger than its fear." Although I can't explain how his psychic powers work, any more than I can explain how little Timmy knew what apartments his mother would see, I've seen the brother's sixth sense in action often enough to know it's real. On some cases he's told us the layout of an apartment he's never been to or identified where the "portal," or opening, the demonic force used to gain entry to the home was located.

Once he even read *my* mind. I was visiting the St. Paul Society and brought some pastries with me. Brother Andrew tore into the Linzer torte I offered him with surprising gusto. I was standing behind him as he ate and couldn't help thinking, *Don't they ever feed these guys?* He turned around as if I'd spoken out loud and said, "Fuck you, Ralph!" We were laughing about it all night.

Sometimes Brother Andrew reminded me of Father Martin: They were both worldly men and spoke in everyday language, including some vulgarities. That made it easy to be with them: You didn't feel like you were in church but with a friend. Each had remarkable psychic powers and a real gift for empathy. In Brother Andrew's case, the gift was so strong that it was almost a curse: He couldn't walk into a 7-Eleven without the cashier blurting out all her troubles to him. I also confided a great deal in him, but if I'd ask him what the future held for me, he'd say, "Just let it happen, Ralph."

He once told me about a marvelous vision he had of a big golden cube that gave off a strong feeling of love. Next to it was a big black hole—a spirit portal—that gave off such over-powering evil that he felt he'd be engulfed, disappear, and die. That's when he made the decision to go into religious life. He'd felt the force of God's love and the absolute evil of the demonic.

While he couldn't actually see the evil spirit in this house because it was hiding itself, he could feel its fear and hatred.

"Command it to leave," I urged.

In a loud, assertive tone, Brother Andrew gave the order: "In the name of Jesus Christ I command to you to go where the Lord sends you, harming no one along the way!" He repeated these words twice more, even louder and more forcefully, then shook his head. "It won't go—it doesn't want to leave!"

We gathered up our supplies for the exorcism: holy water; St. Benedict medals for everyone in the house, including the cat; blessed salt and blessed incense. We were just setting the video camera up when the missing tenant strolled downstairs—with a can of Budweiser in his hand. Taking a noisy slurp, this overweight, disheveled man reeked of both beer and bad attitude. I was talking to Jill when I heard Joe say, "Could you put the beer away, please? We're having a religious ceremony here."

Predictably, since I've met a million idiots like this while on patrol, Bill started getting in Joe's face. "It's my home and I'll drink beer anywhere I damn well want," he said in a nasty tone. I could feel my temper rising, but since I was here to pray, not mix it up with some wiseass, I let the other tenants try to reason with their neighbor. Ignoring their cajoling, he continued to stand there, guzzling his beer, as if waiting for the show to begin. Well, there was nothing in the Bible to prevent me from subduing him with a hard-eyed cop stare, so that's what I did.

"Listen up, buddy," I told him. "If you don't put your beer away, take it back to your apartment and deal with your problem yourself."

He looked me up and down, then said in a surly tone, "Fine. Good-bye." Letting out a loud belch, he slowly retreated to his apartment.

"Have a good night—if you can," I called after him, knowing that what was in that house was likely to head straight for that man's apartment—and it would be extremely pissed off when it got there. He didn't seem too worried—and actually had the nerve to turn on his stereo and play the rock band Black Sabbath at full blast.

Resistance is all part of the demonic's M.O., so none of the investigators really expected the case to go smoothly. Satanic forces are always looking for ways to screw up our investigations, and this fool was playing right into their hands. If he'd been the only person in the house, I would have packed up and left then. We'd all risked ourselves—for no pay, since we don't take money to do this Work—to deal with *his* problem, and now he was giving us a hard time.

Although I knew that conducting the ritual at this point would be like putting a Band-Aid on a broken leg, two kids were counting on us, so we forged ahead, with Black Sabbath blaring overhead. First, we lighted blessed incense and let the sweet smell fill each room, making sure that no dark space went unpurified. Brother Andrew and I took turns reading prayers, while Joe and Phil did the same thing in the basement apartment. Over the years we've discovered that it's best to hold simultaneous rituals on the different floors of the house, so the demon can't flee to another floor.

As I read the Pope Leo XIII prayer, I also held up my relic of the True Cross. I always keep it over my bed, except when I need it for a case. You might say it's the equivalent of a cop's gun, since there's nothing more powerful against Satan's forces.

We were about to start the next step, sprinkling holy water in every corner of the room, when the Black Sabbath music suddenly stopped. The second-floor tenant came downstairs, pale and shaken. Not only was there no beer can this time, but his entire attitude had done a complete 180. He was now eager—even desperate—to cooperate in any way he could. When my partner questioned him about his dramatic change of heart, he refused to say what had happened. "Let's just get on with it," he muttered.

That was OK with me; we were happy to finally get full access to the rest of the premises. Quickly, in case he changed his mind again, we resumed the ritual, cleansing his apartment with incense and prayer. Then it was time for the holy water. We hit all the corners to consecrate the room, then sprinkled it in every enclosed space, no matter how small, so no demon could hide there. Holy water is part of the Pope Leo XIII prayer, but we take it one step further. As the final coup de grâce to Satan and his henchmen, we used blessed salt in the same way we had used the holy water.

It was around midnight, when we finally finished the entire house. Brother Andrew said he could see a black shape moving around the house at a high rate of speed. The demon was looking for a hiding place, but we'd done our job well: There was none. Repelled at every turn by the holiness with which we'd anointed the house, the black shape moved faster and faster, until Brother Andrew discerned that it had disappeared.

Once Brother Andrew told us it was gone, I spoke to all the tenants about what they could expect. "In a few days you may experience some supernatural phenomena as a residual effect of our ritual tonight. Sometimes a demon will return just to harass you, but if this happens, you're to use the holy water and blessed salt we're about to give you. Most important, you must pray and bring God into your lives. I must also ask you not to discuss what you've experienced here, because talking about these events gives the demon recognition—and could draw it back to your home."

They all thanked us, even Bill. Walking outside in the clean, frigid air was wonderful after being in that house for four hours, but now we had to travel on icy roads after dealing with a demonic spirit. Since Tommy and Brother Andrew had the longest ride, I prayed they'd make it home safely.

That should have been the end of the story, but there was a curious sequel. The next day Brother Andrew got a call from a close friend who lived three thousand miles away in California. Around 9:00 P.M. Pacific time (midnight in New York), just as Brother Andrew completed the exorcism, this woman was asleep on her couch and had a chilling nightmare. In her mind's eye, she saw Brother Andrew surrounded by evil. The dream was so vivid that she woke up shaking and went to her kitchen to make some soothing herb tea.

While she was pouring water into a cup, she had the unmistakable feeling she was being watched.

She whirled around and saw a very hairy creature, about five feet tall, glaring at her and gnashing its horrible yellow teeth. The feeling of hatred the beast gave off was frightening beyond anything she'd ever experienced. But she had the presence of mind to do what Brother Andrew had taught her: command it in the name of Jesus Christ to leave. It immediately vanished, but she was so distraught she didn't sleep at all that night, and called Brother Andrew first thing in the morning to see if he was all right.

He told her he was involved in a case of demonic infestation at that very time and this is what happened: Just as the demon was leaving the house by the graveyard, the woman was thinking of Brother Andrew, because she sensed he was in danger. When you think about someone, you form a psychic connection with the person, because thought has substance, just as when you pray, you connect to God. When the demon departed, it followed that thought connection to her and, in its diabolical rage, manifested itself in her home until her command banished it back to where it belonged—Hell!

5

THE INCUBUS ATTACK

Lightning cracked overhead and sheets of rain lashed at my car as I set off on the five-hour drive to my next case. My partner Joe couldn't get the day off from work, so I was alone and on edge, well aware that the people I was about to meet were being assaulted by forces far more perilous than this torrential downpour. I'd seen the McKenzie family profiled on the TV show *Sightings*, which reports on real-life cases of supernatural activity. As soon as I heard what kind of phenomena this family was experiencing, I knew they were being oppressed by demons. I called Ed Warren, knowing he had contacts at the show, but he said he wasn't comfortable soliciting a case. "If God wants this family to get our help," he said, "He will lead them to us."

A few months later I was chatting with Ed over the phone. "Hey, Ralph, I got a call from *Sightings* the other day," he told me. "They want Lorraine and me to look into a case in Washington, D.C." I knew immediately that it was the same case I'd called him about, but Ed had forgotten our discussion until I reminded him. "You should come too," he urged.

If what the McKenzie family said on TV was true, then they were in the clutches of a very powerful demon. By the time I reached Washington and stopped at a pay phone to let my wife know I'd arrived safely, the wind was near gale force. Jen is very tough and tried to hide her anxiety, but I was worried too, being so far from home if my own family should need me.

Running through the rain to my car, I saw a large branch crash to the ground on the other side of the street. *Was I nuts to drive two hundred miles through a raging storm to help people I don't even know?* You might think so, but how much crazier is this than risking my life every night on street patrol? Officers a lot tougher and braver than I'll ever be have been killed in the line of duty; young men like Kevin Gillespie, a comrade from the midnight-to-eight shift, who was gunned down by murderous carjackers a few years ago—despite a bulletproof vest. Like me, he was a married man and had small children. His seven-year-old son, Danny, wrote a letter that was read during his father's funeral mass: "I love the police. Someday I will be one."

Now his green metal locker at the station house stands as a somber memorial, with a plaque reading "In memory of police officer Kevin Gillespie, shield #4503. He made the ultimate sacrifice by giving his life in the line of duty on March 14, 1996." Below are inscribed two words he often said to me and other officers: "Be safe."

The children in this D.C. case had suffered the same shattering loss as Kevin's son had. Just three days after they moved into their new home, their dad was diagnosed with inoperable cancer; he died a month later. I didn't feel that the demonic had anything to do with it: It was probably just coincidence, but the number three always figures in these cases.

Their house didn't *look* particularly spooky: It wasn't a

drafty old castle or ruined mansion you'd see in the movies, but a very pretty, vine-covered colonial on a quiet suburban street. I didn't detect anything hostile or malignant as I rang the bell.

"Are you the exorcist?" I instantly recognized this thin teenager with huge, haunted eyes as Monique McKenzie, the oldest daughter, from seeing her talk on TV about the unimaginably grotesque horrors they'd endured.

"No, but I'm here to help as best I can," I assured her, then made small talk with the family, who were all huddled together in the living room. None of them wanted to be alone in that house, even in the middle of the day. While I waited for the Warrens to arrive, I took a walk around the spotless, spacious rooms, to see if I could sense anything out of the ordinary. I knew already that the house had a sinister secret, a sordid past.

According to the family, a policeman had told them that the previous owner of the house was a Satanist. This man's wife worked nights and left their two young sons with their father. Nothing wrong with that, except that he and his satanic coven were sexually molesting the boys. As if that weren't horrible enough, the group began sacrificing living creatures to their god, the Devil. Right in front of the little boys, they slaughtered a frog. Now, some of you may scoff at that, thinking "A frog? Who cares about a frog?"

While killing a frog would be more than enough to terrorize two children, I saw this act for what it was, a practice run for something infinitely worse. Eventually the group allegedly killed a baby. No, it was never proven, but the police detective who investigated was convinced it really did happen. But the law is set up so that if no evidence or body is found, no crime has been committed—which is just what these

Satanists counted on. The only people who saw the ritual murder were two kids, and in the eyes of the law, little children don't make good witnesses. The boys told police that the infant was stabbed repeatedly, put into a box, and thrown in a creek down the street. Cops found the box, but no blood or mutilated corpse, so ultimately they had to close the case, after a thorough search failed to turn up a body.

I suspected that these devil-worshippers were what we call "organized Satanists." Organized Satanists will go to great lengths to hide the bodies of their victims, to avoid detection and prosecution. This is easily done, since these Satanists are often professional people—doctors, lawyers, politicians, men and women who are well off in the money department, or even judges and police officers. So these groups have all sorts of resources at their disposal to evade justice, at least on Earth.

Now, all this is conjecture—and it's perfectly possible that no baby was ever murdered. Either way, the police had enough probable cause to lock their animal of a dad up for child abuse—and get him away from both society and his own flesh and blood. What he'd done, however, was wicked enough to draw one of the evil spirits that prowl this world—seeking the doom of souls—and turn another innocent family into the Devil's prey.

I checked the entire first floor, then made my way to the basement. At the bottom of the stairs was Monique's room: a typical girl's bedroom, with everything frilly and nice. I wandered into other areas of the basement, which was very large and divided into several rooms. The main one had a television and a bar in the corner, and was as immaculate as the rest of the house. Off to the side was a laundry room. As soon as I entered, I stopped dead in my tracks, gripped by an overpowering dread. The atmosphere of menace was so overpowering that every hair on my head stood on end. I got the hell out of there, fast.

You can sense evil: Your whole body responds to it. The demonic know how to create the maximum amount of terror in each person, because they know your weaknesses. In this case, the room was just an ordinary laundry room in appearance, but the feeling of terror and hatred was overpowering. I'm not psychic like Brother Andrew, but most of the time I *can* sense the presence of the demonic: It's an unnatural feeling that assaults your senses. A lot of people describe it as an eerie or creepy feeling that something is very wrong.

Later in the investigation, I learned the police detective had told the family that this was the room used by the satanic coven. I didn't need anybody to tell *me* that: Something in that room had already put my entire body on red alert. My adrenaline pumping, I hurried out of the basement but was drawn again to the bedroom by the stairs, which now reeked of a sickeningly sweet perfume. Upstairs, I asked Monique if she or anyone else had just been down there.

She said no, then got very excited when I mentioned the heavy scent in her room. In a triumphant tone, as if this were all the proof anyone would need to believe the horrors in her house were real, she said, "You smelled it too? That happens to us all the time!"

I was touched by her obvious sincerity—and felt certain that this was not a case of infestation, but of *oppression*, the second phase of the demonic M.O. The fiendish objective of this stage is to literally scare people out of their wits with a bombardment of unbearably frightening phenomena designed to dehumanize the demonic's hapless targets, until they can no longer fight off the evil spirit that is trying to possess them. Oppression is infestation multiplied by a thousand: Where there were formerly little scratchings or tappings, you now have deafening poundings that literally shake the entire house. No longer is one person singled out for supernatural assaults; the whole family is affected. Phase two of the diabolical strategy goes well beyond instilling doubt and fear in a single family member; the entire house feels hostile to all who enter.

Infestation is an external assault: It causes physical phenomena as the demonic manipulate objects. Oppression has two parts: While the outward manifestations continue and intensify, there's also a more sinister aspect that's not visible to the eye. Infestation affects the physical house; oppression goes beyond and "haunts" those who live there. No one escapes the torments. Oppression is an all-out assault on the senses that makes terror a constant companion in the very place where you expect to feel safest: your home. Sleep becomes virtually impossible. Large, potentially dangerous objects, like washing machines or refrigerators, may be lifted up and flung at you by invisible hands. Not only will footsteps be heard, but they'll walk right by the people in the house, brushing your body with a chill that's colder than cold.

Then, just as it seems that things can't possibly get any worse, they do. Your loved ones are assaulted even when they leave the home. The car seems to develop a mind of its own, causing accidents and harrowing close calls. Horrifying phenomena start occurring at work—if you have the strength to go to your job at all. The people in your house suffer the physical fury of the infernal force: They may be slapped, punched, scratched, bitten, knocked to the ground, burned, or battered with flying objects. Should your family try to flee, the demonic assailant will stick to you like a second shadow and raise unholy havoc wherever you go. Your relatives cease to exist as distinct individuals within this hell on Earth—instead, your entire being is constantly fighting a desperate battle for survival.

This is just the *beginning* of oppression. During the initial stage of demonic invasion, the attacks are external: unsettling noises, acts of supernatural vandalism, and malicious mischief. Later on, however, the satanic power turns to savage psychological warfare: Objects vanish before your eyes, you gag as your room fills with a revolting stench of rotting flesh or excrement; and you tremble as hideous wraiths manifest in front of you. Your belongings are not only moved around but are smashed in front of your eyes. The world of nightmares becomes your reality: Not a day goes by without some ghastly new horror.

You—or a family member—experience a degrading change in personality: You may develop an aversion to church and anything sacred. Sinful urges become stronger, more frequent, and all but impossible to resist. Maybe you're plunged into behavior that's both strangely gratifying and unspeakably shameful. In a futile effort to evade the ever-present demon, you may drink to excess, turn to drugs, or try to lose yourself in promiscuous sex, each time giving the diabolical force another foothold into your soul. Or perhaps another family member crumbles under the unendurable stress: A once-loving spouse or child becomes increasingly withdrawn, turns cold and hateful, or is suddenly beset by violent, uncontrollable rages. This person may even experience transient possession—transient because his or her will has not yet broken down enough for full possession to occur. While under the sway of the satanic spirit, he or she may brutally attack family members or inflict horrifying injuries on him- or herself, including suicide.

The demonic are brilliant manipulators and will exploit any moral, emotional, or mental weakness in the humans they prey on. Some specialize in a particular sin, primarily the deadly seven: anger, envy, pride, sloth, gluttony, avarice, and lust. With diabolical ingenuity, these forces of darkness seize on our basest instincts and worst temptations and twist them around into attacks of stunning power and perversity.

By now Ed and Lorraine had arrived, with one of their students from Connecticut. A few minutes later Monique's grandmother, Maggie, who lived nearby, dropped by to lend moral support. As I set up the video camera, the Warrens introduced themselves to the six residents of the house: Claudia, who managed a hotel; her live-in boyfriend, Artie, who worked as a moving man; her fifteen-year-old niece, Jessica; and her three daughters: seventeen-year-old Monique, and thirteen-year-old twins, Carolyn and Marybeth. While you'd expect twins to look alike, all four girls had an uncanny resemblance to each other, like those Russian dolls that open up to reveal smaller and smaller versions of the same figure.

Unlike the young widow, who was blonde and disguised her distress under elaborate makeup, you had to wonder when any of these kids had last pulled a comb through her unruly brown hair, or taken a shower. Of course that's not necessarily abnormal for a teenager, but the expression on their faces was definitely disturbing. I'd seen it dozens of times before on victims of both human and inhuman crimes: a vacant, thousand-yard stare.

To encourage these tortured, traumatized souls to talk, Ed decided to question each of them privately in the family room, while I moved around the house, sometimes escorting family members up and down from the basement and sometimes keeping them company in the kitchen as they awaited their turn.

Monique spoke first, explaining that the trouble began just before her first Christmas without her father—a time when demonic activity typically peaks, because evil spirits are enraged and inflamed by the holiness of the season. There was nothing subtle about the spirit's opening salvo: raucous pounding on her night table, as if an unseen force were sending Morse code messages: three violent thumps, then a series of rhythmic raps. "I thought someone had broken into the house and was going to kill me," the teenager said in a hollow, expressionless voice. "I broke out in a sweat and was afraid to open my eyes."

This isn't typical of infestation, I thought. There was nothing subtle about this. *It seemed that this demon was so powerful that it had skipped right to oppression.*

Squirming shyly on the couch, in agonies of teenaged embarrassment at what she was about to reveal, the girl reported that she had heard—and felt—something breathing heavily on her ear as she lay in bed. "In a raspy, decrepit voice that sounded thousands of years old, it said, 'I want to make love to you!' It scared me so bad I ran to my mother's room for help."

Shame-faced, Claudia admitted that she hadn't believed a word her daughter said. "I was certain this was a nightmare, so calmed her down and sent her back to bed."

"But *you* knew it wasn't a nightmare," Ed said to the daughter in a kindly tone.

"No one could convince me it was just a dream," Monique replied, looking Ed firmly in the eye for the first time. "Not my mother, not you, not anybody in the world!" Her big eyes challenged anyone to disagree. I didn't doubt her truthfulness for a second.

Warm weather brought a brief peace to the house, and Claudia said she'd completely forgotten her daughter's "bad dream" until she had a horrendous experience of her own the following winter. "I was sleeping by myself—my boyfriend was away—when something came into my room. I felt it breathing loudly on my ear. Then I felt myself falling forever and kept thinking 'God help me!' I was paralyzed with terror but knew whatever was in the room with me was pure evil. I was fighting the evil feeling with everything I had."

I knew this wasn't sleep paralysis, a rare medical condition that usually starts in childhood and causes people to become temporarily unable to move or speak, either while they're falling asleep or as they're waking up. Not only was everyone in the house affected, but terrifying phenomena were also taking place during the day, while the family was awake.

Closing her eyes briefly, as if to consult images on her eyelids, Claudia resumed her story. "I thought I got out of bed at this point and saw my children flickering on the walls as if they were floating. I tried to speak to Carolyn and Marybeth, but no sound came out of my mouth. The furniture looked all wavy and transparent. When I got to the kitchen telephone, I dialed my mother's number, but the person who picked up was my dead husband! 'Hello,' he said, and I screamed, 'Hurry home and help me!' As soon as I spoke, I was back in bed again."

Watching Ed closely, trying to gauge his reaction, she asked, "Do you think this was an out-of-body experience?"

Ed agreed it might be, but felt he had to make an important point. "The voice you heard was *not* your late husband! It was a demon *speaking* in his voice." The evil force was using a frightening, but also oddly reassuring disguise for its malevolent intentions. I've heard of this happening in other cases, where the phone would ring and the voice of a dead relative would be heard on the line. This is a most cruel and confusing tactic of the demonic.

When I returned to the kitchen, something peculiar happened. I was facing the dining room, where double doors led out to the patio. Since it was now dark, the glass doors were like a mirror, reflecting everything in the room. A sudden movement caught my eye: A shapeless black mass glided from right to left inside the room, right in front of these doors, then disappeared through the wall. True to my police training, I immediately went out on the patio to search for an intruder. There was no one—no one human, anyway.

That wasn't the first time I'd seen a strange shadow like this. People often ask if I ever saw any ghosts or demons when I was growing up. Actually, it was only after I entered the Work that I started having preternatural experiences. Once you give the demonic recognition, you draw them to you—something I didn't realize when I began this Work. Now I understand that when you get involved in investigations, you cross a line, and once you cross it, you can never go back. The chances are high that you will be disturbed and harassed in your own home, because the demonic never forget and never stop seeking revenge.

That revenge comes in ways you'd never expect. In the winter of 1992, my wife had a harrowing encounter in our home. I was off on a case and she was watching TV, while Christina slept. Suddenly Jen saw something out of the corner of her eye: a huge black shape about eight feet tall, with no features at all. She felt a terrible chill and every hair on her body stood on end. The shadow was at the doorway of our baby's room! Paralyzed with fear, she watched as it glided down the hall and vanished. As soon as she recovered enough to move, she crept cautiously into our bedroom, got one of the bottles of holy water that's always present, and sprinkled it everywhere.

By the time I got home, she'd gotten over her fright and was boiling mad. "You go off on these cases and bad things happen when you leave," she shouted. "I'm scared to death being here all alone with a baby. Am I supposed to spend the rest of my life worrying about shadows and creepy stuff I don't even like to talk about?"

Her words were like a kick in the balls. I'd signed on for the Work, but my family hadn't. Why should they be subjected to harassment from Hell? It was like having somebody I'd arrested show up at my door or threaten my family. I did my best to calm her, then got another bottle of holy water and performed an exorcism of my own home, with the Pope Leo XIII prayer. We fell asleep in each other's arms around dawn, under the relic of the True Cross that hangs over our bed.

Not satisfied with scaring the shit out of my wife, this demonic spirit showed up again a month or so later. This time I was home, lounging on my living room sofa in front of the TV, when I saw movement in my peripheral vision. A big black shape was moving away from Christina's crib! Although the room was dark, the shadow was blacker than darkness. I have often heard people I've interviewd describe shapes they could see clearly in the dark, things so unnatural that they appeared to be swallowing up darkness. Now I knew exactly what they were talking about. I got off the sofa like a madman—I don't think my feet even hit the floor—and ran to my daughter. To my relief, she was sleeping peacefully, but the feeling I had was utter terror. Even after using holy water, I couldn't sleep all night, knowing that a demon had been so close to my baby girl.

The worst incident of all was in 1995. Christina, who was then five, peeked into her baby sister's room and screamed. "I saw something that was all wavy, like it was melting," she told me later. "It *was leaning over Daniella's crib like it was going to pick her up. I yelled to Mommy, 'One of those things you and Daddy see is here—and it's getting Daniella!'"* Jen raced into the room and saw the shadow hovering over the crib. Just as she frantically picked up the baby, the formless mass vanished. My wife and daughters fled the room, with Christina in tears, slamming the door behind them.

I was wild with rage when I got home from work and heard about this. When I entered the Work, I knew that anyone who goes up against the Devil pays a price. I'd expected that for myself, but not for Daniella, who is now four and weighs all of twenty-five pounds, most of it her long silky hair; or for Christina, nine, a sturdy little athlete who loves soccer and horror movies, just as I did as a kid. Yet I've discovered in case after case that's exactly the M.O. of satanic spirits: One of the cruelest ways they get at people is by attacking their children. This raises the fear factor much higher than if I were the sole target, and has caused me to feel tremendous stress and guilt.

To safeguard against satanic attacks, I've done my utmost to make our home extremely repellent to evil spirits, just as my burglar alarm and gun make it hostile to thugs of the human variety. It's not just holy water and blessed salt that I rely on, but I have made God—not the Devil—the center of my life. I avoid dwelling on demonology. In my everyday life, my focus is on being a husband and father. Even when I'm actively involved in a case, as I was here in D.C., I devote attention to it only during the investigation or when I'm writing up my report on it. To obsess over occult horrors is unhealthy and dangerous to the soul; lifting up your eyes to the wonder and majesty of God's creations is the cure. It's only through His mercy that we can survive dark nights of evil.

When I returned from my search of the patio, none of the McKenzies said a word to me, yet I could tell they'd seen the shape too. They just nodded their heads in grim satisfaction, as if to say "See, we told you so!"

In the family room, Claudia was describing the times when they could actually hear the demon entering their basement. The portal—the opening in the spirit plane that lets a fiend from Hell enter our world—was the laundry room, the site of the satanic rituals. The family could always sense when the spirit was coming. Your body will react to pure evil, even if you may not understand what you're feeling. Sometimes the spirit crept up the stairs silently, as the family members' bodies instinctively broke out in icy sweats; other times its steps were so loud that it sounded like someone was running with cinder blocks on his feet. The footsteps always started in the basement, and the family's terror would mount as they pounded up the stairs toward them. The noise provoked terrible fear, since the family members never knew what horrible thing would happen next.

Ed asked Claudia to pound on the wall to show what the steps were like. He'd done this in other cases, so we could get an idea of what the noises sounded like to the family, but no one can ever really reproduce exactly what was heard. The mother slammed her fist into the wall three times, and with each blow her kids and boyfriend upstairs literally jumped out of their chairs. That's how thoroughly the demon had trained them in terror. I comforted them by explaining it was just Claudia, demonstrating the sound for Ed, and they settled nervously back in their seats.

Next, Artie told his tale—a brief one, since he'd had few encounters with the unearthly force. Well into middle age, he had the beefy build of a man who made his living through manual labor and drank a lot of beer afterward. He was wearing worn blue jeans and a T-shirt with the sleeves ripped off to reveal tattoos on both of his massive biceps. Having spent some time under the tattoo needle myself, I admired the intricate workmanship of the fire-breathing dragon on his left arm. For all his size, he seemed a bit shy and mumbled his words, perhaps because his speech was rough and uneducated. "One time I thought I heard one of the twins crying and went into her bedroom to tease her back into a good mood. There wasn't nobody in the room, but when I looked at the bed, I seen a baby doll lying on the pillow—with real tears in its eyes. It wasn't the kind of doll that cries, just a regular plastic doll. I don't know how to explain it."

The next occult episode was at 4:30 A.M., the hour this hard-working man customarily got up on weekdays, since he had to be at his job by six. "I came out of our bedroom and seen what looked like a monster. There ain't nothing else I can call it. It had rough fur sticking up all over its body, and was hunkered down like it was hiding. I looked at it and just kept on walking, hoping it wouldn't see me. It vanished." He had one other run-in with the spirit a few months later: This time it took the shape of a man's shadow, much larger than Artie's own, and moved along the floor beside him, deliberately keeping step with him. Strangely—or perhaps not so strangely—one of his coworkers sensed that he was having problems and gave him a rosary when he got to work that day.

Claudia confirmed that she'd also heard a baby's cry, as had several other family members and visitors. The bizarre phenomena didn't stop there, she added. "We'd just come back from church with our friend Jamie, and sat down to say some special prayers, when my younger twin, Marybeth, said her stomach was burning, as if she'd just been scratched. I lifted her shirt and she'd been clawed from hipbone to hipbone, in a wide red line that was welting up. I was in awe and didn't know what to do."

She, Marybeth, and Jamie folded their hands and resumed their prayers for a few minutes, until Marybeth let out a loud yelp of pain. "Mommy, my face is burning," she cried, and Claudia saw *three* side-by-side scratches appear on her daughter's cheek. There was that number again, the calling card of the demonic.

"All I could think was that *it* was angry that we were praying," Claudia said. Obviously worried that we might have doubts about such an incredible incident, she quickly added, "Marybeth couldn't have done it to herself, because her hands were in a praying position the entire time. Then my friend Jamie cried out: *She* was getting scratched too! We all heard growls and saw red marks appear on her face, her forearms, and her chest."

The attacks became increasingly physical. The next day Claudia's niece, Jessica, felt the demon's claws, which raked her face and arms so hard that she bled. "The kids looked like battered children," Claudia said. "I felt we had to get out of that house, so we went to my brother's home."

There the family discovered that they could run, but they couldn't hide. "*It* followed us," Claudia explained, "and the children were attacked again. Marybeth was scratched right in front of me, on the face. It burned her, and she was looking pretty bad. It was a horrible feeling that as a parent, I couldn't protect my own child. I put her in between me and my boyfriend, and we put our arms around her, but she *still* got scratched."

Not satisfied with these cruelties—or the abject terror it had already aroused—the demon showed an even more sadistic streak when they returned home. That night it told the terrified twin that it had a special plan just for her—a girl's ultimate nightmare. As Marybeth sat sobbing in the living room, with tears and blood streaming down her ravaged face, she saw a terrible sight—so horrible that she could barely describe it to us. With her eyes fixed on the floor, the thirteen-year-old told us, "I looked through the bedroom door, and it was lying on the waterbed, with its legs open."

She stopped there and gave her mother a pitiful, imploring stare, as if to say "Do I really have to go on?"

"We've all seen it differently," the mother interjected. "To me, it looks like a beast with short black fur."

"No, it was hairy and huge, like Bigfoot," the teen insisted. "And it was saying really vulgar things." She hesitated again and buried her face against her mother's bosom.

Almost inaudibly, she added, "It was masturbating!"

"I thought she was going to have a nervous breakdown," Claudia said. "She was crying her eyes out."

Summoning up every ounce of nerve she had, the girl continued, so softly that we could barely hear her murmuring into her mother's chest. "In this really ancient voice, it said, 'You can kiss your family good-bye, because your ass is mine tonight!'"

"She was completely hysterical," Claudia said. "She told me she *knew* it was going to rape and kill her that very night."

Was such an unspeakable atrocity even possible? As a cop and a father myself, there's nothing I loathe more than a child molester. I could hardly imagine the dread that threats of revolting violation and death must have evoked in this timid, haunted girl! Each time I think I have finally grasped the evil of which these demons are capable, they reveal new depths of hatred and depravity that stagger the mind.

Yet I wasn't entirely shocked that this diabolical force was attacking sexually, given the unnatural lust that originally drew it to this house: the brutal molestation of two little boys. Demonic spirits have no gender—they are neither male nor female—but are still capable of rape because they can assume the shape of a person of either sex, complete with genitalia. A demon that takes female form to violate a human male is called a "succubus"; one that sexually oppresses women is an "incubus." That's what was lurking in this house of women, wantonly exposing itself to a little girl in full sight of her mother!

It's often said that rape isn't a crime of sex but of violence—and that's certainly true for the demonic. They derive no pleasure from the sex act, because the damned never feel joy or delight of any kind. They're doomed to eternal misery and suffering, but they mount incubus or succubus attacks to degrade, humiliate, and further terrify their victims. It's also an insult to God, who created us male and female so we can be fruitful and multiply. Joining as one flesh is part of holy matrimony—and the demonic are driven by a relentless hatred of anything holy.

Any supernatural attack is horrifying, but this has to be the worst. Imagine being sexually assaulted by a hairy brute or a shapeless creature you can't even see. Such an intimate violation is enough to drive you insane. At times, when the attack is over, the victim will have a sticky and vile-smelling substance on his or her skin—the foulest mark of the devil.

While Claudia didn't know all this, she was scared witless by her daughter's plight. With desperate courage, she addressed the incubus. "I'm begging you, as a mother, not to take my child tonight! Whatever cursed thing you are, don't hurt my daughter—hurt *me*, if you must! I'd die right here and now to save my child."

The only reply was mocking laughter that shook the house. Hoping for divine protection, the single mom called a minister from the Baptist church the family occasionally attended. He referred her to a Catholic priest, saying that what they needed was an exorcism.

The priest, however, wasn't very sympathetic. "How dare you call me at this hour?" he demanded peevishly, even though it was only 9:30 P.M. After hearing about the growls, baby cries, bloody scratches, and lewd threats from the beyond, his only comment was "Maybe this is God's way of getting you back to church."

He hung up, leaving Claudia clutching a dead phone. The savior she'd counted on had refused her. *Who else could she possibly call, if even a man of God couldn't—or wouldn't—help?*

6

THE SATANIC STALKER

Truly, this was a family under siege—attacked at every turn, in ever more horrifying ways. What could they have possibly done to deserve such ghastly punishment? As far as I could tell, their only mistake was buying the wrong house. I didn't believe that they were singled out for satanic wrath for not going to church often enough, as the priest had heartlessly—and erroneously—suggested. After all, there are legions of outright atheists out there—and most of them don't have any problem with the demonic. It was true that Claudia, a widow, was living in sin with her lover, but the world is full of people whose sins are far greater than that but are still spared diabolical retribution. And what about her sweet, scared children—what offense could they have conceivably committed? None that I could see. Yet I also knew that the Devil couldn't possess or oppress anyone without God's permission, since He has ultimate authority over the forces of darkness.

People have often asked me why God allows the demonic to do anything at all, especially to good people. Since I'm a cop—not a theologian—I'll rely on Bishop McKenna's explanation. He points out that the Old Testament addresses the issue of unfair suffering in the story of Job, a virtuous, God-fearing man who was blessed with many children and great wealth. Satan, however, asked if he could tempt Job, and was allowed to strike him down with one misfortune after another—first killing Job's cattle and camels, then all of his children. Although devastated by these losses, Job said, "The Lord gave and the Lord has taken away; blessed be the name of the Lord."

Again the Devil tempted this innocent man to curse God, by covering him with boils from head to toe. Plunged into despair, Job wished he'd never been born, but remained steadfast in his faith. Three of his friends told him he must be sinful indeed to be so horribly afflicted, prompting him to question God. Out of a whirlwind, the Lord reminded Job of His infinite power and wondrous creations. "Were you there when I founded the earth? . . . Have you ever, in your lifetime, commanded the morning, and shown the dawn its place?" Humbly, Job repented of doubting the divine plan and was rewarded with a new family, double the riches he'd lost, and an extraordinarily long life.

Beyond that, I can't explain why this particular family was subjected to such trials: It's one of God's mysteries. I simply put my fate in His hands and my faith in His loving protection, knowing that it's only by the grace of God that we can stand in the presence of pure evil and survive.

The hour was growing late and Claudia felt utterly helpless. She had to do something to protect her daughter Marybeth from harm, but what? She'd already tried the prayers her minister recommended, to no avail. Not only was this particular demon so powerful that it could withstand holy words, but it was actually provoked to greater viciousness when she invoked God's name—choosing that moment to slash its mark on Marybeth's smooth face. Fleeing to her brother's house hadn't helped either, and it would be pointless to call the priest again.

When it seemed like there was nowhere to turn, Claudia remembered one final refuge: a place where she'd always felt safe and protected from danger, where there was always someone to soothe away her fears and worries with calm words and comforting arms. Although she was forty years old, had borne three children and buried a husband, Claudia picked up the phone and called her first protector—her mother Maggie. "I know it's almost midnight, but we're coming over," she said, her voice breaking like a frightened child's. "Please, it's an emergency."

The demon decided to let loose with some spectral sound effects: first the anguished wail of a baby in unendurable agony, then hideous laughter that rattled the house like an earthquake.

On the other end of the phone, an unseen force bludgeoned Maggie. "The cigarette I was smoking was knocked right out of my mouth and flipped through the air. Outside, I heard unbelievably loud whistling, and something struck the side of the house. There was a tremendous crash, and I saw that a large sculpture of an angel I'd owned for many years had been flung off its shelf and was lying in pieces on the floor. Then a chill went right through me. Three times I felt it, and each time it felt like the chill of death."

By now mother and daughter were sobbing together over the phone. Like Claudia, the older woman was overcome by the impotent grief and despair of a mother who sees her beloved child in desperate danger but can do nothing to help.

The fiend wasn't finished with Maggie. Her weeping turned

into horrible choking gasps, as invisible hands suddenly grabbed her by the throat. "I couldn't breathe, and my eyes were bulging out. I could hear a roaring in my ears and a lot of noise, like heavy furniture was being moved around. I thought I was going to die!"

Just as the older woman was on the verge of passing out, the satanic force released her. She collapsed back in her chair, struggling to catch her breath. At last she could speak again, and told her daughter what had happened.

"Mom, are you okay?" Claudia asked anxiously, and felt somewhat reassured when she heard a breathless yes and the familiar sound of her mother lighting a cigarette. *Taking her kids to her mom's house would be a terrible mistake,* Claudia realized. *Her childhood home was no longer a safe haven. Merely by talking about going there, she'd inadvertently put yet another family member in peril! Was there no limit to this foul creature's malevolence that it could terrorize in two places at once?*

As I listened to this story, I was struck by the eerie parallels to another mother-daughter situation—a strange attack on my sister, Lisa, in our mom's house. Soon after I got involved in the Work, my mother and my sister moved to a new house on Long Island. One night Lisa was home alone and would be spending the night by herself. No problem, my then twenty-six-year-old sister thought, since she was a big girl and knew how to handle herself. But this night really put her courage to the test. Jen and I had been by earlier, and neither of us saw or felt anything out of the ordinary. Nor did Lisa feel there was anything to fear when she went into the living room around 9:00 P.M., hardly an hour you'd expect the demonic to attack. Yet 9:00 P.M. to 6:00 A.M. are considered the "psychic hours," because that's when supernatural energy is at its peak.

That's me as a young—but very serious—baseball
player with the CYO Robbins . . .
(Ralph Sarchie Sr.)

. . . and as a rookie cop in PSA (Police Service Area) #4.
Yes, I had an attitude. Still do. (Ralph Sarchie)

Me, with Lorraine Warren, Bill Ramsey (who was possessed by a demonic spirit that exhibited the characteristics of a werewolf) and Ed Warren. (Jennifer Sarchie)

My partner in the Work, Joe Forrester, and me. (Jennifer Sarchie)

Me with Fr. Malachi Martin, at my home. (Joe Forrester)

Bishop Robert McKenna. (Courtesy Bishop Robert McKenna)

Our Lady of the Rosary Chapel in Monroe, Connecticut. (Joe Forrester)

This photo was taken in Queens; it was not a part of an investigation. The day before, my wife, Jen, had fallen at the location
and broken her arm. We came back to photograph the site so we
could claim her disability benefits. What a surprise we got when
we developed the film! You can clearly see the shape of a person
and a smaller shape to the left of that.
(Ralph Sarchie)

This photo was taken
of my sister on New
Year's Day. She was
attacked by the demonic
a few days later.
(Jennifer Sarchie)

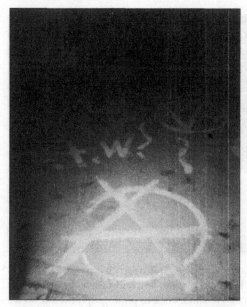

This photo was taken in an abandoned house in the Bronx. The "Anarchy A" is commonly associated with Satanism. "F.t.W." stands for "F___ the World." (Ralph Sarchie)

Also taken in the Bronx, this time at a playground. The Pentagram and the Sign of the Beast—666—speak for themselves. (Ralph Sarchie)

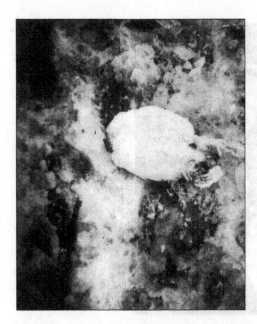

Photo taken in front of PSA #2, East New York, Brooklyn. This headless chicken was placed in front of the Command. (Ralph Sarchie)

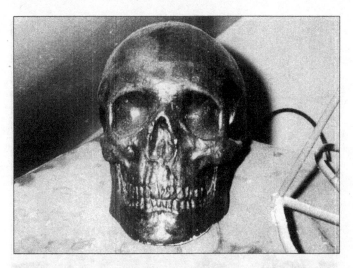

This skull was connected to a case of demonic infestation that I handled. When its owner denied being involved in the occult, I walked away from the case. (Ralph Sarchie)

Christina and Daniella with me at 1 Police Plaza on the day I was promoted to Sergeant. (Jennifer Sarchie)

The girls and me at Bear Mountain State Park. We love Bear Mountain. (Ralph Sarchie)

So there was Lisa, unwinding in front of the TV, when suddenly she heard a loud bang coming from the basement. It scared the hell out of her, and she froze in her chair, not daring to go downstairs to investigate. The pounding continued for about five minutes, then abruptly stopped. Finally she convinced herself it was the boiler, went to her bedroom, locked the door, and eventually fell asleep. In the safety of daylight, she got up her nerve and went down to the basement. What she found was extremely unsettling. The basement door, which could be locked or unlocked only with a key, was wide open. The sound she heard must have been the door crashing back and forth—but there was no wind that night!

Naturally, she called me. I was angry that she hadn't contacted me the night before, when she was trembling in her living room chair, but I rushed over to help. I found the door and its lock to be working perfectly, and questioned her about different ways it might have gotten unlocked. She was 100 percent positive that no one had unlocked it—and knowing how security-conscious my mother was, I felt sure it was firmly bolted at all times. I also found no signs of forced entry—and believe me, I've seen lots of burglaries in my time. Still, I wasn't sure if supernatural forces were responsible. Despite the Work, I'm *not* inclined to blame every unexplained event on the demonic. To play it safe, I put some extra locks on the door.

What happened a few nights later left no doubt of diabolic intent. Although my sister steered far clear of the Work and always cut me off if I mentioned a case, saying "I don't want to hear about *that*," she still fell prey to an evil power. She was sound asleep when something—she didn't know what—woke her in the night. Such was its fury that it grabbed the back of her head and shoved her face into the pillow. To her utter horror, she felt her bed lift off the floor. Too scared even to scream, she thought she'd die right there with our mother sleeping in the next room!

But as suddenly as it started, the attack stopped. With the frantic strength of fear, she leapt from her bed and flicked on the light. There was nobody in the room! After lying awake all night, with every light blazing, she called me first thing in the morning. Now certain that my own sister had been assaulted by a satanic spirit, I again hurried to her house—with, as backup, Bob, a police lieutenant I worked with in East New York who was interested in the Work. Although not a Catholic, he was a very good man and kept watch while I read the Pope Leo XIII prayer in the house. When I got to Lisa's room, the temperature turned very cold. Bob shivered and said, "Ralph, do you feel that?" I nodded, never stopping the prayer. After the final amen, there were no more problems in that house.

There was an odd sequel to this story a few days later. My wife is forever taking photos, and had taken some pictures of my sister in her bedroom before the nightmarish attack. After Jen got them developed, she spent a long time studying one of them. Finally she handed it to me and said, "What is this?" I took a look and almost fell off my chair. The photo showed Lisa and our daughter Christina—and something else. You can see spirit energy that is extremely bright and moving from left to right. At the very top of the energy is a shadowy figure starting to manifest itself. I never thought Lisa was imagining things, but here was physical proof that she'd been stalked by a sinister spirit. Thank God she escaped relatively unscathed!

My mother-in-law, Carol, had a similar but even more harrowing experience, also when she was sleeping. I can hear the skeptics and debunkers out there saying "Hey, they were asleep, so it was just a dream." But consider this: The demonic love to terrorize people when they are most vulnerable, and what better time to do that than when they're asleep in their own beds? I've had nightmares where I've literally woken up soaked in sweat, but I *knew* those were dreams, just as my sister and mother-in-law *knew* their experiences were real. The same thing happened to the McKenzie women: When they told their story on TV, a nonbeliever suggested that they were just sexually frustrated women who only dreamed they were stalked by an incubus. I couldn't believe this debunker was so cruel and mean-spirited. Would he tell the teenaged victim of a *human* pervert that she only imagined being attacked because she was starved for sex? That's just plain sick.

Here's my mother-in-law's true story, exactly as she told it to me. She was awakened one night by a suffocating pressure on her chest. When she opened her eyes, she saw a hooded specter. Its body appeared solid, but when she looked where the face should have been, there was only blackness. It looked like a monk, but its words were full of unholy menace: "I'm going to kill you!"

Beyond fear or even dread, Carol turned to prayer and began to recite the Hail Mary. The pressure on her chest grew more and more intense, and after reaching the words "Holy Mary, Mother of God, pray for us sinners now and at the hour of our death," she lost consciousness. Her plea for help was heard, and she woke up the next morning to the sound of birds singing. She used the holy water I'd given her, and over the next several days, it slowly washed her terror away.

The McKenzie family, however, was still trapped in a web of fear. Convinced that the demon would hunt them down wherever they fled—or be lying in wait when they arrived there—Claudia and the exhausted children all huddled together on Jessica's waterbed like cornered animals. Even with every light blazing and big, muscular Artie standing watch at the door, no one could sleep. Their hearts pounded, and their nerves were so on edge that if one of them moved, everyone jumped. Periodically, the house made some tiny creak, and they all screamed.

The incubus, however, didn't attack that night or the next. For the next month it did absolutely nothing, except let the family marinate in their own terror, not knowing when—or how—it would next assail them. You might say it was toying with them, playing a cat-and-mouse game. With bestial cruelty, it was waiting for its prey to be lulled into a false sense of security.

Gradually the family let down their guard and resumed their old sleeping arrangements, except that the children now slept two to a bed, with the twins in one room and Monique in her cousin's room on the first floor. That's when the predator from Hell pounced.

"It was a Sunday," Jessica explained. "Sunday is never a good day in this house—and on a scale of one to ten, this Sunday was a ten! I woke up sweating and looked at the clock. It was three o'clock in the morning. That's when a lot of horrible things happen here."

Her cousins, the twins, also woke up drenched in sweat. "We heard crashing footsteps, looked at each other, and said, 'It's coming!'" Carolyn added. To their incredible relief, the steps ran past their door and stopped.

Jessica, who'd been sleeping on the waterbed with Monique, shouted, "It's at *our* door!" Astonishingly, the locked door swung open, and a huge dark shape oozed into the room.

"I felt it land on the bed," the cousin continued. "It was

leaning over us, and the waterbed went crazy! It was shaking like the ocean during a storm. I was thrown against something, maybe its chest. The thing was roaring at us so loudly that I could feel my whole body vibrating from the noise. I was scared to death."

Claudia was jolted from the first sound sleep she'd had for a month. "The children were screaming hysterically, and over the din I heard Monique shrieking at the top of her lungs 'Mom, it's getting Jessica!' I fell out of bed, trying to run to them. It felt like I was running in slow motion and would never get there in time. My legs felt like lead."

It seemed like an eternity before she reached Jessica and Monique. "Their room was as cold as a refrigerator. I threw my body across theirs and saw something running out of the room. It looked like a blur, it was moving so fast."

The twins began shrieking in terror. *The beast was now standing at the foot of their bed!*

"I pulled the covers over my head to hide," Marybeth said, "but the thing got on top of me. It was screaming horrible things in a male voice. What it was saying was so awful I couldn't possibly repeat it, but I thought I'd die of fear! I tried to scream, talk, anything, but I couldn't even whimper. It was all over me like a blanket, and I was suffocating."

Wild with rage and terror, Claudia burst into the room, ready to take on ten demons with her bare hands, if that's what it took to save her child. Once again the satanic stalker departed, in a blur of black. "None of us could stay in that house another second, so we got in the car at 3:00 A.M., and went to my mom's house. I hated to do it, but there was nowhere else to go. Can you understand that? Nowhere to run!"

Mercifully, Claudia's elderly mother and the rest of the family were spared any further torments that night. They dozed fitfully, reliving their ordeal in grotesque dreams. The next morning, the widow reluctantly drove the girls home, fearing what might happen to her mother if the family stayed in her house too long.

Monique was the most deeply affected by the nightmarish attacks. "When I was cooking, I'd get strange urges to pick up a bottle or knife and attack the rest of the family. Was I losing my mind? I was afraid of myself, and told my mother that this just wasn't me."

Jessica was also buckling under the stress. "My hand kept moving from side to side, against my will. I had a constant feeling of horror, as if I was splitting into a good side and a bad side. My hands felt like they had claws—and I wanted to scratch someone." She stared at her hands in disbelief, as if they might betray her at any moment. I noticed that she'd clipped her nails very short.

Were these bizarre thoughts signs of possible possession? Actually, horrible visions or disturbing impulses are common during oppression and even can occur during infestation, as I'd already seen in the graveyard case, where the young mother was frightened by sudden, overpowering feelings of rage, hostility, and hatred. This is a form of psychological warfare, the internal aspect of oppression, where the demonic amplify a person's negative emotions. It's only natural that Monique and Jessica would be angry about their dreadful ordeal and might wish, at times, that someone would be punished for putting them through all this. With fiendish cunning, the demon eagerly seized on these fleeting feelings and turned up the volume until the children's own thoughts became all but unrecognizable to them.

Yet what made these violent urges so peculiarly distressing was that they weren't *completely* foreign to these girls. On

some deep unconscious level, they did want to hurt somebody, just as they'd been hurt, scratched, and terrorized in
their own beds. Who wouldn't? We all have a dark side: A
psychiatrist once wrote that "bad men do what good men
dream." With savage brilliance, the demon had confronted
these children with the worst thoughts they'd ever had, during the worst time of their life, as if to say "See how vile and
evil *you* are." No wonder Monique questioned her sanity, feeling that only a monster would fantasize about stabbing her
relatives!

Strange as it may sound, I was actually quite impressed at
how *well* these kids were holding up to the mental and physical abuse they'd suffered. By the time oppression sets in, most
families are quite dysfunctional. The people usually become
extremely despondent and go off in their own little worlds—or
turn on each other and quarrel constantly. This family, however, had the psychological fortitude to band together in their
supernatural adversity instead of letting it break them apart.
Perhaps it was because this was a house full of women, ac-
customed to sharing their feelings and fears with each other.

Suspecting that her family's reactions might sound demented to outsiders like us, Claudia emphasized that they
were normal people, caught up in a highly abnormal situation. "If anyone had told me ten years ago that this would
happen to us, I would have thought they were totally insane.
I didn't believe in demons—or the Devil. I thought it was just
superstition. But after living in *this* house, and all the awful
things my family and I have seen and felt here, I not only believe in the Devil—I'm convinced he's here in my house."

The demon greedily drank in the family's terrible dread
and gained strength for its next rampage.

Not waiting for the witching hour of 3:00 A.M. this time, it crept into the twins' bedroom around midnight a few weeks later. Although its feet made no sound that a human ear could hear, both girls woke up, instantly sensing that the malevolent force was stalking them. Too intimidated to open her eyes and confirm that it was there, Carolyn feigned sleep, while Marybeth peeked cautiously out from under the covers. "I saw a tall dark figure standing by the door. It was thin, like a shadow, and darker than the darkness of the room. It came at me in a rush: It was at the end of the bed, then it was on top of me!" To her unimaginable horror, she realized she couldn't move or speak. "I felt a tingling, pins-and-needles feeling all over me and especially up my legs. It was even *inside* me! The sensation was so intense that every part of my body was lit up like an electrical current was running through me."

Frozen helplessly in her bed, she felt an immense weight on her chest, belly, and thighs, as if a large, dangerous animal were settling on top of her. "It was pushing on me so hard, I felt like I was being pushed *through* the bed or maybe pulled into it with a magnet. The more it pressed, the harder and harder it was to breathe: For about a minute, I was smothering, then I somehow got my breath back and yelled for my mother."

Claudia and Jessica rushed to her aid, as Carolyn pounded the bed with the only weapon at hand—the pillow. "Go away," she shouted. "Stop hurting my sister!"

Hoping there was safety in numbers, all of the women piled on the bed and held Marybeth in their arms. Incredibly, she said, "it started happening again, right in front of everybody: the feeling of paralysis, of unnatural energy in the bed. It started raining outside, really hard, and I was more frightened than ever. I started hearing beeps like a StairMaster or a heart monitor when someone dies; and we all heard a woman gasping for air. The noise sounded like it was coming from nowhere and everywhere at the same time. As soon as I could move, it was gone."

The demon's deviancy didn't stop there, however. Over the next several months, it stalked the other females of the family, one by one.

Next was the oldest daughter, Monique. It wasn't silent, stealthy footsteps that woke her in the middle of the night but unbearable noise. Mysteriously, no one else in the house heard it. I've seen this before: The Devil can project a sound to the intended victim, which only she will be affected by, while the rest of the family is totally unaware of what's going on. The person singled out for this attack may attempt to wake her relatives but sometimes is unable to rouse them from sleep. It's another example of how the demonic can ratchet up the terror, by making the person feel alone and isolated.

"The noise sounded like someone was banging the walls and floor with a sledgehammer," Monique told us. "At the end of the bed was the outline of a man, looking at me as I slept. I had the sense of something really evil and scary, like it wanted to kill me. It flopped forward, on top of me, and I actually felt it enter my body." She blushed and paused for a minute. "You know, sexual intercourse. It hurt really bad, like I was being ripped open."

Worse even than the physical rape, the thin teenager explained, was the mental rape. "I also felt a presence in my mind, full of evil and obscene thoughts. It was worse than pornography—it was sickening beyond belief. I wish I could erase the things I saw from my mind—they're like a stain that won't go away. Even though I couldn't move a muscle, my mind was fighting these visions the entire time, because I felt if I gave in, I'd die."

Her cousin was the demon's third victim—and the most reluctant to tell her story. "I was real restless that night and couldn't sleep at all. I couldn't get comfortable and kept tossing and turning. Finally I was going to get up and have some milk, when I saw a dark shadow in the chair. It was laughing weirdly and walked toward the bed in a staggering, wavy motion. The whole room looked distorted, crooked in some way I can't explain. The corners were wrong, or something. The shadow also looked strange, not quite like a person. It had something red and glowing on it." Jessica broke off her account and opened a can of Diet Coke.

After taking several sips, she started speaking again. "It jumped on me. I was fighting, flailing, convulsing, but . . . I wasn't really moving. I was lying on my stomach, soaked in sweat from *trying* to move, but something was pinning me down to the bed. It was heavy and nasty! I couldn't see what was holding me down, but I felt it on my legs and back, pushing me into the mattress. The pillow was pressing on my face and I was suffocating!"

She interrupted herself and tried to distract us with descriptions of frightening phenomena she'd experienced on other occasions. "We've seen a lot of stuff: heart-pounding sounds coming upstairs. You get so afraid that you're going under, losing yourself. It messes with us in so many different ways. I was being scratched; I was a real wreck and looked like an abused child. Sometimes I had big, wide, burning scratches."

I sensed that she was being defensive, anticipating that we would blame her for whatever had happened in that bed, just as rape victims sometimes accuse themselves of dressing too provocatively, failing to heed some subtle signal of their attacker's intentions, or not fighting hard enough. Nobody pressured her to continue. We just waited patiently to see what else she might say.

Finally the words exploded from her. "It sodomized me!" She grabbed her soda, spilling some in her haste to get back upstairs to her family.

Claudia got paper towels and fussed over the spot. I'd already noticed her tidying up anything that was even the tiniest bit out of place, and wondered if being such a compulsive housekeeper was her way of trying to regain control of her chaotic, terrifying life. She might not be able to defeat the demon or even keep it away from her kids, but at least she could win the war against dirt.

Or was she scrubbing because her world was so hopelessly soiled? The widow told us of her own nocturnal encounter with the unclean spirit. "One evening I was unusually tired and just had to lie down. I was half asleep when I saw this huge figure in my room. It was dark, hairy, and had tremendously long arms. I saw big hands, with long claws. *My God*, I thought, *it's a beast!* I said, 'Get the fuck away from me!'"

The beast moved closer, and sprang at her. "It was on me and all over me. I heard a noise, weak at first, with a rhythm to it that got louder and more insistent, until the whole room was roaring. My body was vibrating with the roars, but I couldn't move a finger or say a word. The throbbing went up my legs, higher and higher. The sexual part only lasted a moment, but it was very, very painful."

What about the other twin, Carolyn? Strangely, considering that the incubus molested her mother, sisters, and cousin several more times, it never touched her. I can't explain this, except to say that I've been on other cases where one or more family members escaped unscathed from the satanic activity in their homes, such as Dominick Villanova. Perhaps their special cross to bear was simply knowing how much the people they loved most were suffering, while they themselves were left unharmed.

Hearing the anguish in Carolyn's voice, however, I couldn't imagine how this family had managed to live in this house of horror for six years. I'd only been there six hours, and have never felt such an oppressive place in my life.

Although the very last thing on Earth I wanted to do was *see* this demon in whatever ghastly guise it might assume, Ed and Lorraine felt it was time to try "religious provocation," a technique they frequently use. They asked me to gather the family, then darken the room. "We're going to ask the demon to show itself, in the name of Jesus Christ," Ed told them. "Claudia, command it to come."

Forgetting to mention Jesus, Claudia said, "I command you to come," a potentially dangerous mistake Ed was quick to correct, since ordering an evil spirit around in your own name is just asking for trouble. It's like slapping the biggest bully in the world right in the face. The demonic aren't going to walk away from a challenge by some puny human—it's only the power of God that keeps them in check.

"In the name of Jesus Christ, I command you to come," Claudia intoned nervously, then exclaimed, "It's right by the doorway! I feel its presence: It's here!"

Although I didn't see or feel a thing myself, I was having a problem with this whole procedure. Why the hell would I want the demonic to show itself? If it did, we'd just throw holy water on it and command it to leave in God's name. So why expose ourselves to pure evil unnecessarily? The only answer I can give, and it's a weak one, is "proof." But satanic forces don't want us to prove they exist: If more people realized the Devil is real, churches would be a lot more crowded than they are today, and that's hardly Satan's objective. As Archbishop Fulton Sheen once said, "The Devil is most powerful when he's denied."

Another downside is that once you command a demon in Jesus' name to reveal its identity, it doesn't have to show itself then and there. There is no time frame in the spirit world, so it could reveal itself at a later time, such as when it's 3:00 A.M. and you're nice and snug in your bed, dreaming that you won the lottery. Or it may reveal itself to my wife or children, or to me while I'm driving home from a case.

The only reason I was doing religious provocation at this house was because Ed was the boss, and that's how he wanted it. Only God knows why I was able to walk out of there in one piece. I was profoundly grateful when religious provocation *failed* to draw the demon into the open. Now it was time to get to the heart of the investigation, casting out the enemy.

Doing an exorcism alone isn't my idea of fun, but Ed and Lorraine decided to stay in the basement with the family. I didn't want to ask Ted, the student from Connecticut, to help. I'd never met this well-dressed blond man before, so I had no way of knowing how powerful his belief in God was—or if he even believed at all. Nor did I know if he was in a state of grace. If he wasn't, I'd just be putting him and myself at risk. I always try to discourage people from getting involved in the Work unless their motives are pure and their faith is very strong. Mere curiosity won't cut it. It's human nature to wonder about the spirit world and the occult, but if that were your only reason for trying the Work, you'd endanger yourself and others. And if that were your attitude, I certainly wouldn't want you watching *my* back!

I told everyone to remain seated throughout the ritual, no matter what they heard or saw. I didn't want anyone wandering around during the exorcism. I went upstairs to prepare, while Ed told the family what I would be doing. My senses were ablaze as I went from room to room, burning blessed incense. Not only was I conducting the ritual all by myself, but I knew an extremely powerful demon had been entrenched in this house for years, terrorizing the family whenever the whim struck. I was ready for anything: I fully expected to meet the demon face-to-face, not as the anonymous black shape I'd already seen but in some ghastly manifestation drawn from my worst nightmares or the horrifying visions I've sometimes had during exorcisms.

My sight became unnaturally keen—I was hypervigilant for any tiny movement, any disturbance that might signal the approach of the diabolical force. I've always had excellent eyesight, but everything looked even sharper than usual. More profound still was my hearing as I strained for any sound indicating that the evil spirit was reacting to the incense. Just bringing blessed objects, whether incense, holy water, or relics, into a house like this can be a form of religious provocation—and you should take extreme care doing it. That's why I like to have a partner present, in case I get attacked.

As I listened intently, I was reminded of the time when I was a rookie on Manhattan's notoriously crime-ridden Lower East Side. Part of my patrol assignment was checking roof landings and rooftops for the many junkies, robbers, and rapists who were attracted to these deserted locations like moths to a flame. On that particular night, it was 4:00 A.M. and I was on solo patrol, much as I was in this house, checking a rooftop that had been the scene of many violent crimes. I was vigilant for any sound that might warn of danger as I circled the outside of the elevator room, searching for intruders. All of a sudden, there was a loud *click*. Not realizing that one of the tenants had pressed the button that activates the elevator, I jumped out of my boots in fright because in my alert state, the sound was magnified ten times louder than normal.

I'm no superman. I do get scared, like anyone else. The day I *stop* being scared will be the day when I retire from the police force—and the Work. Apparently, this wasn't that day, because a few minutes later I got the fright of my life. I was standing by the doorway to the kitchen, getting ready to start the Pope Leo XIII prayer, when the refrigerator abruptly decided it was time to chill the food inside. It turned on with a loud *click* that just about scared the pants off me! I think I aged ten years in a single moment. If the Devil could enjoy a good laugh, he would be laughing his ass off at that very moment—at least until I started the prayer.

I went from room to room reading the Pope Leo prayer with my relic of the True Cross in my hand. I was concentrating on the holy words and at the same time making sure that the Devil didn't go on the attack. Going up against an enemy that is both incredibly powerful and invisible is nerve-racking, to say the least, but I took great comfort in knowing that my faith would see me through.

I got through the entire exorcism and showered everything with plenty of holy water. Although I couldn't tell if the evil spirit had left or not, I wasn't frustrated. I've learned to accept that not all cases end with an outward sign of success. I'd done all I possibly could to evict the demon, but ultimately it was God's choice whether the ritual would work. When I went downstairs to check on the family, they were still very nervous. They'd been afraid so long that they didn't know what to expect after the exorcism. After wishing them the best, I said my good-byes and left Ed and Lorraine to wrap things up with the family.

It was close to midnight when I got all my gear packed up in my car. I was physically and spiritually drained. I'd spent ten hours in that house, which was the longest investigation I'd ever done. Four hours is the average. The most exhausting aspect was the exorcism itself. In order for the prayers to be effective, they must be said with energy. That's one of the reasons why you must be in a state of grace. Not only do you need the spiritual protection of a strong, healthy aura, but being in a good relationship with God gives your prayers the positive power that's essential for defeating evil.

I'd put everything I had into helping these people, and now it was time to make the long trip home. My wife had asked me to promise one thing when I began the Work: that I'd never spend the night in a demonically infested home. The very thought of me being in this house overnight terrified her, so I honored her wishes, well aware that she had made enough sacrifices by marrying a demonologist. So, even though I was exhausted and would be driving until dawn, I sat in my car and prayed for a few minutes, thanking God for a safe conclusion to the case. It was time to head for home—and Jen.

As I do with all my cases, I put this one out of my mind. I knew that if I was not successful the family would contact the Warrens and we'd return with a whole team of investigators. I heard nothing more about the McKenzies for an entire year, then learned that they'd called the Warrens to say that all was well, and the incubus was gone. I was delighted that they could finally live in peace but knew that somewhere out there is an extremely angry demon who hates love and loves to hate.

7

CAUGHT BY THE OCCULT

The busy season in the Work starts around Halloween and intensifies until after Christmas, when the celebration of the miracle of Jesus' virgin birth seems to inflame the demonic. It was near the end of October 1994 when I got a call from an extremely soft-spoken young man named Tony Petri, who had a problem. At that time, I was no longer working with Joe Forrester because of an argument we'd had the month before, in September—a month that has been an ongoing source of trouble for me. Tension built up between us because he wanted to leave the Warrens and start his own group, the St. Joseph Society (named after Jesus' father, described in the Catholic Litany of Saints as the "terror of demons"), while I wanted to keep on working with Ed and Lorraine.

At first, we continued doing investigations together and didn't let this issue get in the way. We'd always worked well together, complementing each other's knowledge of the demonic—and we never had any disagreements about how to handle cases. We were very open to each other's ideas and had developed mutual respect. But our conflicting views about the Warrens were fraying our friendship more than we realized. It just took one more difficulty to snap the bond, though, thank God, not for good. The problem occurred when we were driving to a case Ed and Lorraine had asked us to handle. Since we had several investigators, some from Connecticut and some from our New York chapter, we went in two cars. Joe took Scott, Phil, and my equipment in his car, while the rest of us went with Ritchie, a very thin Jewish man from the Connecticut group.

Joe was following Ritchie, but somewhere along the way we became separated. I assumed there was no problem, since each car had written directions and Scott had been to this house at least three times before. A half hour after I arrived at the residence, Joe called, sounding very agitated. He'd gotten lost and was at a diner. I knew where the diner was and gave him detailed directions to the house. In an annoyed tone, he insisted I come to the diner and lead him to the house. Since we were already way behind schedule, I was reluctant but did as he asked. When I arrived, Joe was pissed off, to say the least. We had a big argument right there in the parking lot.

"Get your equipment out of my car," he shouted. As soon as I did, he and Phil drove off, leaving Scott behind with me. I can tell you I was very hot under the collar at being treated this way. I don't like to handle cases when I'm pissed off, but we'd come all this way and people were counting on us, so I went back to the house and did the investigation.

Joe and I didn't speak for months, which led to the disbanding of the group we'd started, the New York City chapter of the New England Society for Psychic Research. A few of our investigators, including Phil, joined Joe's society. Young Chris, however, stuck with me for a while, then got married and went on to other interests. Other people left the Work entirely. I could understand that: When you're battling the Devil, you can get hammered in all kinds of scary and dis-

turbing ways. Yet I was determined to continue the fight
against evil, even if I had to do it alone.

The Warrens continued to refer New York cases to me,
which is how Tony Petri got my phone number. In such a
quiet voice that I kept having to ask him to speak up, he explained that he'd been dabbling in the occult for years but
also believed in God and attended church. Somewhere along
the way he said, "My life became hellish. I didn't feel like myself anymore: My mind was bombarded with alien thoughts.
I know I need help, because something is terribly wrong."
While it was too soon to say if the demonic was involved, I
was impressed by the young man's obvious sincerity and made
an appointment to meet him in his Bronx home.

Don't get me wrong. I'm not infallible by any means and
have occasionally been deceived by people who concoct a
seemingly convincing story on the phone yet turn out to be
liars or lunatics when I meet them in person. Since I don't
charge money for my services, people have nothing to lose by
wasting my time, for whatever reason. A few years ago, for
example, I got a call from a middle-aged man in the Bronx,
who sounded normal enough on the phone, at least to me,
since I hear about strange stuff all the time. He described a
creepy sensation of being watched in his condo and followed
by something he couldn't see. He was also hearing voices but
couldn't make out their words—a phenomenon we call "magical whisperings."

All of this could have a supernatural explanation, so Joe
and I went to check it out. It was a beautiful autumn evening
when we arrived at the condo and rang the bell, with no idea
what might await us on the other side of the door. No one
answered. Joe was puzzled and told me he'd confirmed the
appointment earlier that day. He pressed the buzzer again,

and after several long rings, the door finally opened to reveal a man wearing a tattered terry-cloth bathrobe. Joe and I looked at each other, knowing something was definitely off. We introduced ourselves and asked if he was Stuart Butterman, figuring we must have the wrong apartment. "Yes," he said, sounding a bit annoyed when we said we'd wait outside until he was properly dressed.

Five minutes later we were finally ushered into an exquisitely decorated living room. Not a thing was out of place, except Stuart, who was oddly dressed and repeated the same story he'd told on the phone, much less believably this time. With a wild flourish of his hands, he added that he had angelic powers and could communicate with spirits. "Is there anyone dead you'd like to speak to?" he asked. I glanced at Joe and could see his bullshit detector was on red alert. Although neither of us is psychic, I knew what my partner was thinking: *This guy isn't just eccentric—he's a nut job!*

"No, thank you," Joe replied politely. I cautioned Mr. Butterman that if he really was in touch with the dead, he should give it up immediately as this practice is extremely dangerous. He gave a demented laugh, and we left.

Now I was about to walk through the door of a new case. As always, I felt an indescribable mix of excitement and apprehension as I parked outside Tony's home. *What would go on inside?* I tried not to think of the possibilities, because I like to start an investigation with an open mind. As I got out of my car, I felt a little jolt at the back of my head. Thinking it might be a bug, I felt to see if anything was in my hair. Finding nothing, I didn't give it a second thought and continued up the walk. Once I got inside, I felt it again, a subtle poke. Tucking what had just happened away, I introduced myself and set up my video camera, anxious to get on with the interview, since I was due at my police job by midnight.

Tony looked just like his voice: small and so delicately built that a strong breeze might blow him away. He was in his twenties, with a full head of brown hair and a neatly trimmed goatee. His large brown eyes were soft and soulful, just what you'd expect for a blues musician. Although he didn't appear to be rich, I got the impression that this young pianist wasn't hurting for money. He was neatly dressed in a flannel shirt, slim-fitting black jeans, and well-worn black sneakers. From the nervous way he plucked at his clothes and what he'd told me so far, I sensed he was in deep trouble. I also felt he was a good-hearted, honest person, and liked him right away.

He lived in a basement apartment in his mother's house. Though small, it was a perfect bachelor pad. The place was very neat and clean with starkly modern furniture I suspected had been selected more for the elegance of its design than for comfort. Several framed posters of jazz and blues musicians hung on the walls.

After offering me a cup of freshly brewed coffee, Tony explained that his difficulties had begun, quite innocently, when he was a high school senior. "I had a girlfriend who said she was at a party where they'd played a most interesting game. 'So what was it?' I asked, and she went to her room and got a Ouija board. I'd never seen one before, and thought it was a toy. We played, and that thing in the middle just zoomed around on its own accord."

My face darkened at this. *There ought to be a law against these evil, occult "toys"!* Keeping my feelings in check, I told Tony that the object he was describing was called a planchette.

"Nothing exciting happened," he continued. "We asked it questions and it gave us the answers, but they weren't very interesting or dramatic."

A few days later he learned that his girlfriend's father was seriously ill. Tony was very close with this man and, being such a sensitive person, got extremely upset. Like many teenagers, he began to wonder about life and death.

A woman he met a few days later claimed she had the answer, and started to tell him about Christian Science. He brushed her off at first but later read the literature she gave him. Christian Scientists believe that Jesus came to save us not just from sin but also from illness and death. According to this religion, the methods Christ and His disciples used to heal the sick and raise the dead can be used in modern times, so followers of this faith shouldn't go to a doctor but to a Christian Science practitioner to regain health or to solve any personal or financial problems they might have.

That resonated with Tony, now that his girlfriend's father was so ill. He tried to will the old man back to health, but when that didn't work—and the father died—he was bitterly disappointed and turned away from Christian Science.

But Tony was still spiritually hungry, and wanted more than ever to know what the world was all about. He felt that something was missing from his own existence and was thus captivated when he saw an ad in a magazine proclaiming "Learn the Mysteries of Life!" This was precisely his goal, so he sent money to the address in the ad and received "initiation" instructions from the Rosicrucians, also known as the Ancient and Mystical Order Rosae Crucis (Latin for "rose cross"). Headquartered in California, this group promises to unlock secret wisdom from the ages, banish fears and frustration, enrich the human spirit, and open the door to self-mastery. They claim to accomplish this by revealing the workings of mysterious natural laws through which an initiate can turn wishes and daydreams into reality. If that's not grandiose enough, they also tout their teachings as the path to improve memory, increase health, influence other people, learn the truth about reincarnation, decipher ancient symbols, and ultimately obtain cosmic consciousness.

The training course Tony received advised studying "first-degree" Rosicrucian doctrine for six weeks, then initiating himself into the order with a secret rite. He was told to darken a room, surround himself with lighted candles, and stare into a mirror. As instructed, he then traced a five-inch cross on the glass while intoning "Hail Holy Cross." This was followed by precisely three minutes of meditation. The use of a looking glass for mystical rituals is known as "crystalmancy," or "magic mirror" divination, and has a long history. St. Augustine wrote of witches who wrote prophecies on mirrors in human blood, and ancient Roman oracles used reflective surfaces in a rite called "speculum" to forecast the victors in upcoming battles. Magic mirrors have also been used for sorcery—and are now sold over the Internet.

By dabbling in the occult, Tony was attempting to fill a void—and soon enough, his gnawing, adolescent hunger *was* filled, by a demon. He didn't think he had anything to fear, though. "I felt it was safe to play around with these things, because at the church I went to, they told us the Devil doesn't exist."

After completing the initiation ritual, he sat down to his calculus homework—and was overcome by bizarre sensations: "I suddenly felt like I'd been injected with a drug. When I looked at the sheet of paper I'd been writing on, it wasn't a sheet of paper anymore. It seemed like I was looking *through* it and seeing the infinite makeup of that piece of paper and all of creation. I remember thinking 'Where am I?' But it seemed so ridiculous. Was I going crazy? I knew I *wasn't* crazy: I was a good student, getting good grades. I was involved in music, making recordings, and should be happy, since I was doing everything that pleased me."

I didn't doubt that Tony was telling me the truth, but I saw that he was a troubled person who had gone down some dark roads in his quest for answers. He had more to say about that experience in his room. "My mind was bombarded with questions, but they weren't my *own* questions."

What were they? Tugging at his clothing more anxiously than ever, he said, "They were questions like 'How is it that matter exists? How is it that *anything* exists?'" He said he considered these legitimate questions, but only if they actually came from his own intellect. "But these questions were alien and frightening. I even questioned the existence of God. I felt I was being programmed like a computer, by whom or what I didn't know."

Tony's words were setting off alarm bells. Maybe this man really didn't know, but I did. I saw a strong correlation with a case Father Malachi Martin had written about in *Hostage to the Devil*. This man, called Carl V. in the book, was a psychologist who opened himself up to possession by delving into parapsychology to learn about the true origins of Christianity. The parallel between the two cases was the method the evil spirit used to attack. Like Tony, Carl V. was engaged in his studies when his consciousness changed in a single moment. He lost all physical sense of his surroundings: He was no longer *looking* at them but somehow *participating* in them. As he described it, he *knew* every object he saw in its entirety, just as Tony *knew* the "infinite makeup" of a sheet of paper.

The difference was in the two men's desires. While Tony longed to know the mysteries of life, Carl V. wanted to know the mysteries of Christianity. The psychologist's experiences, however, were more profound than the young musician's, because Carl V. had uncanny psychic abilities, bestowed on him not by God but by the Devil. Both men, however, had the distinct feeling of losing "self." Their total being was swallowed up by a diabolical force. While neither gave up complete control at this point, by involving themselves in the occult, they unwittingly invited demonic possession.

After the homework episode, the "hellish" period of Tony's life began. For several years afterward, as he attended college and then launched a career as a musician, he could function fairly normally, but he kept having bouts where he couldn't think straight and felt alienated from himself.

A friend suggested he try transcendental meditation (TM), which is not a religion. The instructors say it can be practiced by people of any faith, including clergy. TM in itself isn't evil, but it can have very negative side effects, as Tony's story illustrates. Its devotees say that this form of meditation releases stress and purifies the mind, body, and emotions of the person who does it. This phrasing bothers me, because it sounds like a deliberate attempt to exclude any reference to the human soul. In speaking of "natural law," TM also ignores God and focuses solely on the "self." For someone who is already troubled and vulnerable, like the young pianist, opening up his mind this way can admit supernatural forces that seek only to destroy. Instead, I urge anyone interested in meditation to focus solely on thoughts of God, who will grant inner peace and relieve stress.

Tony was very impressed with TM. After trying it for a few months, he had another extraordinary experience: "My consciousness was again transformed, but in completely the opposite way as before. It was a very positive turnaround, and the terrible feelings of the past years melted away in a single moment. I was filled with peace and joy." This set off alarm bells for me: I could see that, at this point, he was being drawn in even further.

Since he was a Catholic, Tony asked two priests about TM, and both gave their approval. I was extremely disturbed by this: Priests are in the service of God, and should have been directing his spiritual life toward prayer and the holy sacraments, not nonreligious meditation. After Tony's so-called uplifting experience, and with these priests' OK, he signed up for an advanced course in TM, which led him further down the path to possession.

This course, as Tony explained it, was called the Sidhi. Sidhi are a group of mantras (focus words) that one intones during a long meditation. Each of these mantras was associated with different powers. Tony decided to concentrate on the one for levitation. Nothing remarkable happened for several weeks, then he felt electric energy and lightness enter his spine. "At times I would feel the energy go into my shoulders and rise into my head. I would be sitting in the lotus position and lift right off the floor. I would go higher and higher without doing anything; and the energy kept getting stronger and stronger."

I questioned Tony further about this because I've seen practitioners of TM attempting to levitate. It looks pretty comical, watching these people bouncing up and down on the floor. But Tony assured me he did nothing to lift himself up—it just happened.

Although he believed he'd opened the doors of perception, he discovered darkness on the other side. "What came along with the energy was a babbling of words from my mouth, words I didn't understand. This disturbed me terribly, so I spoke with both the TM instructor and a priest. I got similar explanations, sort of."

His teacher said energy rises from the base of the spine and opens the chakra points—the body's power sources—which gives rise to levitating, sometimes called "yogic flying." Yogic flying is a wonderful thing, the instructor added, showing that Tony had risen to a higher plane of consciousness, both mentally and physically. "I thought *Great, but why am I babbling words I can't understand?* The teacher said it was just stress coming out in 'articulated words.'"

The priest took a different view and suggested that Tony was "speaking in tongues." To back up his theory, he cited a number of Biblical references, none of which advocated incoherent, meaningless babble. (In some religions, such as Pentacostalism and charismatic Catholicism, participants speak in tongues, but only as part of their prayers.) The holy man's words made Tony believe he was having an important spiritual experience. *Although I hate to criticize a priest, I felt this one just didn't have a clue. It made me sick to think that Tony had been led further astray by this misguided interpretation of his behavior.*

Despite the young man's increasingly strange state of mind, his career was taking off. Just as he was about to perform in his first concert, he fell under the influence of yet another friend with off-the-wall spiritual notions. This man, an antiques dealer with an interest in the occult, gave the pianist a rock he claimed had great power—and would assure Tony's success in the music world. Called a "yoni stone," it was shaped like an egg, with the outline of an eye in green. I'd never seen anything like it, but it was hard to imagine that nature came up with something like this. The friend told Tony that if he kept it in his room and looked at it once a day, his fondest wish would come true.

I've dealt with many weird things in the Work, but "yoni stones" weren't among them, so I asked Brother Andrew, if he was familiar with them. He explained that they were of Tibetan origin and used in fertility rites. I was confused by this, since Tony's troubles had nothing to do with what this rock was meant for. When I researched further, I discovered, to my amusement, that "yoni" refers to female genitalia! So much for Tony's occult buddy. I guess he had had rocks in his head, since he certainly didn't know his stones.

A short time later Tony was hit with the same terrifying feelings he'd had in high school, except that they were much more intense. His mind was overwhelmed with turmoil, as the alien thoughts he'd hoped he'd banished for good with TM came back in full force. "I had the sense my soul was being plucked out of me," he whispered in a quivering voice.

I asked if he always turned to the occult for answers. He admitted he did, but swore he was now willing to do anything it took to get the help he so desperately desired from God. That was the first step I needed him to take. During the interview, I was struck by the eerie atmosphere in his home—and I'm not talking about the yoni stone. I detected a peculiar aura around Tony's head: a ring of yellow studded with ominous black dots.

Putting that thought aside, I explained to him that he'd been taken over by a demon so thoroughly that he could no longer distinguish between his own consciousness and that of the evil spirit. He'd made the first move to getting rid of it, by reaching out to God, but the infernal force had been there for so long and had such a grip on him that expelling it would be difficult indeed. Tony meekly agreed with everything I said, but I could tell he was so confused and desperate that he probably would have agreed that the moon was made of green cheese if that's what it took to get my help.

Despite all the painful and peculiar events he'd been subjected to, he still didn't grasp that he truly was possessed. Yet everything he said was further proof: A few minutes later he mentioned a dreadful experience he'd recently had during a Catholic healing mass. His head began turning violently from side to side and against his will he shouted out "Nayacota"—a nonsense word—in the middle of the service. "I knew I was saying 'no,'" he explained, "because something in me was provoked."

Hoping to bring him some relief from his suffering, I also tried praying over the young musician. As I'd feared, however, the evil spirit was again provoked. The previously calm, soft-spoken man became increasingly agitated, flailing from the holy words as if they were burning his skin. His mouth developed an anguished tic, and he let out a blood-curdling shriek of pain when I held up a cross. I quickly finished the prayer with an emphatic "Amen," knowing I was likely to be attacked if I enraged the demon any further.

Tony immediately quieted down and listened intently as I once again explained that he was possessed by a demonic spirit. He didn't know much about demons and the Devil— and didn't really believe in that stuff. "Are you sure?" he asked.

"I can understand why you're confused about what's happening to you," I replied. "But from what you're telling me, something alien is causing your problems, something that's not you. I'm certain that this 'something' is a demon. When one of these spirits enters a person, he often finds it impossible to pray. That's why you behaved that way at the healing mass."

How could I tell that Tony was possessed? The Catholic Church's Roman Ritual of Exorcism lists signs to look for: speaking in a language the person has never studied and shouldn't know; levitation; superhuman strength or feats far beyond someone's normal abilities; being physically unable to enter a house of worship; giving off a foul, repugnant odor; harboring hatred of Jesus Christ or anything holy; and prophesying future events or having inexplicable knowledge of the past, usually other people's embarrassing, un-confessed sins that they have never revealed to a living soul. Naturally, the demonic will try to conceal themselves from someone like me, who is there to expose them for the foul fiends they are. It's not that the Devil fears me, or any human being, but he fears faith, exorcism, and, most of all, God.

Also confusing the issue is the possibility that the person isn't possessed but mentally ill. Some forms of insanity can mimic signs of possession, since schizophrenia causes bizarre ideas and hallucinations; paranoia creates delusions of being persecuted, possibly by imagined evil spirits; and dissociative disorders can provoke sudden, drastic changes in consciousness or multiple personalities that are *not* demonic. What guides me in making the determination is both divine revelation, which I receive through prayer, and observing how well the person functions in daily life. When someone is possessed, the demon doesn't control the person twenty-four hours a day, so he or she will behave normally most of the time, always knowing that something isn't quite right, as Tony did, when he felt an alien presence "reprogramming" his mind.

I could tell the musician still didn't really understand the true cause of his problem. "Are you willing to undergo an exorcism?" I asked. He immediately said yes.

The interview was now over, so I put my videocamera

away and prepared to leave. Offhandedly, Tony remarked, "I don't see things like everyone else does." Although it was getting late, and I was due at work soon, I encouraged him to elaborate. Rather mysteriously, he added, "I see things as if I have a veil over my eyes." I had no idea what this meant, but stored it away. Every investigation, I learn something new.

When I reviewed the videotape the next day, I noticed something I hadn't seen with my own eyes. On two separate places on the tape, I saw "spirit energy," the same perfectly round, transparent balls I've seen on photos taken in homes infested with satanic spirits. Spirit energy looks very different from artifacts created by light sources, which are generally octagonal in shape. The balls of spirit energy were actually moving across the screen with such pronounced speed that I stopped the tape to look at them again.

I also showed the video to Brother Andrew, not telling him anything about the case so he could make an unbiased psychic assessment. He too remarked on the spirit energy, then added, "There's something very curious about this man. He's possessed by a demon, but I notice something else too. I can't really see his face. It's hidden under some kind of veil."

Three of the Warrens' investigators came to Our Lady of the Rosary Chapel to help with the exorcism. Although I'd seen this church many times before, my spirit was still refreshed by the beauty of this wonderful old chapel, with its brilliant stained-glass windows and colorful religious statues. Built in the nineteenth century by Methodists, it was subsequently purchased by the late Father Francis Fenton, who founded the Orthodox Roman Catholic Movement (another name for Traditionalist Catholicism). Bishop Robert McKenna, an ordained Dominican priest and exorcist, was put in charge of the chapel in 1972, and has officiated there ever since, conducting traditional Latin masses and sacraments.

These assistants were all very experienced, devout men I'd worked with many times before. Ed and Lorraine's nephew, John, has been in the Work most of his life. Although he's in his forties, he has a boyish face, with a goatee similar to Tony's. Despite his thick glasses, his eyes are extremely alert and blaze with intelligence. You get the feeling that very little escapes his keen gaze. And he's certainly not a man it's easy to keep a secret from!

Scott is a six-foot-tall martial arts champion with long blond hair. He's the most fearless person I've ever met—ask him to charge into a demonically infested basement and he'd do it without a second's hesitation. Hell, he'd do it if the Devil himself were waiting there, that's how brave he is. But despite being such a dedicated warrior, he's extremely polite. He always treats Ed and Lorraine with the utmost respect, invariably addressing them as "Mr. and Mrs. Warren." He's happy to call me "Ralph," though, and has been a frequent guest at my home.

The final member of our group was Joe Z. Like me, he's a cop. He works in a quiet Connecticut town. A very muscular, brown-haired man in his late thirties, he's a fun person to be around. He has a wicked sense of humor and can keep you laughing all night long. A lot of people think the Work is always deadly serious, but we do laugh and joke around at times on investigations, if we feel this would help put the affected person or family at ease. Although a Protestant, Joe Z. is perfectly comfortable coming to a Catholic church to help the bishop with exorcisms, and has often done so.

While we waited for Bishop McKenna, I talked to Tony Petri. I couldn't help but like this man and sympathize with what he was going through. But I was very careful about what I said to him, since I didn't want to put any ideas in his head about what might happen. I needed him to see for himself that it was an evil spirit—and not his own intellect—that was causing his problem. This understanding was essential to him being freed of the demon, since he had to reject it out of his own free will.

Tony was quiet and reserved as I explained that for his safety and ours, we would be putting him in restraints. He nodded that this was okay with him. I then told him we'd be videotaping his exorcism, but the film would never be shown in public. It was for documentary purposes and to help train future investigators. He said that he understood and wanted to proceed.

Sitting next to Tony, waiting for his exorcism to begin, I felt very small and insignificant in comparison to what was about to take place—the clash of two powers mighty beyond all comprehension, one driven by relentless hatred and evil, the other by boundless love and goodness. It was awesome to be even a foot soldier in this eternal war between the ultimate adversaries, and although I was anxious, I put my faith in God, confident that He'd get us through.

Each exorcism is different, I've found. I thought about Father Martin's extensive studies of the subject. According to his research, each year some 800 to 1,300 major exorcisms—and several thousand minor ones—are performed around the world. After interviewing many priests who have conducted these rituals, he concluded there are usually six distinct phases, which he termed *presence*, *pretense*, *breakpoint*, *voice*, *clash*, and *expulsion*. Not all of the twenty-one exorcisms I've participated in followed this pattern. When I discussed this with Joe, he told me that Father Martin said sometimes these stages come all at once, since the demonic aren't bound by anything except God. Just as some satanic spirits can skip one or more of the three stages of demonic activity—infestation, oppression, and possession—stages can be passed over during an exorcism.

In any genuine case of possession, the demonic *presence* is unmistakable during an exorcism. Everyone in the room can feel the evil spirit because it is so horribly different from anything human. In fact, it is the opposite of humanity. You can't see it, but your whole body responds to it with revulsion. I've found that you'll experience the satanic presence to different degrees, depending on the demon's power. At times the presence will retreat or come in spurts. It may be as subtle, as Father Martin says, as "a hiss in the brain," but once you feel it, you can never forget it.

Bishop McKenna told me it's been the same for him. "In every case I've had, there's always been a definite sign of a demonic presence, but sometimes it's so low-key that the Devil hardly makes himself audible or never speaks through the possessed at all. He may show himself by controlling people's bodies, so they growl or thrash, or obsess and torment them mentally rather than physically. Other times the change in the person when the Devil takes over is so violent and dramatic it's like a dual personality: You reel from it and fear for your life."

Only the most powerful religious belief, like that of the bishop, can get a priest through such an exorcism, because trying to cast out a demon without faith would be like committing slow suicide. Even then the exorcist must keep his mind on God at all times and be aware of his own weaknesses, since that's where the demonic will attack him. He should not shy away or stray from questioning the infernal force but must ask only what is truly pertinent. He also must remember that the evil spirit will lie and tell the truth only under duress, when compelled to do so by the name of Jesus Christ.

The exorcist must perform the ritual with great authority and with great contempt. As soon as he sees that the demon is being tormented by his prayers, he must double the attack. We are dealing with a being that would, if God permitted, destroy humanity because of its extreme hatred. The Roman Ritual instructs that there must be no quarter offered here, no mercy given to the once-beautiful and perfect creature God created as one of His original angels—a spirit that, like us, was given free will but chose the path of sin and eternal damnation. These foul fiends show no pity on the children of God and must be given no mercy in return.

Once the demon is forced forward—and it *must* be forced, since it won't come out on its own—the stage of *pretense* begins. This is the most confusing stage of exorcism, since the demon will try to hide behind the personality of the exorcee. Using the person's own voice, it will make the possessed person act naturally, exhibiting no sign of what it is actually up to. This is an attempt to make the exorcist unsure or doubtful that possession is the problem. During this stage, the person may just sit quietly, doing nothing out of the ordinary. Only experience lets the exorcist penetrate these mind games and manipulations.

This stage, I've found, only occurs when the person doesn't exhibit any of the signs of demonic presence that sometimes take place at the start of an exorcism: uncontrollable shaking, jerky or unnatural body movements, evidence of extreme pain, or a look of complete and utter hatred that everyone involved in the Work has seen. As a cop, I've gotten plenty of murderous glares from people I've arrested, and knew they wouldn't hesitate to blow me away if they got the chance. Chilling as these glares have been, they pale in comparison to the malevolent look only a demon can provoke, which takes loathing to a new level—the depths of Hell. Yet the demons who manifest themselves so early and vividly are also the ones who give up the fight the fastest: They're the low-level forces: "the brutes," which have limited powers of resistance, don't speak during exorcisms, except perhaps in growls or gibberish, and are usually quick to flee from the power of the Cross.

Pretense, if it occurs, must be shattered as quickly as possible, because as long as the demon conceals itself, the exorcism can proceed no further. The exorcist must compel and adjure the satanic power, in the name of Our Savior, to reveal its name. The demon will resist this because once it answers, the charade is over. If it says anything, the evil spirit is losing ground. It is only a small victory in the battle, but a victory nonetheless. In some cases the spirit may stretch the pretense out for hours, trying to stir up doubt and lull everyone into a sense of false security. I have seen exorcisms go from quiet to extreme violence in seconds flat, so I know how hazardous it is to lose concentration.

It's not pretense that's dangerous but what follows. While the demon is trying to fool us into thinking it's not there at all, it *avoids* drama. This stage boils down to a battle of wits between the exorcist and the concealed demon. It's only after the exorcist forces an end to this hide-and-seek game that we reach the next stage, *breakpoint*. This is the stage where the fiend lets loose, sometimes leaping out of hiding and launching an all-out attack.

No one who participates in an exorcism is spared, but the

exorcist bears the brunt of the assault. I look on his job as similar to mine when I'm collaring a criminal. The bad guy knows he's headed for jail—that's the reality—but when you tell him to put his hands behind his back, you have to be prepared for anything. He may stand there obligingly and let you put the cuffs on, or he may fight you with everything he's got. Demonic spirits are criminals of the most sadistic kind: They invade someone's house or, worse still, body. Their terrorism is an offense against humanity and God, so exorcism is the spiritual equivalent of an arrest. The trouble is, you can't grab a demon, throw him down, and punch the daylights out of him if he resists: It is only by the use of prayers, fasting, relics, holy water, and most important of all, the grace of God that a demonic spirit is cast out, to, it is hoped, the ultimate prison, Hell.

When breakpoint is reached, anyone in the church is fair game. Assistants often can be the targets, simply because they're there and determined to free the possessed from the craven creature that has taken him over; and because the demonic hate everybody, even *you*! An analogy I like to use is this: What's the best way to attack someone you hate? The answer is as simple as it is cruel: by attacking his children. Not only do satanic spirits do this literally, by picking on kids in demonic-infested homes, but they also do this figuratively, by attacking humanity—God's children.

One form of suffering evil spirits often inflict on assistants is the mental attack. We all have memories, some good and some bad. Don't think for a minute that the demonic will hesitate to torture you by taking your most joyful recollections and perverting them into something horrible. And as for awful memories you've stuffed in the back of your mind and almost forgotten, they'll come crashing back during an exorcism, with the volume of emotion turned up until it's unbearable. Think for a second of the very worst thing that's ever happened to you; then imagine being bludgeoned with this scene over and over, with each detail as vivid as if you were experiencing it all over again, maybe in agonizingly slow motion, like a nightmare where you know something horrible is going to happen but are powerless to prevent it.

You can also be attacked in other ways. One of the most humiliating is having very personal sins you've committed—and never confessed—be blurted out by the demon for all to hear. Demons, however, have no way of knowing about wicked acts you've confessed and been absolved of, since God has forgiven them. Such sins are invisible to the forces of Hell, because they're no longer attached to your soul. There can be spiritual assaults, a form of torment that's usually reserved for the exorcist, since doubting his faith or questioning God while performing the Roman Ritual actually can be fatal.

Another sign of breakpoint is a change in the exorcee's voice. At times the demon will speak in the person's own voice, and at others, in a harsh, guttural, or unnaturally deep voice, making a woman, for example, speak in the voice of a man. Some demons even fluctuate between different voices, all the better to cause fear and confusion. Even in these instances, you can tell when the evil force is talking because it can't help but reveal it is *not* the exorcee. A satanic spirit may talk of the possessed in the third person and say, "I [or we] took him because he was so good" or "I [or we] cursed her." You get the sense that the satanic spirit thinks of the person as its property and of a human body as a mere container for its evil. The symbolism is obvious: "Back off, priest—this person is *mine* [or ours]!"

Father Martin describes a stage he calls *voice* as a frequent, singularly disturbing offshoot of breakpoint: An unnatural babble begins. "The first syllables seem to be of some word pronounced slowly and thickly—somewhat like a tape recording played at subnormal speed," he explains. "You are just straining to pick up the word and a cold layer of fear has gripped you—you know the sound is alien. But your concentration is shattered and frustrated by an immediate gauntlet of echoes, of tiny, prickly voices echoing each syllable, screaming it, whispering it, laughing it, sneering it, groaning it, following it. They all hit your ear."

I myself have never yet heard the voice, but according to Father Martin it is agonizing to endure. The exorcist must get himself under firm control and command the voice to be silent. His role is to get as much useful information from the demon as possible while demanding that distractions be stopped. Bishop McKenna says that the voice hasn't been a problem in his exorcisms: "Blessedly, I have been spared such molestation or visions of this kind myself. I am in no way psychic, completely lack any sixth sense, and consider myself the opposite of clairvoyant. I focus entirely on the standard, traditional ritual of the Catholic Church for exorcism and ignore any gibberish I might hear from the possessed."

Next in Father Martin's stages is *clash*, a battle of wills that concerns only the exorcist and the demon. Even the possessed person is excluded from this fearsome struggle, where the hellish force tries to engulf and overpower the priest, who, in turn, calls on God to banish and defeat this agent of the Devil. Propelling the exorcist on is his knowledge that he has already won the earlier battles, by forcing the spirit to come forth, give up its pretense, respond to questions, and abandon its techniques of distraction. Now it only remains for the diabolical presence to make its final surrender, in the aptly named stage of *expulsion*.

Departure would be too mild a term for this stage. As in every preceding stage, the demon must be forced, compelled, commanded, and driven to obey God's will, as expressed through the exorcist. In real life, the last act of this diabolical drama is almost an anticlimax: The exorcee will tell us that the evil presence is now gone. Some people's relief and gratitude is so profound that they break down and cry. Others have no memory of their possession and may even be puzzled as to why they're in the church or who we are. Since these reactions also could be a demonic ploy—a new form of pretense—the exorcist will continue to use prayers, relics, and holy water to make sure the demon truly has been expelled.

While a satanic spirit may give an indication that it's leaving, the only one I've seen during a solemn exorcism comes in the form of extreme violence suddenly stopping. I never ask for a sign that the Devil is gone during exorcisms of houses, but sometimes I've gotten one anyway. The sign is usually a loud bang from an empty part of the house. It's one of the ways the demonic let you know they're gone—for now.

I felt very nervous when Bishop McKenna put a crucifix in Tony's hand at the start of the ritual—he'd never done this at any previous exorcism. The figure of Christ on the cross is the symbol of our salvation, but in the hands of the possessed it can become a weapon. In the real-life case later fictionalized in *The Exorcist*, a priest was maimed for life during the exorcism of a child (who was a boy, not a girl as in the film version). During the Roman Ritual, the exorcee yanked a spring out of the mattress he was lying on and used it to slash the exorcist's arm open to the bone. The priest was horribly scarred and never regained use of the limb.

From that moment on, I watched the musician like a hawk, ready to quell any threatening move on his part. I'd assisted at one exorcism a while back where the possessed person constantly tried to scratch and bite the assistants. It was this man's fourth exorcism—and each had become progressively more violent. He was possessed by seven different demons, and each ritual brought a more powerful one forth. During the exorcism I attended, the demon decided to compel the man to tear at his own hands with his teeth, and it took eight of us to save him from serious injury. Today there were only four assistants—and I prayed that would be enough.

The bishop read the Roman Ritual over Tony but got no reaction at all. That's how some exorcisms go—it's a long struggle to force the evil spirit forward. The holy man stopped his prayers to ask the musician how he felt. "I'm getting some pain near the bottom of my spine," he said softly. This is one of the major chakra points—and from what Tony had told me, I knew it was the area through which the demon had entered.

The bishop stood right in front of Tony, a spot I didn't like, since he could be hit before any of us assistants could react. In Latin, he demanded, "Tell me your name, demon!" Getting only silence, he repeated the order in English. The second time, Tony's head jerked and he made a guttural sound. Whether it was a word or not, I couldn't tell, but the battle was definitely on.

Sensing this, the bishop took two steps back, to my relief. Tony began breathing heavily through his nose, and his head and neck jerked wildly from side to side, as if he were afflicted with Tourette's syndrome. The demon was finally showing itself, and the musician muttered something that sounded like "No."

Bishop McKenna reached the point where the ritual calls for the exorcist to drape his stole around the possessed person. He touched a relic to Tony's head, chest, left shoulder, and right shoulder—the sign of the cross. The response was a very loud and distinct scream: "Shit!" The flagrant obscenity was in sharp contrast to Tony's usual mild, soft-spoken manner. "Shit!" he screamed again. No pretense here—the demon wasn't bothering to hide itself.

As the ritual continued, the demon roared its defiance in an unknown language, a Babel of tongues. Sometimes it sounded like Arabic, at others Hindi, but for all I knew it might be an ancient tongue humankind has forgotten or that was never spoken on Earth. The only word I could recognize, if you want to call it a word, was "Nayacota," the nonsense term that Tony had told me was the demon's way of saying "no." I have never come across this expression in any other case, so it was probably unique to this particular evil spirit.

The words became a torrent, but the bishop ignored them, saying "Tell me your name, Devil!" Tony yelled out two completely incomprehensible syllables. "How many are you?" the man of God demanded. He received no reply until he sprinkled holy water on the musician.

"Shit!" the diabolical spirit yelled again, then Tony broke into heart-rending sobs. The priest paid no attention to either the cries or the curses: The demonic have a million tricks to stop the Roman Ritual. As he sternly intoned the prayers, the musician alternated between shouting vulgarities and weeping like a child. Suddenly he turned to me, tears streaming down his cheeks, and asked for a cross to hold. I will not respond to an exorcee during the ritual, but the bishop once again allowed him to hold the crucifix, and Tony grabbed it like a lifeline.

You might think this meant he was freed of the demon, but not so. We could see Tony struggling with the evil spirit, weeping and clutching the cross when he was in control and recoiling from it with dreadful shouts when the Devil regained the upper hand. It was incredible to watch the battle raging inside this man.

Over two hours had gone by, and the bishop was on the third reading of the ritual. Tony's yelling and jerking had subsided, but he was still snared by the satanic force. He whispered that his back was causing him great pain, so I lifted his shirt so that the exorcist could anoint his spine with holy oil and apply relics.

When I lifted Tony's shirt, I couldn't believe my eyes: His vertebrae had actually sunken into his body! It looked like he had no spine at all, just an unseen force holding him up. Stronger measures were needed, so the bishop did something he rarely does during an exorcism: He brought out the Most Holy Eucharist, which is normally taken out of the church during these rituals so it won't be defiled by the demonic.

After placing the body of Christ in a monstrance and safely covering it with a gold cloth, the exorcist showed it to Tony, who just sat there staring. Next the bishop touched Tony's back with relic after relic, each time eliciting a violent jerk.

When the exorcism was finished, Tony was clearly spent. I asked if he was all right, and he whispered yes. His next remark, however, was chilling. "My spine feels very threatened."

He was still possessed—and still refused to admit that a demon dwelled inside him! Instead, he viewed it as part of his own body, not a hostile invader.

We knew then that the exorcism had failed. You may wonder why, after going through all this, Tony couldn't recognize the demon for what it really was. It's because the demonic are masters at masking themselves. Tony was actually holding on to the evil spirit because he didn't understand that it was separate from himself. I was disappointed that the ritual hadn't worked. I realize it's ultimately God's will, but in this case, the problem was that the musician just couldn't see the truth.

I don't blame him for being taken in, but it certainly was frustrating. I told Tony that he needed to pray about the matter as best he could until we could set up another exorcism. He said he would, but I wasn't so sure. I spent a long time talking to him, and every time I reached a point where Tony seemed to be about to admit that a demon was responsible for his situation, he'd say something contrary like "For the life of me, I don't know what's wrong with me."

That's why I was extremely surprised to get a call a few days later from a very excited Tony. The day before, he'd gotten a strong feeling that he should go to a church that was having a twenty-four-hour Adoration of the Blessed Sacrament. There he'd spent two hours sitting in front of the Most Holy Eucharist, commanding the demon to leave in the name of Jesus Christ, just as the bishop had done. Immediately after he'd left us, he explained, he'd finally realized that the evil power was a separate—and most unwelcome—presence, and prayed that God would banish it from his body.

As he gazed at the Most Holy Eucharist, he miraculously felt a powerful energy depart from his spine and the veil lift from his eyes. The only explanation I have for this is that, as

I've said, there is no time frame in the spirit world or for getting an answer to prayers. I feel the exorcism *did* work, after all, but its effect wasn't felt until Tony finally grasped his true situation and decided to exercise his free will. That and the power of the Holy Eucharist were too much for the demon to withstand, which is why it was finally expelled.

Although Tony was positive that he'd been freed, I urged him to go through with the second exorcism anyway. He assured me he didn't need it. I had to go along with him, since I couldn't very well drag him to the church. As we talked, I discerned a change in his voice—it didn't sound so weak and defeated anymore—and in how he described the evil force. For the first time he spoke of the demon in the third person, using the word "it." That's when I truly believed he *was* freed.

He thanked me over and over for our help. Marveling over this astonishing news, I called the bishop, who pronounced it a miracle. The holy man didn't sound the least bit surprised, however. "God works in mysterious ways," he said. "You know that, Ralph."

8

THE WEREWOLF

The message on my machine was garbled and indistinct. "Help me!" were the only two words I could make out. I could tell immediately that it wasn't a prank call: It was a case, and, by the sound of it, an urgent one. Earlier that day the Warrens had appeared on *The Richard Bey Show,* a daytime TV talk show, to discuss Bill Ramsey's demonic possession. Bill's remarkable life story is chronicled in a book he wrote with Ed and Lorraine: *Werewolf.* I'd also been asked to go on the show but couldn't get the day off from work. At the end of the program, the producers flashed Joe's name and phone number and mine on the screen as the investigators to contact. Not knowing what terrible emergency my mysterious caller was facing, I just about went crazy playing the message tape over and over, but I couldn't figure out who'd called or what number he'd left.

A couple of hours later Joe called. "Ralph, you wouldn't believe the call I got a little while ago. This guy was on his car phone, calling from somewhere on the Long Island Expressway. He was in a real panic. He has strange seizures that terrify him and his family—and had just had one right there on the highway! He said he'd almost crashed his car before pulling off the road to call me. Then he told me that things are so bad he can't live like this any longer."

Joe managed to calm the near-suicidal caller and offered to contact the man's wife, Lucinda. He was just about to dial her number when *she* called him. Although she didn't know about her husband's terrifying attack on the freeway, she wasn't at all surprised to hear about it. "That's why I'm calling you, Mr. Forrester," she said. "Greg—that's my husband—has been having these fits for almost twenty-five years."

Like my mother, Lucinda Morton was a beautician who cut people's hair in her home to earn extra cash. Earlier that day, when she was between appointments, she flicked on the TV and happened to see *The Richard Bey Show*. Her jaw dropped when the Warrens discussed Bill Ramsey's case, because it had such astonishing parallels to her husband's problems. She immediately called her husband at work to give him Joe's and my phone numbers, then decided to call my partner herself. "I know this may sound really far-fetched," she told him, "but I think Greg might be a werewolf, like that guy your friends were talking about on TV."

Given Greg's desperate frame of mind, Joe made an appointment for us to meet with the Mortons that very night. Right off we noticed something peculiar when we parked at the couple's Long Island home. Although the driveway was relatively new, the asphalt was oddly scarred in several places, as if someone had attacked it with a rake. The house itself was a very attractive white stucco Tudor, with red roses growing on a trellis around the front door.

Lucinda, who was about fifty, was holding a small, yapping poodle in her arms when she opened the door. She was living proof that some people grow to look like their dogs, because both she and her pet had big puffs of fluffy black hair on their heads. The beautician's hair was teased and sprayed into a gravity-defying beehive that resembled black cotton candy and her full mouth was generously coated with glossy purple lipstick. She wore a turquoise pants suit and several pieces of chunky gold jewelry. I liked her immediately. Despite a rather anxious, fluttering manner, she was very friendly and seemed delighted to see us. She led us into a well-lit living room decorated in flowery patterns, where her husband was waiting.

There was absolutely nothing wolfish about Greg Morton's appearance, by day or night. Far from being abnormally hairy, he was actually bald, with a bland, moon-shaped face, and he wore thick glasses to correct his nearsightedness. Oddly enough, when I met Bill Ramsey, he was also balding, clean-shaven, and looked like a million other middle-aged men. If you passed either of these guys on the street, you wouldn't give him a second glance.

Since Joe had already heard part of the Mortons' amazing story from the beautician, he took charge of the interview. "Lucinda, why don't you tell Ralph what you told me on the phone?"

Running her long, manicured fingernails through the poodle's fluffy fur as she spoke, she said, "Well, this is going to sound really peculiar. For many years, Greg has been having these spells where he acts like an animal."

"You're not speaking figuratively, are you?" my partner asked.

"Not at all. It started one night when we were in bed, sleeping. All of sudden, my husband sat bolt upright in the middle of the night. I woke up and asked what was wrong, but he didn't answer. His eyes were open, but he didn't even blink. He was just staring off into space, like he was in a trance. Then he let out a loud growl that didn't sound human at all."

"Did it sound like a wolf?" I wondered, thinking of the Ramsey case, which Joe had helped the Warrens investigate a few years before I got involved in the Work.

"No," she said. "It was more like a large cat or a tiger. It didn't sound like it was coming from his lips but from deep inside his body, kind of a rumbling roar that scared me half to death. I kept screaming my husband's name, but he couldn't hear me. I felt like a stranger was in our bed, because he didn't seem like himself at all. It was as if someone else had taken over his body. Then he started talking in a different voice, ranting and raving in a language I'd never heard before! I almost had a heart attack, I was so frightened!"

"Had anything unusual happened in Greg's life before this episode?" Joe queried.

Both Mortons shook their heads. "No, everything was normal," Greg said. "A few years before that I'd started my contracting company and was working hard to build up my business. We didn't have that much money then, but we were happy."

Greg's experiences had eerie similarities to the Ramsey case, except that Bill's first attack took place when he was a nine-year-old boy in England, his native country. He describes it in his book by asking "Have you ever walked into a meat locker right after you've been outside on a hot day? That's what this was like. I was playing and . . . it felt like my body temperature dropped a good twenty degrees. Sweat froze on me. And my whole body started shaking. It was as if I'd opened this door and stepped inside to another dimension."

A very violent dimension, he soon discovered. Although

the uncanny chill—and an incredibly rank odor that accompanied it—faded away later in the day, he felt irrevocably marked with "a coldness at his very center" that set him apart from other children. As he hurried toward his house to have dinner, he stubbed his toe on a fence post and flew into a frenzied rage. Like Greg, young Bill let out terrible growls that rose from deep inside his body. Filled with supernatural strength far beyond that of any normal nine-year-old, he ripped the offending fence post right out of the ground and swung it overhead like a baseball bat—with its wires still attached. Although his maniacal rage soon subsided, the experience transformed him. "Something had entered my soul . . . something that didn't belong there," Bill recalled years later.

Greg, on the other hand, had no memory at all of his nighttime fit. Just as suddenly as the spell came over him, it left him, and he lay back down, fast asleep, leaving Lucinda to stare at him in horror all night long. *Who was this man she'd married? Had he gone insane? Or was he just in the throes of a bizarre nightmare?* Her peacefully snoring husband had no answers, either that night or the next morning. When he woke, he refused to believe the incident had actually happened.

"He said it was probably just my imagination—or a dream I'd had," Lucinda said. "I knew it wasn't." She found herself fearing her usually mild-mannered husband. Days went by, and Greg acted just like his old self, heading off to his renovation business at 8:00 A.M. as always and returning at the stroke of 5:00 P.M.

Here again was an odd echo of Bill's story, since he also behaved completely normally after his strange frenzy. In fact, Bill did nothing out of the ordinary for nearly two decades, as he grew up, got married, and, like Greg, entered the building trade, as a carpenter. Like his American counterpart, he had three children—and some very peculiar problems in the bedroom. First, he began having a recurring nightmare where he'd call his wife's name, and when she turned to look at him, she'd recoil in horror, as if she'd seen a monster. One night he suddenly sat up in bed, just as the Long Island contractor did, and let out a ghastly growl. That's when his nightmare came true: Just as he'd so often dreamed, his wife opened her eyes in real life, took one look at him—and screamed.

Greg's wife had almost convinced herself that the peculiar incident was some strange fluke when her husband had a second spell, also in the middle of the night. This time he got out of bed and walked on all fours, like a wild animal, growling that deep growl. He moved with a catlike grace, similar to that of a large predatory panther. Clutching the sheets to her chest in abject terror, his wife watched him claw savagely at the wood paneling in their bedroom, ripping it apart with his bare, bleeding hands. Again he flopped back down on the bed, slept like a dead man all night long, and woke with no memory of his berserk frenzy.

Lucinda, however, now had tangible proof of his nighttime rampages—and showed him the hole in their bedroom wall. The otherwise inexplicable injuries to his hands also testified to the truth of her words, although Greg still found it hard to believe he'd behaved this way. At his wife's urging, he consulted their family doctor the next day. After a complete physical, the M.D. found no evidence of epilepsy or a seizure disorder of any kind. Nor did the tests show any other physical ailment. Except for his scratched-up hands—and two peculiar fits—Greg was the picture of health.

"The doctor prescribed tranquilizers," Greg explained. "That didn't help at all."

Naturally, the next stop was a therapist. The shrink also

did a battery of tests, but found no signs of mental illness in this hard-working businessman who, rather ironically in view of his propensity to destroy his home, repaired other people's houses. During the day, Greg behaved completely normally: He was a perfect father to his three kids. You might say he was a loving family man who happened to have one bad habit: From time to time, at totally unpredictable intervals, he turned into a beast and tore his home apart.

Over the years, the pattern changed, Greg told us. For a while, the attacks lessened, and his business thrived. "Then the fits of madness, or whatever you want to call them, started happening in the daytime, when I was awake. I could actually feel the frenzy coming on. It was like a roaring in my brain. For the safety of my family, I'd lock myself in the bathroom when I felt this way, because after this force took hold of me, I'd lose all control."

With an embarrassed expression, he told us that during these episodes, he'd dig at the bathroom tiles until his fingers bled. The fits became so frequent that he'd sometimes go completely berserk and run from his house to rip up the asphalt driveway, leaving the marks we'd observed when we parked. Understandably, he went back to the psychiatrist, but once again, the doctor was no help. Greg was simply sent home with a stronger prescription for tranquilizers that did nothing to tame his rages.

Greg and his wife were now haunted by horrifying questions: *What if he attacked his family—or someone else? Just how dangerous was he? Could he kill someone during one of these episodes? And what was the cause of his terrifying affliction?*

I could understand his fear, given what happened to Bill Ramsey: Roaring in the night led to horrifying daytime rampages. In the throes of one seizure, Bill brutalized a nurse, tearing at her arm with his teeth and drinking her blood. Police found him on all fours, his face contorted into a hideous, bestial expression, growling with inhuman fury. The officers wrestled him into a straitjacket and took "the wolfman," as the British press later dubbed him, to a mental hospital. When Bill came to his senses later that day, he had no memory of his behavior but told the psychiatrists he felt there was a beast inside him. After his release from the hospital, he went on to attack several other people, including a prostitute and an entire police station full of cops.

Having met Bill Ramsey myself and spoken to him at length about these events, I was particularly struck by how both he and several witnesses said that he really had taken on some physical traits of a wolf during these seizures, mainly in his facial expressions, body movements, and especially his clenched, clawlike hands. He also told me he'd feel drawn to the window when there was a full moon outside, to howl at it like a wolf. In demonological terms, we call this "lycanthropy", from the Greek *lykoi* (wolf) and *anthropos* (man).

I'm not saying that either Bill or Greg was a werewolf, because if I did it would be pure b.s. The truth is that both men were possessed by demons with some of the *characteristics* of a beast, whether a wolf, a panther, or another fierce predator. Making Bill howl at the moon was a *ploy* the evil spirit used to conceal its nature and create confusion. Think about it: Anyone who knows anything about wolves knows they really don't howl at the moon. That's just legend. They howl to communicate with each other, whether the moon is full or not. So Bill wasn't acting like a wolf at all: He was being attacked in a way that fit his notion of lupine behavior, leading him to conclude that he'd turned into a werewolf.

Through his involvement with the Ramsey case, my

partner Joe has studied lycanthropy, a fascinating condition that's inspired strange legends all over the world. The ancient Romans believed that certain magic spells or herbs could transform a human into a wolf, while the Greeks of antiquity had a wolf cult that held an annual orgy of human sacrifice and cannibalism. During the Middle Ages, people who were suspected of being werewolves were actually burned at the stake. Among the Gypsies, the view is that shape-shifters, or werewolves, are under a curse. Father Martin felt there may be some truth to this, as he knew of cases where lycanthropy was passed down from generation to generation, like a family curse. But with God's grace this hellish cycle of possession could be broken. Navajo shamans hold that evil witches called "brujas" can change themselves into coyotes, while Japanese folklore speaks of people who turn into foxes. In India and China, legend has it that humans can shift their shape to that of the most dangerous beast in that part of the world, the tiger. A Nigerian priest reports that some tribes in his area have crocodile or leopard cults, where the members are said to become transfigured into these much-dreaded creatures through magic rituals. And, of course, the Devil is often pictured as half-man, half-beast, with cloven hooves, a long barbed tail, and a pair of horns.

What do Joe and I think about all this? We think a lot of it is superstition. What legends leave out is the role of the demonic. From my personal experience in the Work, I know that diabolical forces definitely have the power to induce grotesque visions in humans through a process called "telepathic hypnosis." Such fiendishly inspired hallucinations could certainly account for the centuries-old tales of werewolves and other shape-shifters, since demonic possession has been with us since God created humanity. Or it may be that some demons really can cause animalistic changes in the people whose bodies they inhabit, though I've never seen such a thing myself. As Father Martin once said, "Confusion, it would seem, is a prime weapon of evil." And what could be more confusing than a man who changes into a beast, and back?

Joe and I have seen many cases where possessed people will go through periods of normalcy, as Greg and Bill did, and function as usual in everyday life. The demon doesn't seize control twenty-four hours a day. Most of the time, the victims are in command of themselves. In nine out of ten cases, people suffer blackouts lasting an hour, a day, or weeks on end where their personality undergoes a drastic change. They may become violent, abuse their loved ones, destroy property, become sexually promiscuous, or act in other depraved ways. This amnesia is merciful: Sometimes God allows the demonic to so oppress these people's souls that they aren't aware of their repugnant behavior.

Others, however, know what takes place but are powerless to do anything about it. They'll say that it's like watching a movie—something else is in complete control and moving their bodies. I've seen the same thing with exorcisms: Some people have no memory of the ritual, and others remember everything. Even in their lucid intervals, possessed people always sense an alien presence. Often, however, they don't understand the true nature of the evil spirit inside them. Because belief in the Devil has declined so much, most people aren't familiar with the signs of demonic possession. Greg didn't realize what speaking in a foreign language he'd never studied really meant, nor did Bill realize that his supernatural strength was a red flag. All they knew was that something was terribly wrong: Greg was so tormented that he actually told us he thought he'd be better off dead.

I could understand his despair. Being possessed is like having cancer. The longer a person has it, the more the malignancy spreads. Yet the person's spirit is never totally obliterated by the darkness inside him. Even when a demon has been digging in for decades, there's always a part of the victim that refuses to yield completely to the assault. When someone is taken over by an evil spirit, most people think that means the Devil owns that person's soul. That's incorrect. Even if Greg had died while possessed, he wouldn't automatically be destined for Hell.

Satan has no claim over a person's soul—all a demon can do is take over the physical body, while the soul continues to belong to God. The only exception is when someone makes an actual pact with the Devil and *gives* his soul away. This is called "perfect possession." The difference between regular and perfect possession involves free will. If an evil spirit breaks down your resistance until you can no longer fight off possession, you won't lose your soul because you didn't give yourself over voluntarily. As long as even one little piece of your being is resisting, exorcism can work.

Another common misconception is that while a demon is inside someone, its torments are lessened. That's untrue because the demonic are spirit and cannot remove themselves from the torments of Hell, no matter where they go. The reason they don't want to vacate the "home" they've found when they possess someone isn't that they're comfortable or happy there but due to their extreme loathing of humanity. They fight like hell out of hatred.

A very striking feature of both Greg and Bill's cases, however, was how suddenly and savagely the demon attacked. This wasn't what Joe and I usually see when a satanic spirit takes someone over; there were no mysterious whisperings, shadowy shapes, or eerie bumps in the night here. Neither man experienced any infestation or oppression, no gradual breaking down of the will. Instead, it was straight to possession with just one knockout punch from the demonic.

Even though they lived half a world apart, on opposite sides of the Atlantic Ocean, their stories mirror each other so closely that they may have been taken over by the same satanic spirit. Since the demonic have vast powers and aren't subject to the physical laws of time and space, there's no reason why one demon couldn't take over two people, or even several people, at the same time. It's also possible that there were two different fiends at work, using a virtually identical M.O.

Whether it was one demon or two, the method these satanic forces used to attack told me what kind of demon I was dealing with. I'm a firm believer in the science of "profiling," a technique the FBI developed to create psychological portraits of vicious criminals whose identity is unknown. Profiling helps police predict what a serial killer, mad bomber, or rapist might do next; narrow the list of suspects; and figure out the best way to catch the perpetrator. I use the same method in my work as a demonologist and have identified several categories of satanic offenders.

First are the *intellectuals*. This is the type of demon that attacked Tony Petri, the young musician. So cleverly did it insinuate itself into his consciousness that, for years, he couldn't recognize that the evil force was separate from himself. It was only after he finally realized the spirit wasn't part of his psyche that he was freed from possession. Sometimes these demons gain a foothold through someone's spirituality, by giving their assault the overtones of a religious experience. The goal is to become such an integral part of the person's life that he doesn't even seek exorcism, a torment that the demonic find worse than the torments of Hell.

Another type of demon, the *con artists*, cunningly preys on people's emotions, the technique the spirit that called itself "Virginia" used to captivate Gabby Villanova. The evil force may be drawn by the human weaknesses that lead us to sin. The incubus in the Washington, D.C., case was drawn to that particular house by the unnatural lust of its previous tenants. Violent behavior of any kind—child abuse, rape, domestic violence, assault, murder—can all be a lure for the demonic. But human weaknesses or viciousness doesn't necessarily result in possession. There must also be an "invitation" that brings evil forces on the scene: occult practices, moving into a house where the demonic are already present, or a curse directed at the person, which can sometimes cause instantaneous possession if it's sent by a very powerful sorcerer.

The diabolical force in Greg and Bill's case came from a distinctly different group of evil spirits I call *the brutes*. These low-level demons are quite different from the shrewd spirit that captivated Tony Petri by appealing to his hunger to know the secrets of life. Rather than attacking through a person's intellect or emotions, brutes operate on a visceral, animalistic level. There's nothing subtle about these diabolical perps: They don't go for your brain, they just grab you by the throat. In the criminal world, they'd be muggers who hit you over the head and rip the rings off your fingers, not white-collar swindlers who surreptitiously embezzle from your bank account.

I explained to Greg that he was possessed by a demonic spirit and that the only way to expel it was by an exorcism. Although he wasn't a Catholic or even particularly religious, he was so frightened by what he'd become—and the terrible danger his family faced from him—that he not only embraced this offer of salvation but asked to have the ritual performed as quickly as possible. Joe and I put him in touch with Bishop McKenna, who was extremely familiar with this particular demon, having served as Bill Ramsey's exorcist. Bill had learned of the bishops through the Warrens, who were visiting England at the time.

Initially Greg had the same view that Bill did about the ritual: It's something you read about in books or see in the movies, a last resort for the truly desperate. Yet the more the two men thought about it, the more *right* it seemed that faith should be the cure for a curse that all the doctors and psychiatrists they'd seen were powerless against. Their decades of affliction didn't have its roots in medicine. Nor could their problems be explained by science: They originated far outside the realm of reason and physical laws. To a scientist or doctor, these events sounded insane, even impossible, the stuff of legends and myth. Possession does not fit into their neat little view of the world. To them, it must be mental illness.

These two men knew better than that. Their terrible fits sprang from humanity's most ancient and wily enemy; and the solution surely lay in our infinitely old and powerful ally, God. Since both men prayed, at least occasionally, each prayed that his exorcism would be successful.

From what Joe had told me about the Ramsey exorcism—and my own knowledge of how demonic brutes act—I anticipated that Greg's ritual might be extremely violent. Shortly before Bill's exorcism, he'd assaulted both his wife and his dog. His hands shaped themselves into claws, so frightening his little terrier that the pet growled at him. Enraged, the carpenter flung his dog against a wall. Its pitiful whimpering halted him from further abuse. "I got right up to the edge of the craziness that usually overtook me," he said. Bill was able to make it to America, but the worst was yet to come.

The night before the exorcism, the Ramseys were staying in a Connecticut hotel. Relieved that her husband's ordeal might soon be over, Nina Ramsey slept soundly, then woke in the wee hours of the night to a chilling sound. Although Bill was asleep, the demon wasn't. A loud growl reverberated through Bill's body, then his hands reached for Nina. She tried to escape, but the brute moved even faster. Filled with superhuman strength, Bill overpowered her. But just as his hands wrapped around her throat, Nina found the ultimate antidote to demonic hate. "Bill, I love you," she whispered bravely. Her words seemed puny compared to Bill's incessant growls, but their effect was potent: He released her and made the same appeal Greg had left on my answering machine: "Help me!"

During the exorcism, Bill's face twisted into a horrible grimace of rage. His hands clawed at the air in front of him, as if he wanted to rip at Bishop McKenna and stop the prayers that were tormenting the demon inside him. When the exorcist held up a crucifix, the carpenter lunged at him, snarling furiously. Although many possessed people have tried to attack the bishop, he's never been injured during an exorcism. I'll tell you why: He's one of the living saints and wears his holiness around him like a bulletproof vest to deflect evil. The demonic brute was no match for the pious bishop, and Bill was finally freed of the demon that had enslaved him.

I prepared for Greg's exorcism the same way I always do. In the Scriptures, Jesus tells us that some demons can be exorcised only through prayer and fasting. The "black fast" is mainly for the exorcist, but I feel it doesn't hurt if the assistants do it too. Prayer is a must before an exorcism. I can never emphasize this enough to people. As a Catholic, I believe that to really worship God, you also need to show a devotion to the Virgin Mary. I pray the rosary every day, whether I have a case or not. I like to walk around while I'm praying, so I sometimes stroll around my neighborhood early in the morning, after I get off patrol, with my rosary in hand. It's very peaceful at this time. Even though I live in the city, one morning I saw a mother raccoon and her babies when I finished my prayers. Since I love animals, it was like a blessing for me to enjoy the sight of these charming creatures of God.

When I pray the rosary, I don't ask for any special favors. I just offer my prayers up to God to use as He sees fit. But before an exorcism, I offer them up to Him for the person who is possessed. Great miracles have happened by showing devotion to the Mother of God and the holy saints. This is the mercy of God because He knows each of us better than we know ourselves. He gave us His Son, Jesus Christ, who became a man and was nailed to the cross for us. This happened in front of his mother, whose suffering must have been unimaginable. Jesus gave us all the Virgin Mary as our mother that day on Calvary, even as he was dying on the cross for us, which is why I pay her tribute and hope her intervention will help the person who is suffering on this earth from possession.

On the way to Greg's exorcism, I prayed again for its success. Since Joe and I knew we would be up against a demonic brute, we made sure to have plenty of strong assistants at hand. Greg was about five foot ten and 185 pounds. There were eight of us to keep him under control: Joe and myself, Phil, Scott, Ritchie, John, and Joe Z. and his wife, Donna. All of us were as big or bigger than Greg. Joe and I both have martial arts training—and Scott is a karate champion—though we have never had to use it during an exorcism. I also felt good about our spiritual strength. As Jesus said, "When two or more people are gathered together in My name, I am with them."

For our safety, Greg consented to wear a straitjacket. If he hadn't agreed, I don't think any of us in the church that day would have wanted to be there, because this was one nasty, dangerous demon. We secured him as tightly as possible, carefully fastening the straps, then tied a thick nylon rope around his ankles to further immobilize him. He sat quietly on the front pew. He knew from past experience that he could go berserk at any moment, even though that wasn't his true nature. He told us to do whatever we thought best: He just wanted the nightmare to end.

Lucinda was extremely nervous and practically quivering from the strain. Stress was written all over her face. She had no idea what was about to take place, since Joe and I tell people as little as possible about an upcoming exorcism, so as not to influence their reactions in any way. Like Greg, she just wanted to be done with this ordeal. Anxiously she asked me what would happen if the exorcism *didn't* work. "This is my last hope for a normal life with the man I love," she emphasized. I just told her to put her faith in God. What else could I say? I couldn't make any guarantees, much as I would have liked to. She gave her husband a kiss, quickly wiped the purplish lipstick print off his cheek, and took her seat at a side pew.

As usual, the bishop began the ceremony with the Litany of the Saints, where he calls upon each and every saint to pray with us. During the litany, Greg quickly began to shake and sweat, then lost consciousness. Joe and I had seen this before, but never at such an early stage of the exorcism. The bishop hadn't even addressed the demon yet, but it already was here—and ready to fight.

The evil spirit gave its battle cry: Low, throaty rumbles that seemed to come from everywhere in Greg's body. They didn't sound human or wolfish but like the roars of some unknown beast. The bishop was so intent on the litany, which he recites facing the altar, with his back to the possessed person, that it took him a moment to notice the ghastly roaring.

Whirling around and striding toward Greg with the asp (a sprinkler for holy water used in Catholic churches) in hand, the exorcist threw holy water at him and roared, "Be quiet, Devil!"

Incredibly, Greg started to raise his arm in a threatening gesture, despite the sturdy restraints around him. Scott, who had been present during many exorcisms, seized him, and the rest of us piled out of our seats to help. Even with seven large men holding him down, the contractor actually broke out of the straitjacket, stood to his full height, and let out an even more terrifying roar.

The straitjacket was hanging loosely from Greg's shoulders. After a furious struggle, during which we all marveled at Greg's inhuman strength, his body suddenly went completely rigid, a frequent occurrence during exorcisms. He became as stiff and heavy as iron, and leaned to the left with such extraordinary force that all eight of us were catapulted in that direction.

The sound of metal ripping flooded the small chapel. Greg was tearing the pew from its moorings, even though it was bolted to the floor. We tried with all our might to push Greg back into his seat, but it was impossible. The bishop gave several vigorous shakes of the asp, sprinkling holy water on Greg in an attempt to subdue the demon.

"In the name of Jesus Christ, be still, Devil!"

The evil spirit grudgingly obeyed, and we soon had Greg back in his seat, firmly under control.

Once during an exorcism of a woman, I had a unidirectional microphone on a ledge behind the pew. After a fierce struggle, she managed to grab the mike. I attempted to pry her fingers off it but couldn't so I sprinkled some holy water on her hands. She immediately let go. Such is often the power of holy water against the demonic. The bishop continued with the exorcism but had barely finished his first prayer, when Greg stirred gently as if he were waking up. His lips moved.

Instead of a growl, two soft words came out. "It's gone!" The large man bent over and burst into tears. Through his sobs, he murmured in an awestruck tone. "It's really gone! I don't feel it inside me anymore!"

This had to be the shortest exorcism on record: five minutes. To make sure this wasn't some ruse of the demon to stop the ceremony, the bishop continued with the full ritual. Greg cried throughout, repeating over and over "It's gone! I'm OK!"

Why did the evil spirit leave so quickly? Although it had been inside this man for many years, it was a low-level demon, a brute that gave up the fight easily. With no strength to stand up to the forces of good, it fled the same way it came, like a thief in the night. I could see the change in this man: His face no longer wore an expression of bewilderment and fear but one of joyous surprise.

It was a very touching scene for all of us. After a quarter of a century, the curse of lycanthropy was finally lifted from this man's shoulders. Still weeping, Greg thanked us—and God—

for his freedom, then ran to embrace his wife. Arm-in-arm, they walked out of the chapel, and I prayed they'd find the happiness that had eluded them for so long.

Outside the church, I asked Lucinda to call me in a few days and let me know how things were going. When she did call, a week later, she was worried. "Greg is very depressed. Do you think this is a sign of anything?"

I told her that was a *normal* reaction. After a person is possessed, he's never quite the same again. You can't be touched by evil and go back to the way you were. Just as assistants, Joe and I lose a little piece of our humanity at each exorcism, so you can be damned sure that a demon that has been inside someone for twenty-five years is going to take something with it when it leaves!

While most people do heal in time, it's common for them to experience posttraumatic stress, just as you would if you were released after a long prison sentence. Your mind can't help but remember your time in the cell with fear and feel anxious about a future of freedom. It's a huge adjustment. I wish I knew a therapist I could send people to after an exorcism for religion-based counseling. I'll always be there for them if they choose to call, but it's not my policy to reach out to them. I feel it's best for former victims of possession to think about their ordeal as little as possible for two reasons: They avoid giving the demon recognition that might draw it back into their life and they help themselves move on.

I gave Lucinda my usual prescription for postexorcism depression, which usually fades with time: prayer and a more spiritual lifestyle. She told me they'd started going to church and were praying frequently. I promised to pray for them too. That Christmas my prayers were answered. I received a card from Lucinda, saying "Greg seems to be doing fine. We are attending church regularly and look forward to it every Sunday. Our lives are slowly returning to normal. As you know, this thing was with us for twenty-five years, and I still get very nervous thinking of the terror we survived. Thank God, and Bishop McKenna, that it's finally over."

9

DABBLERS IN THE DAMNED

Two of my investigations took place in the same neighborhood in Queens, and involved people who literally had neighbors from Hell—of both human and inhuman varieties. This middle-class area, which was within walking distance of the apartment my family and I lived in at the time, is home to hard-working people of many ethnic backgrounds, predominately Italian, Irish, German, Jewish, and Hispanic. The tree-lined streets have a mix of small apartment buildings and two- or three-family homes.

In the first case, a family of four was plunged into life-threatening danger after they rented the basement apartment in their home to the wrong people. The new tenants *looked* respectable enough: The husband and wife were gray-haired financial planners in their fifties, who lived with their grown children. But, as Nina and Marco Salvatore soon discovered, this well-dressed family, who frequently entertained groups of equally well-dressed guests, had an unsuspected dark side: They turned out to be practicing Satanists.

The father of this family also had a cocaine problem—and a disturbing habit. While hopped up on his favorite substance, this middle-aged man liked to head over to an Episcopal chapel down the street. He wasn't there to repent of his sins. Instead, he often stood outside and shouted profanities, invoking Satan's name. Cops were called about this several times. Each time they told him to shut up and go home, which he obediently did. This strange behavior isn't typical of serious Satanists, since they usually *avoid* drawing attention to themselves. But then again, embracing evil isn't exactly normal behavior to begin with.

Shouting blasphemies outside a church wasn't this couple's only offense. They actually attempted to draw the Salvatores' fourteen-year-old son, Andrew, into their coven, much to the horror of Nina and Marco, who were devout Catholics. Even that, however, wasn't nearly as upsetting as what happened after the boy emphatically rejected the Satanists' overtures and Nina told them that if they ever bothered her son again, she'd have them arrested.

Soon after, the Salvatores were afflicted by a horrifying ordeal. The wife was friendly with one of my students, Rose, and called her. "There's something evil in my house," Nina said. "We're all really scared. Do you think the people you're working with can help us?"

Nina explained that time and time again, she and her family would get the flesh-crawling sensation that somebody was creeping up behind them on the stairs in their home, yet when they'd whirl around, no one was there. The unseen intruder would often give them an unexpected shove, causing several near-accidents. Although the pushing occurred mainly on the stairs leading up to the second floor, it was felt throughout the house. Even the Salvatores' cats were affected by this, as animals so often are when the demonic is present; they began to avoid certain areas of the home, no matter how much they were coaxed to enter them.

By the sound of it, this was a classic case of demonic infestation that was growing more dangerous by the minute. The family's oldest son, Andrew, was almost killed on the stairs. He had almost reached the second floor when he felt a violent shove against his shins. His legs were knocked out from under him, and he went crashing down the wooden stairs feet first. His body slammed against one step after another, each collision inflicting fresh, agonizing pain.

Finally he landed at the bottom of the stairwell, striking his head so hard against the wall that his vision blurred. Too stunned to shout and too hurt to move, the schoolboy lay helplessly, waiting for the next blow. Like most kids his age, he'd believed himself immortal, but now he felt like easy prey. *Was he going to be killed right here on his own steps, without ever seeing his Mom and Dad again?* The six-foot-tall, powerfully built teenager was so terrified that all he could do was cower and cry. *He didn't want to die!*

As minutes passed and no new assault came, his tears stopped. Grateful to be alive, he timidly wiggled his fingers and then his toes. Miraculously, he wasn't maimed or paralyzed. One ankle was badly sprained, and he was covered with large purple bruises. Blood trickled from his hairline, and when he touched the enormously swollen cut, the pain was excruciating. Staring at the red, bloody smudges on his fingertips, the teenager recovered his voice—and screamed.

Nina heard his shouts and ran to help. She was such a tiny woman that it was hard to imagine how she'd given birth to this huge son, but with a mother's fierce determination, she half carried and half dragged Andrew into the living room, then forced back tears of her own at the sight of his injuries. After bandaging him up, and making sure no bones were broken, this God-fearing woman knelt on the floor to pray.

Deep in her soul, she already knew her son's fall was no accident.

She intoned the reassuring words of the Lord's Prayer but had to stop when she got to "Deliver us from evil." The heavy brass chandelier overhead was swinging wildly from side to side. When she interrupted her prayer to stare, the light ceased arcing back and forth, but immediately resumed its careening if she even thought about saying an "Our Father" or "Hail Mary." Finding it hard to believe such a thing could be happening in her own living room, she tried an experiment. Even though she felt a bit foolish, she moved to the bedroom and began praying again, peeking through the door to see what the light fixture would do.

Like the divining rods used to locate water underground, the chandelier immediately reacted to the holy words, shaking back and forth hard enough to dislodge plaster from the ceiling. Still refusing to believe the evidence she had just seen, Nina went into another room and repeated the test. The light smacked against the ceiling, showering glass from several shattered crystals. Feeling both scared and silly, Nina took the light down, afraid it might break free of its moorings and kill someone. That's what this family was living with: the overwhelming sense that something hostile had invaded their home and was out for their blood!

To find out more, Joe and I prepared for an investigation, and went over to the house with Antonio, who was wearing his usual military camouflage, Rose, and her son Chris. When we arrived at the two-story brownstone, we waited outside for Nina to come out. Instead her two sons came downstairs, looking extremely distraught.

"Mom's in the hospital," Andrew announced in the sullen tone of a troubled teenager, then went back in the house, leaving us standing on the stoop. The younger boy, who was about six, remained at the door, staring at us.

We didn't have to be psychic to sense that we weren't welcome in that house, either by the humans or the satanic trespasser. Since Nina wasn't there to authorize our activities, and Marco wasn't around to invite us in, we left. Joe and I are of the belief that if *you* have a problem and ask us to look into it, then aren't home when we come or change your mind, hey, that's fine with us. Good-bye and good luck! Naturally we were sorry that Nina was sick and prayed for her recovery, but if her family didn't want us, we had other things to do.

When you're dealing with the demonic and you're a threat to them, you encounter obstacles in most of your cases, so we weren't all that surprised. A few weeks later Nina's health rallied a bit, and she called again, still anxious for our help. After apologizing profusely for her son's rudeness when we came to her house, she told me what happened when they asked their parish priest to bless their home.

Unfortunately, the man of God couldn't come for several days, she said. "While we were waiting, we started finding broken stuff around our home. We have several locks on our door, but somehow somebody—or something—kept getting in and destroying our possessions, no matter how carefully we stored them."

True, these were only things, but the effect of having her family heirlooms, wedding china, vacation souvenirs, and other irreplaceable mementos vandalized was devastatingly demoralizing. The invader was strolling through the family's most intimate spaces and violating them. Each shattered teacup or ripped baby photo sent the same chilling warning: *You're not safe in your home, because I can get you where you live,*

*any time I want, and destroy you. And there's not a damned thing
you can do to stop me!*

Amid the chaos of these attacks, there was only one thing
keeping Nina and her family sane: The priest was coming.
Each day she'd sweep up the debris of yet another family
treasure, she said. "We were counting the days because it was
so hard to wait. We were going out of our minds with fear."

At last the much-anticipated day arrived, and the young
priest rang the downstairs bell. Nina eagerly invited him in,
but the man of God stopped just short of the vestibule as if
he'd run into an invisible wall. In an angry tone, she added,
"He mumbled an apology and said he just couldn't stay in my
house another minute. Then he turned around and walked
away—without a word! Can you believe that?"

I could see that Nina was quite upset and wanted my reaction. What could I say? Exorcism isn't for everybody, or every clergyman. Father Martin always said the ritual is rarely
entrusted to a recently ordained priest and is usually reserved
for priests of mature years. Dazzling intellectual brilliance or
sophistication isn't required, nor is a scholarly background.
The best exorcists, he added, are singularly *lacking* in imagination, but rich in moral and religious judgment. The priest
shouldn't have to work hard to develop these qualities; they
should be traits that come to him naturally, from his earliest
years.

While exorcising a home that's demonically infested is far
less arduous than a full-fledged exorcism of a possessed person, I suspect this priest was too unseasoned to handle the
case. His flesh was willing—and he showed up, right on time—
but his spirit didn't have the special grace that Father Martin
so eloquently described. I don't fault him for knowing his
limitations or for his cowardice, since it's very dangerous for

an inexperienced priest to go up against the demonic, but I do consider him negligent for not reaching out to other clergymen and finding someone who could help his terrified parishioners.

The more interesting question, however, is *what* stopped the priest in his tracks and sent him scurrying back to the safety of his rectory. Why had this particular house become so singularly inhospitable that it repelled even a man of God, and terrorized a family of such devout, unswerving faith as the Salvatores? Nina was firmly convinced that the devil-worshippers in the basement had unleashed satanic forces on her family.

"Nina, I'm still willing to help, but I have a few conditions I'd like you to agree to first," I told her. "If we come back, it's going to be the last time we'll come because we don't go where we're not wanted. If your family truly wants our help, I want you or Marco to give us written permission to enter your home and do our Work."

We always make sure to cover ourselves legally in these cases, to limit the possibility of being sued. Hey, the Devil has many avenues of attack—and without being too disrespectful to the legal profession, litigation is certainly one of them. I have heard of many exorcists from all different faiths who ended up in hot water because they didn't cover all the bases or, as we say in the police department, CYA (cover your ass).

Since we'd now covered our asses, and Marco had promised his complete cooperation, I returned a month later with the same team of investigators. We agreed that Joe, Antonio, and I would handle the house, and Rose and Chris would remain outside on the steps, where they felt most comfortable. But when Marco Salvatore answered the door, he looked grim. "My wife's back in the hospital for more tests," he told us. "I sure hope the doctors know what they're doing, because I'm very worried about her. She's very sick."

Joe, Antonio, and I looked at each other. Hearing that Nina was so ill gave us added impetus to cast out the demon in her home and put an end to the infestation if at all possible. Marco was also extremely anxious to resolve the problem before his wife got out of the hospital. "I don't want her or the boys frightened any more. I don't think Nina can take too much more of this—and frankly, neither can I. The last few weeks have been a nightmare for us."

He led us into a rather cluttered and gloomy living room. From the musty odor, I got the feeling he hadn't been doing much housekeeping since his wife got sick. Although it was daytime, heavy brocade drapes blocked most of the light from the windows, and only one lamp was lit, apparently with a 25-watt bulb. I could see damaged plaster on the ceiling where the chandelier that Nina had taken down used to be. The room resembled an antique shop, crammed with old-fashioned mahogany furniture. The armchairs and sofa were upholstered in dark brown velvet and piled with needlepoint pillows. There were also several little tables, some of them covered with crocheted doilies and little knickknacks.

Marco looked quite out of place in this dainty decor, which was what you might expect in an old lady's home. The house, it turned out, was owned by Nina's mother, who had chosen the furnishings. Marco was a rough-and-tumble guy, who'd briefly been a professional boxer and had a battered, Jake LaMotta–like face to prove it. With his rippling muscles and powerful right jab, the former heavyweight feared very little in this world, yet he now feared his own home.

I remembered a story Rose had told me about him. Several months earlier, a mugger had the misfortune of pulling a gun on the ex-boxer in an attempt to relieve him of his hard-earned cash. Even looking down the barrel of a .38-caliber revolver didn't intimidate Marco, who now worked as a nightclub bouncer. He just knocked the mutt out with one well-placed punch to the jaw. Leaving the would-be robber lying in the gutter, he continued on his way. He'd handled it himself, without the police, just as he'd handled every other problem he'd ever been faced with—until now.

I could immediately sense how frustrated this macho guy felt. For all his physical toughness, he was powerless to do anything about the situation he was in now. An evil force had invaded his home, terrorized his wife, and beat up his son. But what good were his quick fists when he was up against an enemy he couldn't even see? This wasn't a problem he could solve with his brawn.

"Did my wife tell you about the fight she had with those Satanists downstairs?" he asked. "They actually tried to re-cruit my son! And that thing that attacks us on the stairs is their doing, I'm sure of it!" He pounded his fist on the coffee table emphatically.

I told him I'd already heard about these problems, but there was something we wanted to know. "When exactly did your wife first get sick? Was it before or after the confronta-tion with your neighbors?"

"It was about a week later. I don't know if the argument had anything to do with it, but believe me, having people like this in your house is enough to make anybody sick!" Marco's face darkened even further.

Joe and I suspected that a curse was at the root of this family's problems. If so, it was urgent to learn everything we could. We needed to break the curse, if at all possible. It's con-ceivable, though very rare, for curses to cause death if the spell isn't broken in time. We wanted to find out how the spell was sent and what kind of black magic was used. The evil arts take many forms, and some covens use an eclectic and highly potent mix of methods. My partner Joe knows all this firsthand, because after taking on a large coven of witches in one of his cases, he became the victim of a curse himself and spent the next three years fighting for his life, as he was struck down by one serious illness after another and was the victim of a near-fatal accident. The only thing that saved him, I believe, was his knowledge of the occult and his strong faith in God.

Curses are typically used to exact revenge. Some magicians attach their evil spells to physical objects that carry the malevolent intention into the victim's home. These are called "contact objects." Just as a religious medal blessed by a priest has a positive charge of holiness and protection, objects cursed by a sorcerer have the opposite effect. They are repositories for negative energy that acts as a catalyst for demonic infestation. Some particularly fiendish occultists spread evil spells by making seemingly religious objects, such as ceramics or pictures with a Christian motif, then adding something extra: a curse. These artworks are then sold at craft shows to spread the germs of evil to the pious, unsuspecting people who buy them.

In one case, a schoolteacher who also did volunteer work at a Catholic organization fell victim to this satanic scam. While celebrating Christmas with her daughter, she heard a terrible explosion. All the glass on her shower door had shattered—not outward, but inward. She called my partner Joe immediately. He noticed a painting over her bed of Our Lady of Guadeloupe, which was so hauntingly beautiful that he couldn't take his eyes off it—or the magnificent black lacquered frame around it.

Proud of her painting, the teacher told Joe how she'd gotten an incredible bargain on this lovely work at a street fair. Joe admired it with her, marveling at the artist's skill at depicting anatomical details. Suddenly he spotted something extremely unsettling. Everything else was correct, but Our Lady of Guadeloupe, who is normally depicted trampling on a two-horned devil, had no feet! That was the tipoff, he explained. "Sometimes a demon will appear as a saint, or even as Christ, but there's always an imperfection. By *leaving out* the Devil and the Lady's feet, that satanic artist, rather ironically, *revealed* his painting's diabolical intent," at least to experts like Joe.

Right after he decoded the painting's secret, sinister message, the temperature in the schoolteacher's bedroom dropped a good twenty-five degrees, he adds. "The demonic spirit was right there in the room with us. I read the ritual, and the room warmed up. Everything was fine, but I had to remove the painting for her own safety." The question was, what to do with it? Explains Joe, "Some sorcerers booby-trap these objects, so if you burn them, another curse with a burning effect hits the victim, and makes her skin feel like it's on fire. What you have to do is either bury the object in ground consecrated with holy water or blessed salt or drop it in deep water. I took the painting to a bridge between Brooklyn and Queens, attached a five-pound weight, and dropped it into the canal with a couple of other cursed objects from other cases."

The power of curses is very real. Many scientific studies show that prayer has the power to produce medical miracles. A recent conference on faith and medicine drew over a thousand American health professionals, who testified to recoveries from illness that science couldn't explain. A Yankelovich poll of family doctors found that 99 percent of the physicians surveyed believe that religion can aid healing, and one-third of medical schools in this country now offer courses on spirituality and health.

A study at Dartmouth College showed that the best predictor of who will survive heart bypass surgery is the degree of the patient's religious faith. Six months after the operation, 12 percent of those who rarely or never attended church had died, while all of those who described themselves as devout were still alive. When Dale Mathews, M.D., reviewed three hundred studies on healing and religion, he found that 75 percent of them confirmed that believing in God or a higher power benefits health, with the deeply religious having lower rates of substance abuse, depression, or anxiety; enhanced quality of life; quicker recovery from disease; and a longer life expectancy. Another study found four times the rate of high blood pressure among atheists as churchgoers, even though the people who were studied from both groups were smokers. And other research shows that spiritual practices can help people overcome infertility, insomnia, chronic pain, and swelling from arthritis.

Since it's been established that invoking God, through prayer, can improve your health, why couldn't invoking the Devil have the opposite effect—and cause harm? The Salvatores didn't believe in curses, but you don't have to believe to be affected by them. Although Nina was only in her forties, wasn't overweight, and didn't smoke or drink, her previously excellent health took a drastic downturn after her confrontation with the Satanists. She was hospitalized repeatedly with heart problems and other ills. As I've already told you, belief in God benefits blood pressure and heart health, so I consider it equally likely that the demonic can attack in these areas. This was a curse.

After Marco told us everything he knew about the Satanists, which wasn't all that much, Joe and I began the exorcism, with Antonio watching our backs. Rose and Chris, who remained outside, were in the right place at the right time to witness a strange event that took place while we were in the house. As we were doing the ritual, burning incense, and reading the Pope Leo XIII prayer, the Satanists below were involved in their own little battle. Soon after we started the prayers, a car pulled up in front of the house and an impeccably groomed man in his late fifties got out. The head of the Satanist family hurried out of the basement with a large, extremely ornate book in his hand and gave it to the man in the car.

While my investigators couldn't see its title, my hunch is that it was the Satanists' "book of shadows," or "grimoire." These are names for a spell book that's often handed down from generation to generation in devil-worshipping families, and contains their personal collection of black magic incantations. Such books—unlike the spell books sold at most bookstores these days—are the hallmark of what we call "organized" or "generational Satanists." As St. Peter wrote in one of his letters, and is still true in modern times, the Devil "prowls around like a lion seeking whom he can devour" and recruits people like this to join his pride.

The two students on the steps heard snatches of the Satanist's remarks. "My wife has a 104-degree fever," he told the man in the car, "but we're leaving immediately." Apparently satisfied by this information, the older man drove off without further conversation. A few minutes later, the Satanists left their apartment in such haste that the wife's hair was a mess, and her clothing was disheveled. They didn't return while we were there. After they left lights started flashing on and off in their apartment but not in the rest of the house.

As we were reading the ritual in the upstairs bedroom, I heard loud, scratching sounds from the corner of the room. "Did you hear that, Joe?" I asked.

Puzzled, he said he didn't hear a thing. This isn't unusual in demonically infested houses, where strange noises may be projected to one person but not heard by the rest. In other cases, one person will see a spectral manifestation while others in the room see nothing, a phenomenon called "telepathic hypnosis."

Shrugging off the eerie sound of claws, I moved down to the first floor, so Joe and I could read the prayers at the bottom of the stairway that had been so dangerous to anyone who walked there. When I positioned myself, I suddenly had the overwhelming sensation that I was going to black out. Blood rushed in my ears and darkness began to close in around me. It started from my peripheral vision and moved around to the front of my eyes. The room was swimming. I asked Joe to "hit" me with some holy water, pronto. That helped, but I still felt shaky and sick to my stomach. When you are in a small or enclosed area during a house exorcism, psychic energy can build up and affect you in all sorts of extremely disagreeable ways. I recovered soon and continued with the ceremony.

We completed the rest of the house and left. When Rose and Chris told us what they'd seen, we went to the basement window to see if we could observe any other supernatural activity. We didn't see anything out of the ordinary, but when we noticed that the window was slightly ajar, Joe threw several handfuls of blessed salt through the crack. *Those Satanists will have a nasty surprise when they get back!* I thought.

We found out later that while we were in the house, doing the exorcism, Nina actually suffered a heart attack. Were she not in a hospital at the time, she never would have made it. Rose spoke to her after she got out of the hospital, and Nina was happy to report that the house had a different feel to it. There was no longer a sinister sense of foreboding. No more feeling of terror on the stairs. Nor were any more family possessions broken or destroyed. She even put the chandelier back up.

But even though we were able to bring the case to a close and the Satanist family was evicted from the house, a few months later Nina lost her battle against the demonically induced disease that had ravaged her heart. Upon hearing the grim news that she'd passed on to her final reward, I bent my head and prayed. *Rest in peace, Nina, where no demon can ever touch you.*

I thought this was the end of my Work in this Queens neighborhood, but I was wrong. A few months later I got a frantic call from one of my investigators, Phil. A friend of his was in terrifying trouble, and once again Satanists were on the scene. To my amazement, the new case was only a few blocks from where Nina's family lived, but it was in a different type of building—a six-family apartment house—and involved a *very* different coven from the one I'd encountered before.

This unsavory group weren't stylish professionals trying to hide their diabolical bent; instead, they flaunted it in the most garish manner imaginable. They looked like gangbangers. Their heads were shaved and they sported satanic tattoos. Each member wore an inverted cross around his neck, and scared the hell out of everyone else in the building, including Phil's unfortunate friend. If the group's appearance wasn't alarming enough, these characters were actually seen catching stray cats around the neighborhood to sacrifice to the Devil. Such behavior marked them as "dabblers" rather than serious Satanists, but made them no less dangerous.

Their activities weren't news to me: I was all too familiar with these particular perpetrators. So were the local cops, who suspected them of spray-painting "666" and satanic slogans on several buildings in the area and of other offenses, ranging from drug dealing to armed robbery. The delegation of tenants from the Satanists' building who had summoned me and Joe also accused them of black magic. To help us handle what sounded like a rather dangerous case, we brought three investigators: Scott, Phil, and Chris.

What made this otherwise quiet neighborhood such a hotbed of satanic infestation? What most people don't realize, until they're threatened by it themselves, is how common Satanism really is. By some estimates there are over eight thousand satanic covens in this country. In just about every American city, black masses are now available on a weekly basis, in a choice of locations; some covens have become so specialized that they limit their membership to pedophiles from the clergy or lesbian ex-nuns. *The Satanic Bible*, by Anton LaVey, has sold over a million copies, and urges those who buy the book to "hold Satan as a symbolic personal savior, who takes care of mundane, fleshy, carnal things." Such messages are finding a ready audience in schools, since most of them now have at least a few self-professed witches among the student body, whether practitioners of white or black magic. Wearing satanic emblems has almost become a fad among today's disaffected youth. No wonder demonic possession is on the rise!

The problem, ironic as it sounds, is the current *lack* of belief in satanic spirits. As Father Martin says, "the belief that [the Devil] doesn't exist at all is an enormous advantage that he has never enjoyed to such a great degree. It is the ultimate camouflage." As priests and ministers are toning down sermons about fire and brimstone, the Devil is quick to capitalize on this situation, by drawing in dabblers who truly have no idea what they're letting themselves in for.

Whether you believe in black magic or not makes no difference to those who seek to use it against us. In fact, the less you believe, the more likely that you won't know how to protect yourself if you're attacked this way. This situation is all the more to the liking of the legions of sorcerers, black magicians, witches, warlocks, Satanists, and other practitioners of the occult.

Or, if you are curious about the dark arts yourself and are tempted to try a spell or two, be warned: The Devil *doesn't* protect his own, since his relentless hatred for humanity extends even to those who profess to serve him. Full of guile and perversity, he and his demons simply bide their time, then swoop down to destroy these people without a second thought.

Like the Salvatores before them, these victims of the second satanic coven also had learned to dread the stairs in their building. The downstairs neighbor heard her three-year-old scream with terror one afternoon while he was playing on the building's steps. "Mommy, he won't let me go," the boy yelled from the second floor. When she ran to help, the child was drenched in sweat, trembling from head to toe, and crying that he'd seen a ghost with big teeth, dressed in a black hooded cloak. "It had no nose," he added—a clue I quickly picked up on, since, as I've said, the demonic, unlike ordinary ghosts, often have some oddity of appearance when they manifest themselves to humans.

While the mother initially dismissed the incident as the product of an overactive imagination, she took it more seriously when her three-year-old spit at a picture of Jesus a few days later. Meanwhile, other tenants were complaining that the building's basement gave them the creeps and stopped using it for storage. A woman on the third floor saw an eerie black shadow float up the stairs at midnight; another tenant woke up in the middle of the night to find a man with a goatee sitting on her sofa and staring at her.

"I was stunned and rubbing my eyes to see if I was still asleep," she told me. "I turned around, and when I looked back he was gone. I went psycho and ran around my apartment saying, 'Whoever you are, go away and stop scaring me!' When I told my neighbor about it to see if I was losing my mind, she said I was describing a man who'd died in the apartment over ten years ago. The next day I put crosses in every room."

After seeing the floating black shadow, the third-floor tenant found herself shaking with fear every time she had to use the stairs to her walk-up at night. "When I go up, I have my back to the wall and cling to the banister, then creep up because you get a feeling that something is right behind you. When I turn around, I don't see anything, but I'm petrified that someone is going to push me down the stairs. There's such a strong presence of evil that my friends tell me that they also go up the stairs with their backs to the wall and feel like something dreadful is lurking there. Some of them won't come over anymore; they're that scared."

To rid the building of its inhuman inhabitants, five of us went over to exorcise its three floors. Cases like this are dangerous because we don't know exactly what kind of black magic we're up against—or how we might be attacked. Even if we were able to clear the building of the things that are there, they won't stay gone, because the Satanists will invite them back. We still wanted to help these people, so we split up and went to different locations around the building to perform our rituals.

I was in the apartment across from where the devil-worshippers lived. Just then the Satanists' leader, a man named Lewis Williams, came up the stairs. Someone had tipped him off to what we were doing, because the daughters of one of these families hung out with these guys. I was purifying the apartment across the hall from his with blessed incense when I heard conversation in the hall. Someone with a heavy New York accent was asking "Who are these people? What denomination are they?"

I looked out in the hall and saw Williams, who was standing at his doorway. He sneered at me, so I sneered back. He was holding a copy of *The Necronomicon*, which is an extremely evil book. On the inside cover there is a warning: "*The Necronomicon*'s magick is nothing to fool around with and may expose you to psychological forces with which you cannot cope. Remember, if you tinker with these incantations, you were warned!" Psychological forces, my ass! What you will be dealing with is demonic spirits, as Lewis Williams later found out.

This book is dedicated to the late Aleister Crowley, a notorious Satanist who was known as "the Beast." The editor of this book goes on to thank a whole group of people, including a demon he mentions by name. Imagine that! Thanking a demon for terrorizing humanity and seeking the ruin of souls! Apparently, this demon wasn't particularly placated by thanks, since the second edition of this book mentions someone associated with its publication who is plagued by "poltergeists." Well now, we all know what poltergeists really are, so why don't these people have the guts to come out and say so?

This preface adds that the group who put out this book have experienced a number of bizarre occurrences that nearly cost them their lives, then hints around about another potential effect of this extraordinarily evil work. In an apparent Freudian slip, the editors say that people who come into "possession" of this book may experience "changes in consciousness." I think it's pretty obvious what those so-called changes would be—and what kind of risk people who read *The Necronomicon* are running. It may be hyped as the ultimate book of spells, or the godfather of grimoires, but I consider it a publication of pestilence.

None of this deterred Williams from standing there, right in front of me, and reading aloud this diabolical book to counter my prayers. It didn't work. He suddenly broke off his reading and actually ran from me. From my years on the street, I've seen assholes like him before. They like to cause fear in people, but I wasn't intimidated in the least. My prayers were a lot more powerful than what he was reading and he knew that. He had been an altar boy in his younger years, and even in his warped mind, he recognized the power of Catholic prayer. He exited the building—fast.

Before he left, I shouted to him, "*The Necronomicon* is a very bad book." He smirked and replied, "That's good."

We resumed the ritual. In order to evict evil spirits in a

building, we need access to every apartment, but that was out of the question in this case. We did our utmost to make the areas we were in extremely hostile to diabolical forces, but the fact that some of the tenants had no desire to rid themselves of evil was a problem. Lewis Williams, for example, was sure to invite it back in. Despite these handicaps, our prayers seemed to contain the malevolence in the building: Phil's friend told him that after our exorcism, the terrifying phenomena stopped.

When we finished our Work, we left the building to find fifteen Satanists standing menacingly outside. Knowing how bad this group's reputation was, I was armed with my gun. I wasn't looking for trouble, but if I'd found it, I was ready for whatever might come. Scott was Connecticut martial arts champ for eight years. I've studied martial arts for twelve years. Joe is a Vietnam vet and knows how to handle himself in a fight. And we had Phil and Chris, who are gutsy guys too.

While we were there to help people spiritually, none of us would back down from these guys. I try very hard to be a good Catholic, but if you slap me in the face, I won't turn the other cheek. I'll probably knock your teeth out. That's the attitude we used to walk out of there without any trouble from the Satanists.

Like my other case in this area, this investigation ended with a death. A week later I got a call from my investigator, saying that Lewis Williams had taken a gun and blown his brains out. He'd told one of the girls who hung out with him that he "couldn't control *it* any more." If only he'd listened when I told him he was reading a dangerous book.

10

BUSTING THE DEVIL

Like police work, exorcism is a dirty, dangerous job. Since most people will never become possessed or even witness an exorcism, it's hard for them to even imagine how foul and dreadful the ritual can be, just as it's impossible for the average person to grasp what it's like actually to investigate a really gruesome crime, instead of just reading about it in the newspaper as you have your morning coffee. Recently I got a radio call about a fire at a school yard. When I arrived on the scene, the odor was overpowering. When I got closer, I found out why. The smoldering object, which initially appeared to be a large pile of rags, was a corpse, so charred that I couldn't tell if it was a man, woman, or, God forbid, a child.

Try, if you can, to imagine how I felt standing there, with my nose filled with the stomach-turning stench of roasting human flesh, looking at what used to be a human face. Most of the features were burned away, except for a mouth forever frozen in its final scream. I hoped like hell that this person was dead *before* he or she was drenched in gasoline and torched like yesterday's trash. The other officers who responded reacted just as I expected, stifling their horror in coarse cop humor. I know this makes us sound like horribly cold sons of bitches, but it's a cop's defense mechanism. Just as doctors in a hospital burn unit distance themselves from their unbearably injured or maimed patients by cracking jokes among themselves about "crispy critters," the officers on the scene dehumanized this victim with sarcastic suggestions about what his or her name might be. "How about Bobbie-Q?" one cop joked, while another said, "Or if it's a girl, what about Suzy-Q?"

I joined the grim camaraderie, just as I did at another horrific crime scene. Responding to a report of shots fired in a Brooklyn project, my partner, whom we affectionately called B-Dog, and I found pools of blood in the lobby and followed the trail up the stairs. We started seeing bloody handprints, showing that some horribly wounded person had crawled or dragged himself upward. We carefully stepped around the handprints, to avoid contaminating the evidence. With each step, the smell of iron got stronger and the blood thicker. When we reached the tenth floor, we found the victim—a young, muscular guy wearing a green Army jacket, lying facedown in a huge pool of blood. He'd been shot several times and died in a crawling position, with one leg bent and one arm still reaching for the next step.

Soon after detectives from the major case squad arrived on the scene, we saw something move. "Look at the size of that fucker," one detective said. We watched the most enormous cockroach we'd ever seen crawl out from under the dead man's belly and walk lazily up the wall. *It must have been feeding on the blood*, I thought, and realized the other cops had just come to the same disgusting conclusion. Naturally, we had to pretend that seeing some poor bastard lying dead in a slum staircase, while roaches feasted on his life's blood, didn't bother us a bit. Instead, we bantered about being late for *our* breakfast when one of the detectives showed up, munching on a bacon and egg sandwich and drinking a cup of coffee. That was how we shrugged it off as just another night's work in the projects.

A lot of macho cops won't admit it, but stuff like this gets to us. Yes, you get hardened to cruel, random death to some extent after seeing it for years, but no matter how much protective armor you put around yourself—or how many hard-boiled cop jokes you tell—some cases leave an indelible mark. I hate to think about the really grisly murders and assaults I've seen, but they haunt me in ways I'd never tell my wife, and I pray my little girls will never discover. That's not to say that the Job has left me broken or burned out, but you can't see things like this night after night and walk away completely unscathed.

An exorcism also stains your soul. It's not for nothing that demons are called "unclean spirits" in the Bible: Their goal is to defile and destroy. If you've never felt the fury and filth of Satan firsthand, as I have, you may be saying "I don't believe in the Devil or demons, so this is just a lot of crap." Believe me, I've heard that plenty of times, as I sat in a stranger's living room, listening to the nightmare that person was recounting. Even victims of the demonic may refuse to believe that the forces of darkness are responsible for what's happening to them: Often their stories begin "You'll think I'm crazy, but . . ."

Perhaps you also feel these people must be nuts, or that exorcism is a medieval remedy for mental or physical illness that has no relevance in the Internet age. If so, score one for the Devil. Denial only makes him more powerful. But if you believe in God at all, are you really willing to dismiss the parables of Jesus casting out demons as mere fables? In Matthew 4:24, the Bible makes a clear distinction between medical and spiritual ailments, telling us that Jesus' followers "carried to him all those afflicted with various diseases and racked with pain: the possessed, the lunatics, the paralyzed. He cured them all."

The Vatican certainly doesn't consider evil obsolete. In 1999 it issued its first update of the Roman Ritual of Exorcism since the rite was originally authorized in 1614. Possibly spurring this move was an earlier report by Father Gabriele Amorth, official exorcist for the diocese of Rome, of an alarming increase in cases of demonic possession over the previous ten years as well as explosive rises in satanic sects and other occult practices. Also fueling the father's concern was what he considered "sins of omission" on the part of the Catholic clergy, many of whom aren't familiar with the practice of exorcism and many of whom even question the existence of the Devil. He urged the Church to intensify its fight against evil, quoting the Second Vatican Council's prophecy that Satan would seek to destroy humanity "until the end of the world." These sentiments struck a chord with Pope John Paul II, who denounced the Devil as a "cosmic liar and murderer." Satan's power is fed, the Pontiff charged, by the public's increasing tolerance of "lies and deceit . . . the idolatry of money . . . [and] the idolatry of sex."

The Vatican document—an eighty-four-page book of prayers and instructions for exorcism—reaffirms that the Devil isn't an abstract notion or a matter of opinion but a very real menace in the modern world, who "goes around like a roaring lion, looking for souls to devour." Unlike the previous draft of the Roman Ritual, the new manual specifically cautions exorcists not to confuse symptoms of mental illness with the acknowledged signs of demonic possession, such as speaking in unknown languages, "discerning distant or hidden things," exhibiting unnatural strength, and developing a vehement aversion to God, the Virgin Mary, the saints, or sacred objects and images. Exorcism, the guidelines emphasize, should be attempted only after "diligent inquiry and after having consulted experts in spiritual matters and, if felt appropriate, experts in medical and psychiatric science."

There are other new stipulations. One is that no one connected with an exorcism shall ever talk about it publicly—and no members of the media are allowed to attend, to keep the ritual from becoming a spectacle. Recordings, video- and audiotapes, and written notes are also banned. In other words, the Church still attempts to keep exorcism in the closet, so to speak. The manual also stresses that no one can legitimately perform an exorcism without the express consent of the bishop of the diocese. Nor can any Christian layperson use the prayer of exorcism against Satan and the fallen angels, for any purpose, especially exorcisms. Bishops are instructed to bring this edict to the attention of the Christian faithful as necessary.

I agree with these stipulations to a certain degree. No layperson should undertake the exorcism of a person, and in that I'm 100 percent compliant. But Pope Leo gave the faithful permission to read his prayer when the Devil is active. That's why I use it in cases of diabolical activity. (The Pope Leo XIII prayer and other prayers I use in the Work are included at the end of the book.) Now, the revised ritual says that Christians should never say the Pope Leo prayer in whole or in part. I have two problems with that. First, no one in the Church has the authority to overturn a decree issued by a Pope except a subsequent Pope, and that hasn't happened in this case, since these revisions were made by the Congregation of the Doctrine of Faith, a group of priests, rather than the Pope himself.

Second—and most important—are the words of Jesus Himself: John said to Him, "Teacher, we saw a man using your name to expel demons and we tried to stop him because he is not of our company." Jesus said in reply, "Do not try to stop him. No man who performs a miracle using my name can at once speak ill of me. Anyone who is not against us is with us" (Mark 9:38–40).

The Vatican's updated ritual has sparked heightened interest in exorcism. In September 2000 the Archdiocese of Chicago announced that it had appointed the first official exorcist in its 160-year history. This priest, whose name was withheld by the archdiocese to protect the privacy of those who consult him, has participated in at least nine exorcisms in Rome and now is evaluating over a dozen possible cases of demonic possession in Chicago. The Reverend James LeBar, one of four exorcists serving the Archdiocese of New York, reports a sudden surge of exorcisms in his city, from none in 1990 to over three hundred in the decade that followed. Overall, the number of full-time Roman Catholic exorcists has risen from just one several years ago to ten, with many other priests performing the ritual as part of their other religious duties, the way Bishop McKenna does.

On September 7, 2000, Pope John Paul II held an exorcism for a nineteen-year-old Italian woman who had been possessed since childhood. The woman flew into a diabolically provoked rage during a public audience with the Pope in St. Peter's Square, screaming in an unknown language. According to Father Amorth, a witness, her voice became "cavernous" and she exhibited superhuman strength during a struggle with security guards—telltale signs of possession. Touched by the woman's suffering, the Pope hugged her and promised that he'd hold a ritual for her the following day. He spent nearly an hour praying over her and commanding the demon to leave but was unable to expel the evil force.

After the papal exorcism failed, Father Amorth, president and founder of the International Association of Exorcists, who had been asked to consult on the case, spent two hours conducting his own exorcism. During the ceremony, the demon jeered at the Pope's efforts, saying "Not even your [church] head can send me away." Nor did the second ritual cure the woman. "This is a case where the possession is very, very strong," Father Amorth reported. "From what can be foreseen by us exorcists, it will take years of exorcisms" to banish such a powerful demon that it could even resist the prayers of the Pope himself. The Pontiff, however, is said to have successfully exorcised another Italian woman in 1982.

Although the Catholic Church has downplayed the role of exorcism in recent years, its revision of the Roman Ritual and the Pope's own willingness to serve as an exorcist have affirmed that the nearly four-hundred-year-old ritual remains a very modern answer to the age-old problem of possession. Yet it can also be a dangerous undertaking because, as Father Martin says, when an exorcism fails—and the demon ultimately triumphs—all who participated in the ritual pay the price.

Still skeptical? Let me tell you about the worst case of diabolic evil I've ever encountered and the toll it took on everyone involved. In May of 1993, my partner Joe was in a terrible mood. He had a very bad headache, had just finished a rather annoying day at work, and was upset by a prediction a psychic we both knew had made a few days earlier: an attempt would be made on his life later that year. When the phone rang, he was greeted by a raspy, uneducated—and extremely familiar—male voice: "Having some problems, Joe?"

Joe immediately went on red alert. Ever since the psychic's prediction, he'd been expecting trouble—and here it was. This particular caller had an uncanny ability to sense when my partner was at a physical, emotional, or spiritual low—and he invariably chose those moments to get in touch. He was a New Jersey housepainter who, rather ironically, had the same name as the saint who drove Lucifer and his fallen angels out of heaven: Michael.

This Michael, however, was anything but angelic: Although he looked like a frail old grandfather—with a thin, bony face; pointy white beard; and pale, almost translucent skin—he'd been possessed by an extremely powerful demon for many years. Joe knew all about Michael's long ordeal since this was one of the first cases he'd investigated after entering the Work in 1986. My partner had also participated in two harrowing exorcisms for the housepainter—and paid a terrible price for his efforts to help, since he was almost killed during the first of these rituals.

In the bland, guarded tone he used for polygraph exams of vicious criminals, Joe asked, "What can I do for you, Michael?"

"I need another exorcism," the painter said. "I'll be in New York for a few days in September, so that would be a good time."

"Have things gotten worse for you?" my partner inquired, aware that the demon inside Michael had tormented him terribly after the previous exorcisms. At times the housepainter would suddenly become frozen in his footsteps, with a hideously contorted expression on his face, as the evil force suddenly seized control of his body—leaving him to stand there like a gargoyle until it released its grip.

"No one would want to switch places with me, that's for

sure," Michael said, then let out a harsh, high-pitched giggle. "Or maybe someone would? I'd do *anything* to be free!"

Joe shivered from a sudden chill. Even over the phone, on a beautiful spring day, a palpable feeling of evil emanated from this man. Although my partner sensed that getting involved with Michael again would be perilous, he didn't hesitate for a second.

"I'll call the bishop," he promised. As soon as he hung up, Joe threw holy water on his phone, his usual practice after Michael called.

To prepare for what we knew would be an extraordinarily grueling and risky ritual, Joe brought audiotapes of Michael's previous exorcisms to our class so our investigators would know what we were up against. Normally, neither Joe nor I will play tapes of any unresolved case, because any time you give the demonic recognition, it's dangerous and can attract evil. Not only that, but this particular satanic force was extraordinarily powerful: so powerful, in fact, that Michael could actually attend church and even take Holy Communion, which is impossible in most cases of diabolical possession, where the person is incapable of praying at home, let alone in the presence of the Most Holy Eucharist.

Before playing the tapes, Joe gave the twelve students who'd gathered in my basement a stern warning. "I know some of you have assisted in exorcisms, but on a scale of one to ten, everything you've seen before is a one or two, and this is a nine. We're dealing with terrible stuff here—it's like the cases you've read about in Father Martin's book. This could be the kind of exorcism where the priest has a heart attack, because this demon is a real soul-killer. Believe me, I'm not being melodramatic when I say that if you choose to get involved in this case, you could literally be putting your life on the line."

These words had a profound effect on our students, who were stunned to hear my normally calm partner speak so passionately. They were riveted to their chairs, hanging on his every word. I could feel their fear, but no one left.

After pausing for a moment, Joe continued. "If you have any physical or spiritual weakness, you could be attacked in those areas. If you have any health problem, it could be exacerbated by your involvement in this case. Or things may go wrong in your life or your marriage. You could be mentally attacked during the exorcism and face terror you can't even imagine. You could even walk out of the church with permanent psychological damage."

Seeing how grim the students looked, Joe felt it was time to offer some encouragement. "Forewarned is forearmed," he emphasized. "This is going to be the Olympics of exorcisms, so you have to do everything in your power to strengthen yourself, especially spiritually. I expect you to go to mass or the services of your faith every week without fail from now on."

His large brown eyes scanned the room. Apparently feeling he was assessing the condition of their souls, a couple of the students looked as embarrassed as if they'd been caught smoking in church. All the people in our class are deeply religious, but they're also human and sometimes have spiritual lapses, like anyone else.

With a benevolent gesture that made Joe look more monkish than usual, my partner brushed his hand through the air as if to say "Don't worry about your past mistakes—just get on the right path now."

I reminded the students that they were to start a black fast three days before the exorcism and go to midweek confession if they were Catholic, even if they'd been absolved of their sins the previous Sunday. "You want to be in a state of grace when you go up against this demon," I said, feeling as if I were giving the patrolmen I supervise at the Four-Six their sector assignments. "And don't forget to pray the rosary—every day, if possible."

I place great value on this form of devotion. During a period of difficulty in my marriage with Jen, I went to Our Lady of the Rosary Chapel to pray about our problems. When I finished, Sister Philomena, one of the nuns there, sensed I was troubled and asked if I prayed the rosary.

I had to admit that I wasn't *that* devout. "No, I don't, Sister," I replied.

"Try it," she said. Since then I've made the rosary part of my daily routine and find it an unfailing source of comfort and strength.

After reminding the students of our religious rules, Joe briefed them about Michael's background, which gave few clues about how the housepainter came to be possessed. Nor did the man himself have any recollection of when or how the demon entered him. Raised in a poor but religious Jewish family in New Jersey, Michael later converted to Catholicism. At eighteen, he enlisted in the Navy, hoping to better himself. He didn't take well to military discipline and often found himself in trouble for drinking, mouthing off to his superior officers, or getting into fights with other enlisted men. After his term of duty was up, he drifted from one menial job to another, eventually settling on a career as a housepainter. Despite being a rather difficult and quarrelsome man who had few friends, he wooed and won the affections of a young nurse, and married her in 1960.

At some point—he has no recollection of exactly when—Michael began feeling alienated from himself. "He told me that some of his thoughts seemed very strange, as if someone else had taken over his mind," Joe told the class. "He also found it harder and harder to control his bad temper, which steadily got worse. To his horror, he became physically and psychologically abusive to his wife and children during these rages. At times he felt so full of hatred that he even frightened himself."

Like many of the people who consult us, Michael tried psychological counseling without success. He also saw many doctors about his frequent, agonizing headaches and the sense of impending doom that sometimes overwhelmed him, but despite extensive medical tests and scans, they found no physical explanation for either ailment. There were also periods when these problems lifted on their own, sometimes for months or even years on end, but the darkness always returned.

Gradually Michael started to see that his problems were in the spiritual realm. As sometimes happens, this demon had attacked without warning, skipping the stages of infestation and oppression. Instead, it invaded like a thief in the night, taking over this man with such stealth that he didn't know exactly when or how it entered him. He consulted clergymen of all denominations, and attended Jewish, Pentecostal, Baptist, and Catholic healing services, none of which helped. Through a priest in Queens who holds this type of healing masses, Michael learned about Joe, who told him about the bishop's frequent success in casting out evil spirits.

My partner's investigation turned up some indications that Michael may have been cursed by his mother-in-law, who was of a different faith, and bitterly opposed his marriage to her daughter. Even many years later this sour, reclusive woman continued to be extremely hostile to him.

"Was she some kind of witch?" asked Chris, our teenaged investigator, who had come to the class with his parents, Rose and Phil.

"I don't know," Joe said. "Since Michael was never invited to her house, he couldn't tell me if any signs of the occult were present. But it's certainly possible."

When he began looking into the housepainter's problems, Joe—who was then a novice at the Work—didn't realize the old man was possessed. A small but telling incident tipped him off, my partner told us. "I had invited Michael to my home for dinner, and as we ate, it started snowing heavily. Because the driving conditions were so bad and this man lived a considerable distance away, I invited him to spend the night. During dinner, he seemed extremely uncomfortable—and now insisted on heading home, despite the blizzard outside. He later told me that the religious articles in my home were causing him actual physical pain, a feeling like spikes were digging into his spine and neck."

Joe encountered what he's convinced is the same demon in another case a few years later, which involved a mother and daughter who had practiced witchcraft. He said, "When several of us, including two psychics, went to their home at the bishop's request, one of the psychics actually felt this demon crawling on her skin: The mental picture she got was of a scorpion with spikes. I suspect that this demon came to her, and possibly Michael, through a curse created during a Brazilian black magic ceremony."

Although not psychic, Joe has also seen this demon in his mind's eye on several occasions. To him, it didn't look like an insect but something even more frightening. "Its face was inhuman. The best word to describe it is reptilian. It resembled a lizard, with big teeth and bat wings. Hatred was all over it."

But why would a South American demon possess a New Jersey housepainter? Joe had a theory: "During her lifetime, Michael's mother-in-law, who died a few years before I met him, owned a business that employed many South American workers. Since many forms of black magic are practiced in these countries, she may have found a sorcerer among these workers and hired him to curse her son-in-law."

When Joe mentioned this, I was reminded of an investigation I was involved in, where a man was possessed by seven demons. We had that many exorcisms, and each time, the bishop would ask the evil spirit, "How many are you?" The answer would always correspond to the number of exorcisms that had been held, because at each ritual, one more demon would be cast out, forcing the next, more powerful demon forward. Each ceremony increased in violence, to the point where we all felt it wise to have a medical doctor on hand. After a frenzied struggle on the part of the possessed lasting well over thirty minutes, the doctor checked the man's vital signs. In an astonished whisper, the physician told me that his patient's heart rate was as calm as if he'd been sitting on a couch watching TV—while every one of the assistants was exhausted from the battle.

Curiously, this case also involved a curse by a relative. This man had an evil stepfather who incited the Devil to attack him, leading to the stepson's possession. As a rather understandable result, the younger man had developed an extreme loathing of his stepfather, which actually amplified the curse, since the demonic gain strength from negative emotions. Due to the intense hatred inside this man, his exorcisms weren't successful until he finally consented to forgive his stepfather. Once he did this, he was finally freed.

While the reason for Michael's possession remained unclear, there was no doubt about the ferocity of the demon inside him. Although my partner wasn't present at this man's first exorcism by Bishop McKenna, he still paid for having set it up, I told the class. At the exact moment when the Roman Ritual was beginning in Connecticut, Joe was walking down a sidewalk in New York City, when a van roared out of a nearby gas station and slammed into him. Fortunately, the blow flung him to the side of the vehicle, so he escaped certain death from its wheels, but he was left with agonizing injuries that took weeks to heal.

Back at the little chapel in Connecticut, Bishop McKenna was also under attack. "We had Michael roped into a chair in front of the altar," the exorcist told me when I reviewed the case with him. "There was a strong sheet wrapped around his arms, but this tiny man slipped out of these bonds as easily as Houdini. Six large men were present to restrain him, but he struggled so furiously that it taxed their strength to the ultimate. Michael had a weak, quavering voice, but when the demon came forth, he spoke in a deep, harsh tone of tremendous menace, making many gruesome threats. 'I'll kill you,' this devil howled—and indeed, he would have done me in, right there in my church, if he could. But in the end, these were vain threats, because the Devil can do no more than God permits.

"I have an audiocassette of this exorcism, and it shocks the wits out of all who hear it. The Devil ranted and roared terrible protests at my prayers, yet as soon as I'd stop exorcising Michael, he'd immediately come to himself and be polite and pleasant. His fury was extreme when I applied relics of St. Dominick, the founder of my order; St. Vincent Ferrer, also a saint from my order; St. Catherine of Siena; and St. Patrick."

Relics, I reminded my students as I shared the bishop's recollections, are extremely potent weapons against the demonic. It's not that Catholics consider bones, ashes, hair, or clothing from saints, or splinters from the cross Jesus died on magical, as some people outside our faith mistakenly argue. Instead, they are holy because they embody miracles of God. The Bible offers several examples of this: The Book of Kings describes a dead man who was brought back to life after his body touched bones from the prophet Elisha, while Acts relates how handkerchiefs and aprons that had touched the body of St. Paul were then used to expel evil spirits or cure the sick. This shows that God sanctions the use of relics to drive out satanic forces in His name.

In Michael's exorcism, one particular relic elicited some extremely revealing remarks from the demon, the bishop recalled. "When I held up a crucifix containing a piece of the True Cross that I wear on my breast and adjured this devil to depart, he pointed a finger at the cross and said something I'll never forget. 'You weren't supposed to die,' the demon shouted, indicating that Satan knew all along that the crucifixion would be his undoing. If the Devil could have prevented Our Savior from sacrificing His life to save mankind, he surely would have."

A picture of the Virgin Mary also had a remarkable effect, the exorcist added. "The demon howled and pointed a finger at Our Blessed Lady. In a low, tormented voice, he said, 'She wasn't supposed to say yes.' This confirmed that I was dealing with an evil spirit—no ordinary human being of faith would ever condemn Mary for having consented to be the

Mother of God. During the Annunciation, when the angel Gabriel told her that she would conceive Our Savior, she replied, to the Devil's eternal torment, 'Behold the handmaiden of the Lord, be done unto me according to Thy word.' By saying yes, as the demon well knew, she brought Jesus Christ to this world, who later became the first exorcist."

No miracles occurred at Michael's first exorcism—or the second, which Joe assisted in. "I'd stayed away from the original exorcism because I'd just started in the Work and didn't feel I was holy enough to be at an exorcism," my partner told the class.

Several students nodded in apparent sympathy, and I remembered feeling the same way myself. Even after I rediscovered my faith and got into the Work, nobody ever accused me of being a saint. "Ralph, you have a lot of rough edges, but so does the Devil," Ed Warren once said. I took that as a compliment. So I could understand why the students—or my partner—would question their spiritual fitness.

For the second exorcism, continued Joe, "The bishop convinced me that as a lifelong Catholic, I *was* up to the job. It was my very first exorcism, so I didn't realize until later how extraordinary Michael's ritual was. At certain points, the back of his head bulged out a good two or three inches and began pulsating. He looked like a space alien with a big, throbbing brain. I've never seen anything like this in my entire life: It was like a Hollywood special effect on *Star Trek*."

During this exorcism, which was tape-recorded, the demon repeatedly babbled in a language no one understood, frequently using a word that sounded like "sarabande." When my partner later played this tape to language professors at a local college, one identified the tongue as a mix of Spanish and Portuguese. Since the only foreign language Michael knew was Hebrew, his otherwise inexplicable knowledge of these languages supported Joe's theory that the curse Michael was under originated in some form of Brazilian sorcery, perhaps based on Bantu or Congo beliefs.

"Years ago an exorcist from the Vatican said that the toughest cases of all involved black magic of this type," my partner said, while the expressions on our investigators' faces became increasingly grave.

Ultimately this exorcism failed, as did five subsequent rituals held over the next few years. Since Joe wasn't at these rituals, I asked the bishop about them. Sounding very tired and sorrowful, the man of God described these epic struggles as the most harrowing he'd ever experienced in all his years as an exorcist. "We had repeated sessions lasting for days on end, all of them so violent as to exhaust those who restrained Michael. I'd go on for many hours at a time trying to exorcise him, because from the way he was acting, I never knew if at the next instant the demon would be gone. I didn't want to give up if there was any chance the Devil was weakening and might leave. Finally Michael's restrainers would plead with me to break if off because their strength was giving out.

"At one session, I had only one nun to help me, yet all by herself she was able to restrain Michael. I was never so frightened in my life as I was that he might break loose and kill me, but the Lord in His providence kept us safe from harm. I'm ever grateful to God for this, but that nun later left our order. Again, as soon as the exorcism stopped, so did the danger because the Devil quieted right down."

Bishop McKenna paused and gave a long sigh before he finished his story. "Unfortunately, I wasn't able to help Michael much or deliver him from the demon."

Nor could several other exorcists of various faiths the

housepainter consulted, all of whom fell victim to the same
curse that afflicted Michael. Each time the Brazilian scorpion
stung in a different way. A Lutheran pastor who worked with
the painter for four futile years developed life-threatening
health problems, while a Catholic priest who planned an exorcism for him had to cancel it after receiving a telegram that
his mother had died—three days before the scheduled ritual.
The Catholic father returned from the funeral and scheduled
a new ceremony only to have his church burn down shortly
before the appointed day.

Yet another clergyman involved in this case lost his min-
istry after being falsely accused of child abuse. A Protestant
preacher suffered many strange calamities and mysteriously
dropped out of sight soon after participating in a deliverance
ritual for Michael. His fate is unknown, but I suspect that his
spirit was broken by the holy war he'd endured.

If all this wasn't enough to scare the wits out of our students, Joe had one final warning. Recounting his phone conversation with the painter, he told the class that Michael's
final remark about wanting to swap places with someone else
might be no joke. "I don't think any of us can truly understand how desperate this man is. I have a hunch that somehow he's made a bargain with the demon for a transference to
take place during the exorcism. If we're not extremely careful,
someone could end up being possessed!"

Our students were clearly shocked—and a bit skeptical.
"Do you really think he'd try to do such a thing?" Rose asked.
"Is it even possible?"

"We have to be prepared for any kind of attack, even an
attempt at possession," Joe emphasized. "There's no evil the
demonic won't stoop to—and this man has endured so much
that his spirit is broken. He wouldn't care if another person

had to suffer in his place, if that meant his suffering would be over. He said he'd do *anything* to be free."

I urged our students to take every spiritual precaution, both for themselves and their families. "Civilians can be attacked too," I cautioned. "If you have a relative whose faith isn't strong, that person could be a weak link in our battle. Help that family member get in a better relationship with God."

The students looked grimmer than ever now that Joe had fully described the dangers they'd be braving, should they decide to assist with Michael's eighth exorcism. During the class, I also got a little "warning" that the Devil didn't like what we were up to. We listened to some of the tapes of Michael's previous exorcisms, but not all. Knowing that any time this particular demon is discussed, creepy phenomena occur, I went upstairs during a break in the class to check on my dog, Max. Jen was out at the movies with Christina.

I found the door of my apartment flung wide open—even though no one else was at home, and I'd locked it myself. Since I have guns in my home, I am extremely careful to keep the door secured at all times, yet unless Max, my dog, had learned to unlock and open doors, I knew I'd just gotten a visit from the demonic. Yes, it was a minor thing, and I thank God for that, but in retrospect, it was also the first hint of the harm and suffering this exorcism would bring me—and everyone else involved. As I was about to discover, the demonic never forget and never stop seeking vengeance.

11

THE SEPTEMBER CURSE

We decided to hold Michael's exorcism over a three-day period, with the last ritual, if needed, to be performed on September 14, a holy day, the Triumph of the Cross. This date commemorates a seventh-century victory where a Christian emperor regained relics of the cross Jesus died on from a Persian ruler who had stolen them. To ready ourselves, Joe and I both purified our bodies and spirits with our usual, pre-exorcism black fast. On the day of the exorcism, we visited our respective churches, confessed our sins, and received Holy Communion, so we'd be in a state of grace.

The exorcism began on a Friday morning. Phil, Antonio, and Scott volunteered to assist, while Rose sat in the back of Our Lady of the Rosary Chapel and supported us with her prayers. I spent the first fifteen minutes of the ritual puking my guts out. I had knelt in front of Michael to check his leg restraints, and when I did, I got a whiff of an incredibly foul odor, one of the signs of possession listed in the Roman Ritual. I won't be melodramatic and say it was worse than rotting flesh—a stench I've had the misfortune to encounter more than once on the Job—but it was close. It's hard to describe what it smelled like, definitely not fire and brimstone, as you might imagine, but sort of like decomposing garbage. After vomiting in the bucket we put out for the exorcee, I went outside so I wouldn't disrupt the ritual. Since I had very little in my stomach after my fast, I stood in the church parking lot dry-heaving all over the place, until I felt that with the next heave my entire stomach would come up.

Finally I returned to the exorcism, making damned sure not to walk in front of the old man. The bishop was still reciting the Litany of the Saints, so I tried to slip inconspicuously into the pew. Michael instantly turned to me with a very nasty grin and said, "Looks like you need an exorcism too!"

I kept silent. No one should speak to a possessed person during an exorcism except the priest. I run my cases like a police operation, and if there's one piece of discipline I particularly impress on my investigators, it's this: Talking to a demon can cause an assistant to be attacked or even become possessed.

Although each exorcism is different, and the Roman Ritual permits the priest to add whatever he feels is necessary to free the possessed, there are certain questions an exorcist always asks, such as, "What is your name, evil spirit?" Being a Traditionalist Catholic, Bishop McKenna always asks them in Latin and then, if there's no reply, in English. I remember how utterly amazed the bishop was at one exorcism when the exorcee, a high school dropout, needed no translation: She gave an appropriate answer in English to each Latin question. More remarkable still was a nearly illiterate farmer, who actually gave his replies in fluent Latin!

At times, the name the demon gives will correspond to its method of attack or a weakness it exploited to take control of the person. Father Martin wrote about a possessed woman whose face was fixed in a ghastly, twisted grin. During her

chilling exorcism, the satanic spirit gave its name as "Smiler."
In sharp contrast to this harmless-sounding name was the effect it had on the priest, who suddenly found himself overcome by supernatural despair, feeling that God, Heaven,
Earth, goodness, and evil were somehow "a cosmic joke on
little men who in their turn are only puny little jokes." As the
demon smirked, the exorcist slipped into the trap of wondering if all of existence was just a meaningless farce, then col-
lected himself—and commanded Smiler to depart.

Some believe that once the evil power gives its name, the
spirit is loosening its grasp and will be cast out. If so, the response when Bishop McKenna asked this question wasn't
encouraging, since the demon said nothing. Nor did it react to
the next question, "When did you enter?" Clearly we'd reached
the pretense stage.

Like an experienced police interrogator, the bishop never
let up the pressure. "Devil, I adjure you, in the name of Jesus
Christ, to reveal *how* you entered."

This question is asked because the demonic often enter
through one of the chakra points: the body's centers of psychic energy, which run in a vertical line from the base of the
spine to the top of the head. From these points flows the aura,
the spiritual protection that surrounds each person. If you are
free from sin, your aura is very strong and intact, but if you
let your faith slip away, it develops breaks and chinks that can
let the demonic in. A weak aura attracts diabolical spirits; a
strong one repels them. If the exorcist can find out which
physical entry point the satanic spirit used, he can then apply
relics to that area and cause the demon great torment that
may spur it to flee.

The same question can, at times, tell us if the person was
cursed. If that proves to be the case, we must discover *how* the

person was attacked. Was the curse attached to a contact object? If the item is ever identified, we can take the correct steps to contain its evil, by reading prayers to lift the curse and disposing of the object in deep water or consecrated ground, so no one else is harmed by its negative charge.

If the evil spell was sent verbally by a sorcerer, we have other prayers to break the curse and send it back to the person who invoked it. Being more of a crafty thinker than I am, Joe has figured out a perfect, Christian way to handle this situation. Rather than fight evil with evil and practice the black arts ourselves by cursing the sorcerer in return, he suggested that we rebuke magicians in God's name, with a special prayer. We ask that the magician will be surrounded by the "Lumen Christi," or Christ light, by visualizing the person, surrounded by a bright, white light from head to toe, forming a protective shield that won't let evil in or out.

That day the demon didn't give anything up about its mode of entry but was finally provoked to say something. The breakpoint had come. In a deep, guttural voice, it told Bishop McKenna, "I'm going to slit your belly and let your guts spill out!"

Refusing to be intimidated, the exorcist continued to recite the ritual in a steady monotone that betrayed not a flicker of fear. I've noticed that when the bishop is really intent on his prayers, his voice will drop to a soft, hypnotic mumble where the Latin words blur into one long, echoing sound of holiness that seems to last forever.

"Stop your prayers," the demon ordered. "I'll rip your heart out and drink your blood! You're a dead man, priest! Dead, dead, dead!"

Ignoring these lurid threats, Bishop McKenna asked calmly, "What keeps you here, Devil?"

The response to this question can alert us if there's a cursed object in the home—or on the person—of the possessed. We also may learn if the exorcee is holding the demon there. Many times, even though the satanic spirit causes people awful suffering, they may be unwilling to let go. This is most common when the force attacks through the intellect, since the victims have a harder time distinguishing between their own thoughts and impulses and those artfully suggested by the demon.

Since in some cases demonic brainwashing goes on for many years before the person's will breaks down, eventually alien ideas can sound familiar and even reasonable. When the attack takes a religious direction, it can be harder still for the people to clearly recognize the dividing line between their own faith and the distorted version the demon has presented, but until this realization comes, the exorcism won't succeed.

The fiend in Michael turned to a new, even more appalling line of attack after its garish threats to disembowel, blind, mutilate, and murder Bishop McKenna had no discernible impact. After yelling for a while in a language we couldn't understand, Michael's eyes fixed on a Dominican sister sitting meekly by the altar, praying silently.

The next time the exorcist held up his cross and commanded the satanic spirit to depart, it offered a grotesque alternative: "I'll leave this one—give me *her*! I want the nun!"

The way the demon uttered these words made them sound so dirty that my skin crawled at the vileness of it. What gave this demon the right to use this hideously lewd tone about a nun? It was an obscenity! Joe's intuition was right. But even though my partner suspected a scheme to transfer Michael's demon into some innocent victim, he never dreamed the target would be a nun!

Even the usually unflappable bishop was taken aback. "What did she ever do to you, Devil?"

"The nun knows. She's going to be mine!"

As the demon's horrible laughter filled the church, I couldn't help but glance at the nun to see how she was reacting. Her expression was as pure and pious as ever, and she betrayed no sign she'd even heard the demon's disgusting insinuations. I admired her faith under fire.

To my surprise, since Bishop McKenna always avoids any idle questions, he pursued this line of questioning, apparently curious as to why the demon had singled out the sister for its abuse. The spirit reveled in the opportunity to further defile the nun with its awful words. "I'll take her because I want her! And you can't stop me, priest!"

The exorcist could stand no more. "Silence, Devil!" he thundered, then issued a torrent of Latin.

In translation, the ritual, which takes about twenty minutes, but can be repeated as many times as the exorcist deems necessary, includes these words to the demon: "I exorcise you, Most Unclean Spirit! Invading enemy! All spirits! Every one of you! In the name of Our Lord Jesus Christ: Be uprooted and expelled from this creature of God. He who commands you is He who ordered you to be thrown down from highest Heaven into the depths of Hell. He who commands you is He who dominated the seas, the wind, and the storms. Hear, therefore, and fear, Satan! Enemy of the Faith! Enemy of the human race! Source of death! Robber of life! Twister of justice! Root of evil! Warp of vices! Seducer of men! Traitor of nations! Inciter of jealousy! Originator of greed! Cause of discord! Creator of agony! Why do you stay and resist, when you know that Christ our Lord has destroyed your plan? Fear Him. . . ."

After several hours of this struggle, the bishop announced

a break. While in the movies exorcisms seem to go on day and night without stopping until the possession is broken, that's not how it's really done. Sometimes we stop, we eat a little lunch, we rest, and then we resume. It is up to the exorcist. If he feels we shouldn't stop, we'll continue as long as necessary.

As was the pattern during Michael's seven previous exorcisms, the painter's behavior immediately returned to normal as soon as the exorcism was halted. I've seen this before. People typically react to the ritual in one of two ways. Some have no memory of the ceremony and take quite a while to come back to their senses at the end of an exorcism; others, like Michael, are aware of everything that takes place. Now that the demon was no longer being tormented by the bishop's words, it retreated and Michael was himself again.

During the break, Joe took Michael to a pizzeria, where an odd incident occurred. After the meal, the old man decided to have a cigarette, so my partner handed him his lighter. Although the lighter hadn't been used all day and wasn't the least bit warm, Michael dropped it as if it were a blazing hot coal and yelped in pain. "Get the fuck away from me," he yelled, his rough language provoking glares from the family in the next booth.

Joe suddenly realized what had happened: He'd been holding a bottle of holy water during the ritual and gotten his hands wet. Although Michael could normally touch holy objects without ill effects, despite his possession, the demon in him was weakening and now howled at the slight trace of holy water Joe's touch had transferred to his lighter.

Despite this promising sign, no further progress was made that afternoon—just more yelling and threats. The second day wasn't much different, except that I began to have horrifying visions during the exorcism. Grim crime scenes I hadn't thought about in years washed my mind with relentless gore. Cockroaches and scorpions marched through rivers of blood, burned bodies rose from the ground like mummies in a horror movie. I began to imagine terrible things happening to my wife and children—thoughts that are so appalling that I refuse to relive them in print. My fondest memories were indelibly tainted by the poison this demon was spewing, and my worst ones were crashing around me. *Don't listen, I kept telling myself, it's not real! The Devil mixes truth with lies and twists it into horrible perversion! This is insanity, a glimpse into Hell! God knows it's not me thinking these things!*

Focusing on God is the best way to arm yourself against mental attacks from the demonic. Because this form of psychological warfare is so common in the Work, I try to push these thoughts out of my mind the moment they enter, before they take hold in my imagination. I don't consider myself dreamy or prone to flights of fancy, but the demonic can seize on any thread of memory or emotion and weave it into something hellish. This has also happened to me during exorcisms of houses—I've read the Pope Leo XIII prayer hundreds of times and know it by heart, but when a mental attack strikes, I'll suddenly start stuttering and lose my place. Having been my partner for so long, Joe knows without my saying so that it's time to spray me with holy water before I lose it completely.

If blocking the thought doesn't work, I picture a big, silvery cross and concentrate only on that. It's similar to the Christ light I mentioned earlier, which can be used for the same purpose. You just imagine yourself surrounded by a pure white light that goes from the top of your head to the bottom of your heels and use it as a shield against evil thoughts.

But even with these comforting images to protect me, by

the end of the second day of Michael's exorcism, I was so mentally drained that my spirituality was at an all-time low. After an exorcism, you just want to get away from it all. I don't mean that I'd lost my faith, but you do take a psychological beating when you go up against pure evil. Once you have felt the demonic invade your mind, even for a moment, you never feel the same again.

The next day was Sunday, which we'd set as our day of rest from the exorcism. As Joe and his wife, Alla, were walking to evening mass, a heavy branch fell from the top of a tree, narrowly missing them. After mass, they met me outside the church, and Joe told me what had happened. It was a calm night, with no wind at all. We walked back to the spot and looked at the branch, which was large and would have certainly killed Joe if it had hit him. There was no sign of rot—it wasn't a dead branch. It had been ripped off the tree with tremendous force. We saw this was a second attempt on Joe's life by the demonic. There was no need to say anything: We both knew the psychic's prediction had just come true.

Since Monday was the day of the Triumph of the Cross, the bishop, Joe, and I brought relics of the True Cross with us. I sat behind and to the right of Michael with my relic at the side of his head, and Joe held his relic to the back of the housepainter's neck. Then Bishop McKenna stepped forward with his relic, for the part of the ritual that goes (in English), "Behold the Cross of the Lord. Depart, Enemies!"

At the simultaneous touch of *three* relics—the number that symbolizes both the demonic and the Holy Trinity—Michael's eyes went wild, darting from side to side. He wouldn't turn his head to look at any of the crosses, but there was no escape from the sight of them. What I saw in his eyes will be with me for the rest of my life: It was the look of a cornered beast that was trapped and frightened, but vicious at the same time. As a cop, I have seen people in all states of rage, anger, hate, pain, and death, but I can't describe his reaction in these terms. They say the eyes are the window of the soul, but what I saw there was not human. It didn't contain one ounce of humanity, and I will never forget it.

This soul-searing moment wasn't a turning point. The end of the third day was the same as the beginning of the first: Michael wasn't freed. For whatever reason, the powerful demon that had him in its grip wouldn't leave. The painter seemed pretty much resigned to ongoing possession, despite the torment it caused him.

"How do you feel?" the bishop asked in a kindly tone.

"I know you did your best, but it's still there." The housepainter sounded weary. "I guess that's just how my life is meant to be."

Although the bishop offered to set up another exorcism, Michael declined, then thanked all of us for our efforts.

"I'll always pray for you," Bishop McKenna said.

"So will I," added Joe, giving Michael's arm a friendly squeeze. "You can always call me."

I also prayed that our efforts might bring him some relief in the future or had helped weaken the demon. Joe refused to be discouraged by the result, pointing out that our efforts may well spare Michael the most heinous form of demonic captivity: perfect possession. In ordinary cases of possession, even though the person's will breaks down and he can no longer fight off the invading demon, his soul—contrary to what most people believe—still belongs to God, not the Devil. Only when the person *voluntarily* surrenders his spiritual essence, by making an actual pact with the Devil, can he suffer perfect possession, lose his immortal soul, and consign himself to eternal damnation. As the great exorcist Father Martin once said, "Ralph, if you ever come in contact with someone who is perfectly possessed, run like hell!"

Michael's exorcism wasn't the end of the case for him—or for me. Every September since then, the demonic has gotten its revenge on me for the moment of sheer terror it felt in the bishop's church. It didn't do this through outward phenomena, such as hideous apparitions or formless black shapes. Instead, it acted under the cover of darkness, with a new form of psychological attack. Every September since this exorcism, my life suddenly becomes a battleground.

Now, the people who know me best will tell you I'm not the easiest person to get along with. You might say there's a touch of Michael in me, because I can be bad-tempered, nasty, and argumentative. Yet even with these combustible traits, the problems I've had in this particular month aren't always my fault. The first September after the exorcism was when Joe and I had our big blowout, after my partner got lost on the way to a case. Our split resulted in the New York organization we'd run together breaking up, which is why I worked alone during some of the supernatural cases I investigated. We didn't speak for six months after this quarrel.

When I finally did call Joe, we got to talking about what happened, and he said, "Ralph, do you know what month we had the fight?"

I replied, "Yeah, it was September."

"Right," he said. "Now remember this: Michael!"

His words hit me like a sledgehammer. The exorcism! I said that all made some sense, but when I'm done with a case and no longer working on it, I forget about it. No point in dwelling on evil, unless I'm giving a class or lecture on the Work. With all the stuff in my life, Jen, my daughters Christina and Daniella, and the Job, I didn't pick up on the connection, but Joe has a more analytical mind than I do and is forever looking at possibilities I'd miss on my own. He's also very inventive about adapting and developing prayers for the different aspects of our Work.

Joe feels that during this exorcism, I may have inadvertently been too casual or gleeful about tormenting such a potent demon with my relic. He suggests that in my zeal to help Michael, I went a step too far and got personal with the satanic spirit, unleashing its undying wrath into my life and relationships. I have to admit that there's something to what he says. Today I'm more relaxed than I used to be, but back then I would yell "Charge!" and run right in rather than standing around thinking things over.

I'm the same way as a cop: It's a wonder that I don't get my ass shot off more often! With his clear, sensible thinking, Joe is always the one who reins me in. And now that he'd figured out that it was the demonic—so rightly described as a "cause of discord" in the Roman Ritual—that had busted up our partnership, we made up and resumed battling Hell's armies together.

The next year, 1995, I had a serious problem on the Job that kept me from being promoted to sergeant. That September I was on foot patrol, alone, in an area notorious for drugs and shootings. While I was checking a rooftop that was a known drug hangout, all of a sudden I saw someone exit a stairway onto the rooftop of the next building. The man drew a gun and started firing at the building across the street. Through a window, I saw kids in an apartment, playing a video game— clearly in danger of being hit or killed by his bullets.

I yelled to him to stop, but he didn't hear me, so I decided to shoot at him to protect those children, or anyone else, from being wounded or worse. Whether I hit him with any of my rounds or not is unknown, but he fled the scene without leaving any blood trail. The department investigated the incident and my firing of my weapon. Fortunately, I was eventually vindicated. It wasn't until five years later, however, that I finally got my sergeant's stripes.

Despite my problem on the Job, 1995 was a happy year on the personal front: On September 29—the Feast of St. Michael, the Archangel—my wife and I were blessed with our second daughter, Daniella. I was a wreck while Jen was in labor because she'd had such a difficult time with Christina, whose umbilical cord was wrapped around her foot and was finally born by emergency C-section. And Jen had had problems with bleeding during this pregnancy. I brought holy water and sprinkled all four corners of the hospital room.

To make sure our newborn got off to a good start in life, I called Father Martin. In his book the father describes a case of demonic possession where the man wasn't properly baptized as a child, leaving a foothold for the Devil to seize on. I didn't want any slipups with my daughter, so arranged the best baptism of all—a christening by the father himself, who performed the ceremony when Daniella was only a few hours old, right there in the hospital.

Amazingly, Father Martin himself was baptized even sooner than that. He was literally christened in the womb, by his father, a very devout Catholic doctor who also delivered him. Because his birth, like Christina's, was difficult, the doctor felt that his child needed all the spiritual protection he could get to arrive safely into this world. It seemed that the Devil knew Father Martin would grow up to be an exorcist and was trying to stop this from happening. Because little Malachi was a breech baby, Dr. Martin had to reach into the uterus to turn him around—and baptized him at that time, as any Christian layperson is allowed to do in an emergency.

I rejoiced that this extremely holy exorcist was baptizing my child, just as his own father had done with him. I felt that God had truly smiled upon me—and Father Martin.

The next year the demonic got another chance to divide and conquer. This time the confrontation was with my mother, and I managed to tick her off so much that I had to apologize from here to eternity before she'd speak to me again. As before, I wasn't aware of the connection until Joe brought September to mind. I was furious with myself that I hadn't taken some steps to prepare myself spiritually and steer clear of disputes.

The year of worst revenge, however, came when the satanic power got around to Jen and me. Now, I hope I don't make her mad again by telling you that she's as temperamental as I am, and our marriage has been a real roller-coaster from the start. The ride that September was straight downhill until we hit bottom. I withdrew into myself and became more and more impossible to live with. Eventually my partner on the Job got so concerned that he actually called Jen to find out what the hell was going on with me. I in turn saw nothing wrong, and didn't realize where my wife and I were headed until it was too late.

For the entire month, we argued night and day about the most trivial matters. I even became enraged at a message one of our close friends left on our answering machine. Because I work the graveyard shift, I sleep during the day. Usually I can sleep through a ringing phone, but when the machine picked up, this friend was in a chatty mood and left a lengthy message. As she talked on, I became more and more enraged. I wanted to rip the phone right out of the wall and throw it out the window! When Jen got home from work, she'd barely taken off her coat before I lit into her like a lunatic about our talkative friend. Naturally, the nastier I was, the madder she got. We fought for hours, and she ended up throwing me out.

Having nowhere else to go, I went home to Mom. Although my mother is a wonderful woman, I was suddenly back to being her "little Ralph." Staying with her was like reliving my childhood all over again, except that I was a grown man of thirty-five and a father myself. Instead of doing the sensible thing and calling Jen to apologize for acting like such an ass, I let the demon of anger mess up my life even further. I spent a few months living with my mother, and when I couldn't stand that anymore, I took a little place of my own.

During this time I let my faith lapse and stopped attending church regularly. I sat around marinating in misery and broke off contact with everyone I knew, including Joe. Although we had two active cases, I left the Work, recognizing that in my angry, hate-filled state, I wasn't emotionally stable enough to help victims of the demonic. To go up against the Devil in this frame of mind could lead to serious mistakes in judgment, potentially endangering myself or others. Nor could I hope to repair something as delicate as a marriage if I exposed myself to satanic influences when I was already in such a spiritually vulnerable frame of mind.

Miserable as I was, I refused to admit that I was giving the spirit that had attacked me through my weaknesses an easy victory. I was now literally hellbent on getting a divorce—and Jen felt the same. At the time I was too distraught to think about the demonic and its role in shattering my personal life. Later on Joe made the connection for me: As we both knew, the Devil hates love—and especially hates holy matrimony, because it's a union made in the eyes of God. Because a strong marriage is an important support system for people like us, who are involved in the Work, Satan's forces will work overtime to destroy our relationships, knowing that an angry, grieving, and emotionally troubled demonologist is likely to be powerless against evil. Just about every investigator I know has experienced marital problems that brought him to the verge of a breakup. Some of these marriages made it, and some didn't. Because I'd let my marriage founder, the Devil now had one less foe in this world.

God hadn't forgotten me, though. One Sunday I actually felt like going to mass, for the first time since the separation. I don't know why I was drawn to church on this particular day, but it's a good thing I was, because the priest seemed to have picked his Gospel reading with me in mind, choosing the text from Matthew 19:4–6: "Have you not read that at the beginning, the Creator made them male and female and declared, 'For this reason a man shall leave his father and mother and cling to his wife, and the two shall be as one'? Thus they are no longer two but one flesh. Therefore let no man separate what God has joined."

From that moment on, I decided that I would do everything in my power to stay married, if that was at all possible. Without my wife and our daughters, I was alone and adrift. Well, it was very hard—and it took a lot of work on both our parts to make ourselves better people—but Jen and I finally patched things up. After eight agonizing months, our separation was over. To celebrate our new life together, we moved to a new apartment and Jen decorated it just the way she wanted it, with angels all over the place. Every room, including the bathroom, is covered with angels. Now when I come home, I feel like I'm in Heaven, in more ways than one.

12

REAL-LIFE GHOST STORIES

In one investigation, my two lives collided. First, as a cop, I was called in on a case that had some occult aspects. Knowing of my interest in the supernatural, the lieutenant I was working under at the time, who is a great guy and one of the few practicing Buddhists on the New York City police force, consulted me about a bizarre incident that had happened on the previous night's late tour. Two Hispanic males had been arrested for unlawful imprisonment, menacing, and assault. While these crimes aren't exactly unheard of in the slums I patrol, the male victim, who was also Hispanic, reported being subjected to an extremely odd ordeal.

According to the "vic," the two perps had set up shop in a condemned building, where they repaired and sold used refrigerators, washing machines, and other appliances. This man said he'd innocently gone there to buy a washing machine, but for reasons he couldn't—or wouldn't—explain, these guys grabbed him, tied him to a chair, and threatened him with a shotgun. They told him that they had a bloodcurdling plan in mind: First, they were going to wash and purify his feet, and then they would cut his heart out! Scared out of his mind, the vic managed to break free and ran for his life.

The story got even stranger. After summoning police and leading them to the perps, the man suddenly clammed up and refused to give any further details of his kidnapping. When I spoke to the victim, he seemed like a decent man, but I had to wonder if he really was an entirely innocent bystander who was just looking to save a few bucks on doing his laundry. I strongly suspected that he knew these guys and could have told us a lot more about why they'd chosen him as a potential human sacrifice.

When I questioned the two perps in their cell, they weren't talking either—but they were obviously terrified of something. Noticing they were both wearing rosary beads, I had a hunch that Santeria or a related form of black magic was involved. Since everybody, even the victim, refused to answer any further questions, we got a warrant so I could search the perps' residence. It was the most horrible place I've ever been—not because of any preternatural happenings, but because it was filthy beyond belief, splattered with urine, and strewn with rotting garbage. The stench in this condemned building was enough to knock you cold, but I poked through everything and came up with one object linked to sorcery: a rather beat-up ritual sword, apparently the weapon the kidnappers meant to use to carry out their gory threats.

When I returned to the station house to voucher the evidence, an assistant district attorney (ADA) was there to oversee the case, as procedure requires when a serious crime has been committed. After the lieutenant introduced me as an expert on the occult, the ADA took me to the side. I had a feeling I knew what was coming—and I was right. "Do you know anything about ghosts?" she asked. "I think my aunt's house is haunted!" I handed her my card, then some intuition told me to give her a second card to keep for herself. Why I did this, I don't know, but it turned out lucky that I did.

A lot of my cases start in a similar way—and the question I have to answer is, *Haunted by what?* Most people think that all supernatural beings are the same, but there are actually three very different types. *Human spirits* are the ghosts of departed people, while *nature spirits*, also called "elementals," are spirits of air, streams, trees, or other living organisms. Joe and I have never run across an elemental in one of our cases, but if we do, we're covered, since my partner's modifications to the Pope Leo XIII prayer command *all* spirits "not in worship to the Trinity" to depart, including nature spirits. Very little is known about these beings. So-called "white witches," usually Wiccans, call upon elementals to help them cast spells, while "black witches" summon diabolical powers for their magic.

Inhuman spirits never walked this Earth in human form. Inhuman spirits can be pure evil (the demonic) or pure virtue (angels), while ghosts come in every flavor in between, depending on the moral character of the person during life. To further confuse matters, satanic powers may pose as ghosts, to prey on their unsuspecting victims' sympathy; or the human spirits of wicked people may draw the demonic to the place they haunt, following the Law of Attraction: "Like attracts like."

Although the demonic's motive for invading our world is obvious—to destroy humanity—you may be wondering: What's the reason for ghosts? An earthbound human spirit is a tragedy: It shouldn't be here. Ghosts have many reasons for lingering among us, however. Some only make one appearance before moving on. This is called a *crisis apparition* and can occur when a living person is lamenting the loss of a friend or relative. To console the mourner, the deceased may manifest himself to show that he or she is not suffering but has found happiness in the next plane. Grieving too long or intensely is unhealthy and can even be somewhat dangerous, since the negative energy could draw a demonic spirit and serve as an invitation to infestation.

To calm and protect those left behind, the departed may come to them in a dream or vision, bearing a message of peace to start them on the road to recovery. In some cases, the spirit may not take on the physical shape of the deceased but leave some other reminder, such as the scent of his or her favorite cologne. The problem is that the demonic also can do this. Many times, during diabolical activity, people will see what appears to be the ghost of a loved one. However, there is usually something subtly, or sometimes flagrantly, wrong with the manifestation, since evil forces can't perfectly reproduce what God has made.

However, in some cases, a human spirit may have an abnormal appearance. The other day, I responded to a homicide where the victim's ex-husband had stabbed her repeatedly in the face, neck, and chest until the woman was almost decapitated. I don't know if this woman's spirit moved on or not. But if her ghost remained earthbound, it might manifest itself with a gash on the throat. So if we heard about a spirit appearing in this condition and knew that a person had been murdered in this manner, we'd suspect that it was a ghost. But it's also possible that such a horrible crime might draw a demon to the scene. To determine what type of spirit was present, we'd take a close look at the phenomena that were taking place.

In one of my cases, which was referred to me through the Archdiocese of New York, a Bronxville woman told her priest that she'd seen a ghost in her apartment shortly after her next-door neighbor died during heart transplant surgery. The specter was only marginally human in appearance: She described it as a semitransparent black shape with only two similarities to her deceased neighbor. Like him, it stood about six feet tall and had broad shoulders, but its head had no face. "I got the sense it was sad and waiting for somebody," she said. "I am the most unbelieving person on the face of this Earth, but when I saw this ghost, I got a good feeling from it: that it was there to look over my life, and was protective." Once the spirit was gone, she was engulfed by a sudden dread—and prayed it wouldn't return.

Her eighty-year-old mother, who lived with her, never considered the spirit benevolent. "I was watching TV and all of a sudden there was movement on the stairway. I saw a tall black figure, swaying slightly. After about half a minute, I got up and walked toward the figure, which suddenly vanished. I got goosebumps, a terrible chill, and an uneasy feeling. I am scared to death to be alone in this place."

Interestingly, both women said the specter had appeared near a crucifix they had hanging on the stairway wall. The daughter added that one other strange thing happened after the spectral visits began. Although they had paid their landlord extra to use a top grade of paint when their apartment was redone, the pure white tint they'd chosen mysteriously turned to a dirty brown a week after it was applied.

The thing on the stairs may have been trying to pass itself off as a ghost, but it certainly wasn't doing a very good job of it. While it had temporarily fooled the daughter, the mother wasn't taken in. The peculiar phenomenon of the paint as well as the decidedly inhuman appearance of the creature were all the telltale signs I needed to recognize it as a demon.

Joe and I exorcised the house. No sooner had I finished the Pope Leo XIII prayer than the case literally ended with a bang. After a thunderous clap from a vacant room on the second floor, the so-called ghost was gone for good.

Human spirits use electromagnetic energy to manifest themselves. They can draw this energy from any living creature, including trees and plants, but need a lot of it before they can show themselves. Some of us, such as psychics or highly intuitive people, have greater amounts of this energy and so are more likely to see, hear, or sense spirits than the rest of us are. Clairvoyants also may detect the presence of ghosts or demons by "reading" the residues of spirit energy these beings leave behind in small, enclosed areas like hallways or small bedrooms.

Supernatural entities can harness the power of nature as well. Horror movies always use a stormy night as the backdrop for spirit manifestations. Hollywood does this for the frightening effect thunder and lightning have on the audience, but there's also reality to this: Spirits are more likely to be seen during stormy, misty, or rainy weather, when the clouds overhead are crackling with electromagnetic energy. When rain and lightning are all around you, you may see a bluish-white ball of "spirit energy."

If the conditions are right, or if you give off enough psychic energy yourself, this ball may grow in size and intensity until you are able to make out a distinct person. Another way a spirit can manifest is by diverting power from a person's aura, the spiritual energy that surrounds all of us. While demonic spirits are drawn to a dull and broken aura, indicating a state of sin, ghosts can take energy from *any* human aura. Both kinds of spirits also can use heat in the room as an energy source, which is why you'll feel a psychic chill during a manifestation. The spirit has sucked the warmth out of the room. At times a spirit that's invisible to the human eye can be captured by a camera—I've taken several such pictures myself and seen balls of light on videotapes I've made during investigations.

While it's terrifying to see a ghost—if it really *is* a ghost— most human spirits don't intend to cause fear. Instead, they usually wander Earth because they have some unfinished business here. Maybe the person died tragically and can't rest in peace: He was murdered, died young in a car crash, committed suicide, or suffered greatly during a long, lingering illness. Or she may not realize that she's dead. Picture a young mother, on her way home from work to her small children, who is suddenly killed in a freak accident. Her spirit continues on home but is bewildered when her family no longer interacts with her. So she tries to get their attention—and ends up scaring the wits out of the survivors.

Because this ghost refuses to leave her family, she remains earthbound, even after the kids grow up and leave the house. Years pass and new tenants move in, but the mother's sorrowful spirit stays on, because, as I've said, there's no time frame in the spirit world. She hovers unhappily in the background, wondering where her physical body is and when she'll finally get home to the life she lost. That's why I say a ghost is a tragedy. I cringe when I meet people who are experiencing ghost-related phenomena and feel that's perfectly fine. They'll say the spirit is doing no harm, causing no negative phenomena, or is even helpful to them, so they have no intention of helping it move on. Or they'll even argue that it has a right to stay.

That ghost may be friendly, but it's definitely not happy being stuck between two planes of existence. It's caught in a void that has no time and no pleasure. The spirit is denied the opportunity to be reunited with all the loved ones who have passed on before that person did and with those who die afterward. And most of all, that spirit won't get the chance to atone for the sins of the past and be reunited with *God*. The best thing you can do for these lost, suffering souls is have a mass said for them, or pray that they will find their way beyond pain and confusion to the Lord.

Although most ghosts are more unhappy than harmful, there are also evil human spirits. Some people are just plain mean in life and remain the same way in death. These angry or hostile forces have an excellent reason for refusing to move to the next plane: They don't want to face the prospect of going to Hell or, at the very least, having a long stay in Purgatory, a hellish place you don't hear much about these days. It is here, according to Catholic and some Protestant churches, that souls ultimately destined for Heaven are either purified of minor sins the person never repented for during life or subjected to a period of punishment for mortal sins. If I get a case involving a wicked ghost, my prescription is the same as for a good ghost: prayer, which can shorten the time a soul must spend atoning for sins or lessen its suffering in Purgatory.

Evil ghosts can oppress the living in much the same way the demonic do. If they're the spirits of people who were addicted to drugs or alcohol, practiced witchcraft, or sinned in other ways, they can influence the people they haunt to turn to these vices. While Dr. Edith Fiore writes in her book, *The Unquiet Dead*, that people can even become possessed by wicked ghosts, I have never seen or heard of a case of human spirit possession in all my years in the Work. Instead, my experience is that wicked ghosts serve as magnets for the demonic, so they open a potential pathway for possession by drawing satanic powers to the location they haunt.

Unlike demons, ghosts aren't subject to exorcism, so it's difficult to get rid of them. What sometimes helps is having a psychic communicate with the spirit and determine its reason for remaining earthbound. The medium should try to convince the spirit that it is no longer a part of the physical world and should stop scaring people. He or she can then try to send the ghost toward the Light of God, where it will find happiness and peace at last. The trouble is, if a ghost doesn't want to go, there's nothing we can do to make it leave, except pray.

Here's a word of warning for both psychics and anyone who wants to make contact with a deceased loved one. Don't open that door unless you have the spiritual knowledge to tell what's on the other side. Unless you're 100 percent sure you're dealing with a ghost, not some con man from Hell, you could put yourself in great peril. If there's any doubt, *don't talk to the spirit—just command it to leave, in the name of Jesus Christ!* Any other communication with a satanic spirit can be extremely dangerous or even lead to possession.

Another factor that makes it hard to tell at the start of a case whether ghosts or demons are involved is that both have the power to manifest themselves, create strange sounds, and manipulate objects. The key to telling the difference between the two types of spirits is taking a close look at what kind of phenomena are occurring. In some cases a demonic presence is unmistakable from the start, while in others, making a determination is quite tricky.

Like the ADA who was worried about the troubles her aunt was having, one of my fellow cops, Tony, also thought his house was haunted and asked for my help. Many strange things had happened to him and his large Italian family. Lights and household appliances would turn on and off all by

themselves. But the phenomena didn't stop there: Once Tony's father was awakened by an odd noise. Usually a heavy
sleeper, he rubbed his eyes and looked around. At the foot of
his bed stood a little girl, watching him sleep. Just as suddenly as he saw her, she disappeared, but not for good. Over
the years he and other family members saw the little spirit
several times.

When Tony invited his future wife home for dinner one
night, the family was regaling her with stories about their
ghost. She didn't believe a word, until a heavy ashtray suddenly slid across the table, as if the spirit were showing off.
That was enough for the family—they had their parish priest
come and bless the house. But the problem didn't stop: Tony
told me that he'd been awakened by the sound of a baby or
small child weeping. I asked if there was anything odd about
the cry, since I've seen several cases where the supposed cry
of a baby was anything but human. He said it sounded perfectly normal—except that it was right there in the room with
him.

By now I thought I was dealing with a human spirit, but
one thing bothered me. Ghosts don't normally have the ability to turn appliances on and off or move objects around.
Could it be the demonic? During the investigation, I learned
that the house was built on a plot of land that was once a
Dutch Reformed cemetery. The mystery was solved, since I
felt there must be more than one human spirit in that house,
intensifying the ghost's powers. My partner and I went over
the house to be sure but found no sign of the demonic. I told
Tony to have a mass said for these lost souls, but from time to
time, that little girl ghost still appears—or a light flickers on
or off when it shouldn't.

Contrast this situation with another eerie story I heard

when I was assigned to what the police call a "fixer post."
Some repairs were being made to an elevator in a dangerous
public housing project, so I was sent there to make sure the
workmen weren't robbed of their money or tools. The owner
of the repair company told me he was renovating his home
and working late into the night. He kept having an unsettling
sense of someone—or something—watching him. The feeling was so overwhelming that he turned around every few
minutes to make sure he really was alone. He'd stop work
when he couldn't take it any longer, only to return the next
night and have the same thing happen all over again.

One night he went downstairs to start work and found his
tools missing. He questioned his kids, but they insisted they
hadn't been in the basement. When he returned to the area he
was renovating, the tools were back in their usual spot. The
kids couldn't have done it, since they were still upstairs. At
this point I knew we were talking about the demonic because
ghosts can only move small objects and can't make things
materialize or dematerialize. The contractor's next words
proved that I was right: When he tore down one of the walls
in his basement, he found crucifixes behind it, suggesting the
former owner had been trying to banish an unholy spirit.

By now I was extremely interested in his case and told
him I investigated happenings of this nature. I gave him my
card but never heard from him again. I found it very strange
that he told me all this stuff, then never contacted me for my
help, but in this Work, the strange is common.

However, the ADA's aunt, whose name was Ginny, was
quick to call about her "ghost." Although she was very frightened, she was also apprehensive about seeking my help. Since
she lived in the Bronx, I suggested she get in touch with Father
Livanos, a priest I've worked with in that borough, and dis-

cuss it with him. She did and was relieved when he told her I was a reputable person of faith who was knowledgeable about these matters and had helped others with similar problems.

Still worried about what she might be letting herself in for, she asked the priest if she'd be doing anything against God by working with me. He told her the prayers and sacramentals I use conform to Catholic doctrine, so there was no cause for concern. I wasn't the least bit offended by her caution—instead, I respected this woman's meticulous devotion to God.

A week or so later, she was back on the phone. By now it was near Christmas, and as is so common at this time of year, the activity had intensified. Hearing her rapid-fire, obviously nervous voice on the phone convinced me it was urgent to set up a formal investigation as quickly as possible. When I arrived at her home the following day, her first remark was a familiar one: "What I'm going to tell you sounds crazy—and if I didn't see it with my own eyes, I wouldn't believe it myself."

"Don't worry about that," I said. "Chances are that whatever you have to say I've heard before. From my conversation with your niece, I already have some idea of what you're up against."

Ginny was a schoolteacher. She'd been teaching for so long that her eyes were permanently set in a steely stare and her mouth in a faint, disapproving frown. You got the feeling that she knew everything naughty you'd ever done—or even *thought* about doing—and was just waiting to get her ruler out and give you a well-deserved smack or two.

Frankly, she reminded me of some of the sterner nuns at my parochial school. Even her clothing had an austere, nunlike appearance, and her face was innocent of makeup.

Although she was about fifty and her hair was heavily streaked with gray, she didn't try to hide it with dye. She was also extremely slim and fit, giving me the impression that her body was so well disciplined that no fat would dare settle on her angular frame.

As we talked, I could see that her daughters were in awe of her. All three of them promptly snapped to attention every time she spoke. While all this may make her sound rather unlikable, a softer side came out when she played and joked with her little grandson. I realized that this doting grandma wasn't nearly as fierce as I'd thought at first. Her only vice seemed to be coffee, which she drank black and bitter, in large quantities during the interview. Around the living room, which was extremely neat, I saw many pretty little statues, some of them of a religious nature, and numerous family photos in silver frames.

Between sips of coffee, she explained that the problem had begun in October, around the time her oldest daughter, Nancy, who was going through a divorce, moved back into the house with her three-year-old son. The little boy started waking up at 3:00 A.M., screaming and pointing at the wall. When his mother would ask him what was wrong, the little boy, who had a very limited vocabulary, would say he'd seen a monster. This went on night after night, but the family didn't believe he'd seen anything and wrote it off to nightmares.

One night the middle daughter was down in the basement, doing her college homework. As she was typing her paper, she heard her younger sister call her name. She turned around, but no one was there. She got back to work, and heard her name called again. It was definitely her sister's voice. By now she was getting mad, thinking her kid sister was playing silly tricks on her when she had an important paper to write. She stormed upstairs to give Sis a piece of her mind—and discovered that her sister wasn't home!

A few weeks later Ginny had an odd experience of her own in the basement. She put a load of laundry in the washer and went back upstairs to continue her housework. When she returned to put the clothes in the dryer, the washing machine had turned completely around, so the water hoses were stretched to the breaking point. And this was a three-hundred-pound machine! Even at this point, she didn't make a connection between all the strange things that were happening in her house. Instead, since the machine was too heavy for her to move back into place by herself, she enlisted the aid of her next-door neighbor, a New York City cop.

He asked her how on earth this had happened and, when she couldn't explain it, suggested that she get a new washer. "But it *is* a new machine," she replied. "And it's never budged an inch before!"

All the bewildered cop could say was, "Pretty weird, if you ask me." *My sentiments exactly: First we bust two seemingly satanic washing machine salesmen—if that's what they really were—and then it turns out that the aunt of the ADA assigned to the case has a washing machine with a decidedly supernatural "spin cycle"!*

Other than the involvement of this ADA, however, I could discover no connection between the two cases, so I figured it was just a rather peculiar coincidence. Despite being in the Work, I'm *not* inclined to see the demonic under every rock or behind every bizarre circumstance. Still, I felt the Lord had moved in a rather mysterious way by sending this particular pair of cases my way.

Over the next several weeks, other odd events took place,

Ginny explained. "It wasn't one strange thing after another but a gradual buildup," she said. "One evening when I was in the living room, I heard a baby crying, but it wasn't a normal cry. I knew it wasn't my grandson—it sounded like a much younger baby, in great pain or fear. Another disturbing thing about the cry was that I couldn't tell *where* it was coming from. I even went outside and looked around, but I didn't see any child or animal that could have made the sound. It sounded horrible and upset me terribly."

More unsettling incidents followed. After looking at her mother as if asking permission to tell her story, Erica, the youngest daughter, who was a senior in high school, said she'd also gotten a scare one night, when she was alone in the house, or so she thought. "All of sudden, I heard loud footsteps walking from room to room upstairs. I thought someone had broken into our house and was so frightened that I ran next door to get our neighbor, the policeman."

The cop grabbed his gun and searched the entire house without finding any burglar—or any evidence of a break-in—while Erica stayed at his house. Having been at the house a month earlier to help with the washing machine, the officer now felt that things were more than "pretty weird" and joked that maybe the house was haunted. More terrified than ever, Erica refused to go home until her mom returned.

Although Ginny was still skeptical about the supernatural and tried to laugh off the cop's theory, it began to make more and more sense to her. Her grandson was still waking up every night at 3:00 A.M. screaming, and she and her kids were getting increasingly jumpy. Reluctant to call her parish priest with such an outlandish story, she finally decided that it wouldn't hurt to put up a crucifix in the child's room, just in case.

He didn't wake up that night, but in the morning, the cross

was lying on the floor, she said, watching me intently for any sign of disbelief. Finding none, she added with great emphasis, *"The nail was still in the wall!"*

The eerie phenomena came to a head, she continued, when she was having a holiday party in her home. "I'd received a Christmas tree made of seashells as a gift and put it up on my mantel, over there. Right in front of my guests, family, and friends, the tree flew off the mantel! No one was near it or had touched it in any way. It just sailed clear across the room all by itself, landed on the floor, and didn't break!"

"And what was the reaction of your guests?" I asked.

"They all witnessed it, but no one said one word. We all just sat there in total silence." Again her eyes raked over me, daring me to make fun of her or question her truthfulness.

Although I *did* dispute this "ghost" story, I waited a beat to see if she had anything to add. She did. "Now, Ralph, this party was on Friday, and I was planning to call you first thing the next morning, when another peculiar thing happened. I'd put your card on the dining room table, but in the morning, it was gone! None of my daughters had taken it or moved it, my grandson can't reach the table, and I even checked the garbage, but it was nowhere to be found." Finally she called her niece, the ADA, who got out the extra card I'd impulsively given her and gave Ginny my number.

"Do you think the ghost took the card?" she asked.

No, I definitely didn't! "Ginny, you *don't* have a ghost," I said. The schoolteacher gave me a withering glare of hurt and betrayal tinged with scorn. *I'd promised to believe her, listened to her whole story, and now I had the nerve to argue with her? I felt like I was about to be sent to the principal's office!*

"Let me explain your problem," I quickly added. "Your home has been invaded by a demonic spirit, which is causing the phenomena you've described. Only a demon can inexplicably move something as heavy as a washing machine or make an object disappear. No human spirit, or ghost, can do that."

As Joe unpacked the items we'd need for our ritual, I moved to the final phase of the investigation. Now that we'd established the *what*, we wanted to find out *why* a demon was here. Since Ginny had lived in this house for over twenty years but only had trouble after her grown daughter had moved back in, I questioned Nancy—and the rest of the family—about occult practices. All of them denied, very convincingly, any dabbling in magic, tarot cards, Ouija boards, table-turning, or other types of séances. Nor had they consulted mediums or psychics.

I then inquired about a practice Father Martin considered particularly insidious: the Enneagram method, which was developed by a now-deceased Asian spiritual leader, who claimed to have learned it from the Sufi masters of Islam. In this method, a nine-pointed figure is inscribed inside a circle to represent the nine supposed variations of human personality. Each type is given special spiritual exercises that purport to perfect the person's character—a form of heresy, the father explains, since humans are born in sin and ascend to Heaven only after God, in His grace, has cleansed and perfected their souls. This family, however, insisted that they knew nothing of this evil method.

My interrogation turned to a new tack. Knowing that Nancy was recently divorced, I asked if she'd had a bitter breakup, speculating that perhaps her ex had cursed her. No, she replied: She and her former spouse had parted amicably, without acrimony over custody or child support. As she explained that she knew of no one, including her former husband, who harbored ill will toward her or her family, I could see that Ginny had something on *her* mind.

Rather defensively, the starchy schoolteacher confessed that she hadn't been the best of Catholics. "I had all my children baptized and confirmed, but I don't go to church all that often. But I do believe in God!"

I didn't consider these lapses the explanation. I wondered if, like the two Santeria-practicing kidnappers I'd left in a police holding cell, Nancy might know more than she was letting on. Or could her former husband be the problem? But I was unable to find out what, if anything, she'd done—or whether her ex or some unknown enemy had done this to her—so Joe and I decided it was time to move on to the exorcism.

We asked the family to stay in their living room, no matter what they saw or heard, then began the Pope Leo XIII prayer. As I'd anticipated, this demon, which had only progressed to low-level infestation, made no noticeable protest when we filled the house with fragrant smoke, holy water, and blessed salt. We gave the family their own supply of these items and several blessed candles to use after we left, so the house would continue to be repellent to the demonic.

"It's now up to you to keep evil spirits out of your home," I explained. "The way to do this is to bring God back into your life with prayer and church attendance." The schoolteacher and her family promised to be more conscientious about practicing their faith. We concluded the ritual by putting blessed oil on the walls in the shape of a cross.

As mysteriously as it had arrived, the demon slipped silently away without so much as a bang or whimper. Although we weren't positive at the time that it really was gone, Ginny later thanked us for giving her the best gift of all: a peaceful, demon-free Christmas with her family. Joe and I felt that we were able to close the case so quickly because Ginny had called us promptly, before the evil spirit had time to get seriously entrenched in her home.

And as for the two bloodthirsty sorcerers who got me started on this case, the ADA solved that one herself. Thanks to her zealous prosecution, both were convicted of their bizarre crimes and spent *their* holidays, and the rest of that year, in that infamous New York hellhole: Rikers Island jail.

13

A DEADLY SIN

Last year I got a call from a woman named JoAnn, who had read an article about me in *The New York Post*. She was a very articulate woman from Brooklyn—I later learned she was a schoolteacher—but the stress in her voice was obvious. "I think my husband is possessed," she said.

I've gotten many calls like this over the years and always start by looking at the facts in a neutral way, just as I would if I were taking a crime report at work. To be perfectly honest, many people who claim that they or their loved ones are possessed are actually suffering from a mental disorder or simply an overactive imagination. Even when I realize that the demonic is not involved, I always take the time to speak to these people at length and try to help them as best I can. If I feel they are emotionally ill, I'll refer them to a doctor or, if their difficulties are in the spiritual realm, to a clergyman.

JoAnn started off by telling me that her husband, Frank, who was in the dry-cleaning business, had just started seeing a psychiatrist. I didn't want to interfere with this because the doctor was going to prescribe medication. Since some mental illnesses can mimic possession, I felt it was best to wait and see if the drug helped. A mentally ill person will respond to medication, at least to some extent, while the demonic spirit inside a possessed person is totally unaffected by it.

Two weeks later, JoAnn was back on the phone, reporting that the psychiatric drugs hadn't done a thing. That's when the real obstacle arose: It turned out that this man not only wasn't a Catholic, but he'd spent years in a religious movement, the Jehovah's Witnesses, that holds a very low opinion of my faith. While he'd left this group a long time ago, he still hung on to this prejudice.

At that point, I had to back off—if Frank refused to let a Catholic help him, then there was nothing more I could do. "You can't force someone to get an exorcism he doesn't want," I told JoAnn. "It's like dealing with a drug problem: A person has to decide *he* wants to kick the habit and get into rehab. Your husband must seek an exorcism of his own free will or the ritual wouldn't work. In fact, it shouldn't even be attempted under these circumstances."

The schoolteacher burst into tears, saying she didn't know where else to turn. I told her I'd run into this problem before, since demons can target anyone, regardless of his or her religion. That's why the bishop, though a staunch Catholic Traditionalist, is willing to perform exorcisms on non-Catholics, feeling that God's help should be given to anyone who sincerely asks for it. Since *Frank* wasn't willing, however, we couldn't proceed any further.

Not surprisingly, since the demonic will seize on anything to stop an exorcism from taking place, when I finally got to speak to Frank on the phone, he was extremely hostile. "I'm only talking to you because my wife wants me to," he announced in a belligerent tone. "I'm not going crawling to any Catholic for help! It's a false religion and I don't want any part of it! Why do you people talk about a Holy Trinity when there's only one God? It's blasphemy!"

Although I was getting mad, I had to bite my tongue to keep from arguing with him, because I wanted to determine what I was dealing with. Was this just prejudice—or could this man be genuinely possessed?

I didn't want to make the same mistake I did in another recent case, that of a man named Pete who had a bizarre complaint: Every time he looked in a mirror, he saw the face of a boa constrictor where his head was supposed to be. After Joe and I did an extensive interview with this man and his father—who was extremely upset by his son's strange behavior—we concluded that Pete was possessed, possibly by a demon named Leviathan, which is said to be represented by a snake.

When we suggested an exorcism with Bishop McKenna, Pete, who was a Baptist, immediately asked us to arrange it for him. When I called the night before the ceremony to confirm, Pete's attitude had turned around completely. He'd developed qualms about getting help from Catholics and no longer wanted the ritual. Remembering how desperate he and his father were during the interview, I spent over an hour trying to change Pete's mind, as he made increasingly insulting remarks about my faith.

At one point during the conversation, the father picked up the phone and implored me to hold the ritual no matter what Pete said. "Please, don't listen to him, Ralph," the older man said. "My son needs help, and you're his only hope. You have no idea how bad things are with him."

Pete, however, was adamant. "No fucking way am I going to let any Catholic put holy water on me," he insisted. "You people are the scourge of this earth!"

By now I was boiling mad. "That's it," I said firmly. "I'm going to terminate this conversation right now. I'm not going to handcuff you and drag you to a Catholic church. If you decide you want God's help, let me know. If not, I have nothing more to say to you."

I could hear his father still pleading with him as Pete slammed down the phone. Still angry and more than a little baffled by the man's abrupt refusal to get the help he so desperately needed, I called Joe and told him the whole story.

"Ralph, don't you realize you were talking to the demon?" my partner asked. *Of course! How could I have been so blind? The demonic always have a list of bullshit reasons why an exorcism is a bad idea and cunningly exploit their victims' fears and biases. While they have no power over someone's free will, their attack is so strong and intricate that they know the best way to exert their sinister influence. The person may even know that what the demon urges is the wrong decision but feels powerless to resist. Until he or she realizes that the evil force is an alien, unwelcome presence—and consciously decides to reject it—the possession will progress deeper and deeper, as the demon's influence grows stronger and stronger. That's what happened to Pete, and it might be the problem with Frank as well.*

Infuriating as Frank's anti-Catholic diatribe was, I listened to him ramble on about the supposed "errors" of my faith. "The cross is a false symbol," he proclaimed in an extremely deep, rumbling baritone. "Jesus died on a pole or a stake. Have you not read in Deuteronomy 7:26 that 'You shall not bring an abominable thing into your house, lest you be doomed with it; loathe and abhor it utterly as a thing that is doomed'? And what about I Corinthians 10:14: 'I am telling you, whom I love, to shun the worship of idols'? Your cross is nothing but idolatry!"

While neither of these biblical passages actually refers to the cross at all, I said that I had no intention of debating theology. "We both worship the same God, Frank, but here's something you should think about: What kind of religion preaches hate? Like it or not, I'm a Catholic and I'm staying one. If you have a problem with that, then good-bye."

I put the phone down but later called JoAnn to say that I couldn't take the case. She was beside herself and couldn't stop apologizing for the way her husband had spoken to me. "This isn't him," she insisted. "He's not a bad person."

"I can't be sure at this point whether the problem is hatred for Catholics or demonic possession," I told her. "I've dealt with this stuff before, and if it is demonic possession, the attacks will step up now, because the evil spirit will be angry that Frank talked to me. Wait a few weeks and see what happens. Your husband knows where to get help if he wants it, so if he changes his mind, give me a call."

Sobbing with frustration, she said she would. A month later she was back on the phone. "Frank wants your help now."

Somewhat skeptically, I told her to put him on the phone. When he spoke, I was amazed by the transformation in both his voice and his attitude. I now had a very cooperative Frank on the line. Nor was I treated to any tirades about the evils of Catholicism or any biblical quotes on idolatry. I gathered from his remarks that he was being attacked more intensely than ever, just as I'd predicted. "It's gotten so bad that I can't take it anymore," he admitted. "My wife says that if I don't get help, she's leaving."

While that's not the reason for which I would have wanted him to seek help, it was a start and I was ready to proceed, now that Frank was. My next step was to set up an interview at the couple's Brooklyn apartment. Surprisingly, JoAnn was extremely resistant to this idea, saying their home was too "messy" for a meeting. "Couldn't we get together at a coffee shop or something?" she asked.

I said no. I need to interview people in their home, so I can gather impressions about their problem. Sometimes I've seen things in people's houses that have given me clues about the kind of demon I'm up against or what might have brought it to this particular location. I also want to get an idea of what the people's lifestyle is like, check for signs of occult activity, and observe their facial expressions as they describe the supernatural events that have taken place.

"Mess doesn't bother me," I assured her. As a cop, I've been in homes—if you want to call them that—that are more disgusting than you could ever imagine. The other night I was called to a public housing project when officers responding to an unrelated 911 call were told that small children were alone in the apartment next door. Although it was 2:00 A.M. when I got there and their home was in one of New York's most dangerous slums, the door was open. Inside, hundreds of cockroaches swarmed on every surface: on the filthy, broken furniture; on the piles of reeking garbage; and on the stained mattress where I found three little girls—twins age nine and a one-year-old baby—sleeping together. On the floor, right next to their bed, was an overflowing ashtray and a cigarette lighter.

Naturally, we followed procedure. We woke the girls up and immediately got them out of the apartment and to a hospital. Their health checked out okay, so we notified Children's Services so they could be placed in foster care. The so-called mother showed up at the Four-Six around 6:00 A.M. screaming that she wanted her kids. We promptly arrested her for endangering the welfare of a minor, three counts.

And then there was the first DOA case I responded to as a

rookie. Apparently this man didn't have a friend in the world, because he'd been dead in his apartment for a month by the time his neighbors got around to reporting a foul odor. Although the man was Caucasian, the body had turned black and was moving in an odd way. Nudging one of the other officers at the scene, I asked, "What's that?"

"Flies," he said. After that, I must have looked pretty comical to the other cops, the way I started leaping around and frantically shooing away any fly that came near me, thinking it might have touched the dead man.

Far worse than the flies was the overpoweringly fetid stench. I didn't see how anyone could stand it for a second, but I'd been ordered to remain in the apartment until the medical examiner arrived, which turned out to be all day. To keep from vomiting, I'd get a deep breath of fresh air in the hallway, then run into the apartment and throw coffee grounds on the burner of the stove. This made the smell barely tolerable for a few minutes, then I'd burn some more coffee grounds. To this day, whenever I smell burnt coffee, I think of my first DOA. The worst part, however, was when the officers lifted the dead man into a body bag. The gases inside the corpse exploded, and the man actually split open.

If I could survive my first DOA, I was pretty sure I could handle whatever mess Frank and JoAnn were harboring in their home. I asked Keith, a cop I'd worked with briefly in East New York, to come along as backup, since Joe was taking a sabbatical from the Work. I could understand why: You can't go balls to the walls against the demonic year after year without taking an occasional break to recharge your spiritual batteries.

This was Keith's first investigation, and I could sense his excitement. A year earlier I'd run into him at Brooklyn

Central Booking, when he was bringing in a female prisoner. I recognized him from PSA (Police Service Area) #2 and said hello. After securing the prisoner, he came over and said, "Don't think I'm crazy, but . . ." I figured he was going to tell me he had a ghost in his home, but I was wrong.

"I've been taking courses in parapsychology," he continued. I couldn't help but wince, since I hate that word—and the supposedly "scientific" approach to the demonic. Keith seemed to recognize that he wasn't striking quite the right chord, because he quickly added. "What I'm really saying is, can *you* teach me about this stuff?"

I immediately tried to discourage him. "You have no idea of what you'd be getting into. Lots of people think the Work sounds exciting, but this isn't a scary movie, where it's fun to be afraid because it's all make-believe. This is reality—and anyone who tries it pays a spiritual price. I've known people who were so frightened on their first case that they were never quite the same again. That's what happened to one of my students a few years ago."

Keith insisted that he was more than tough enough for the Work. He's Italian, in his late thirties, with dark hair and a powerful build. He's a very aggressive street cop, so I knew that he wasn't going to give up and go away just because I said the Work was scary. Hell, that probably heightened his interest, because this was a macho, action-oriented guy. But the factor that made me decide to take him on was his devout Catholic faith. I felt he might have the makings of a good investigator.

Once I accepted him as a student, I let him know exactly what I expected. "On this investigation, your job is to watch my back. If you have questions during the interview, go ahead and ask them. I'll do most of the talking, but feel free to jump in if something's not clear. However, if this man is possessed, and you assist with his exorcism, you're not to open your mouth and speak to him during the ritual—no matter what. And if things get rough, no slugging it out with the possessed! Just take him down if you have to, but no punches. Those are my rules—and if you break them, it's the last exorcism you'll ever be at!"

Keith promised to follow these rules, so we arranged to meet the couple at their Brooklyn condo the following Thursday. As I drove there, I thought about a conversation I'd had with my kids a few days earlier. Knowing that I had a new case and my wife had a new job, nine-year-old Christina announced that she had career plans too. "I want to help people—and punish demons, just like you, Daddy!"

Four-year-old Daniella was quick to agree. "Your work is scary, Daddy, but I want to do it when I grow up. I'm brave: I like to watch scary movies on TV, except when it's dark. I can do it, I know I can do it. You just have to be brave, right?"

As a father, it troubles me to hear my little girls say they'd like to grow up to be demonologists—and to think about how much they've already been frightened in their young lives. One night, while I was holding my class in the basement, Christina and Jen were folding laundry in the bedroom when they had a horrible fright. A dreadful black shape hovered over the end table by the bed, moved across the room, and then went right through the wall! One of my students happened to look out into the basement hallway directly below that wall—and guess what? She saw the same swirling shape my wife and daughter had seen! It was incredibly eerie.

Even little Daniella has had a few encounters with the demonic. She's heard strange knocking on her bedroom walls and was extremely frightened one night, while I was working on this book, when a picture suddenly fell off the living room wall with a loud crash. Writing about the demonic—or even thinking about them—gives evil spirits recognition, which can provoke phenomena. Having a picture flung around is low-level harassment that no longer bothers me, except when it upsets my kids. Daniella was so alarmed that she jumped into bed with Christina, scaring the wits out of my older daughter, who was sound asleep. There was such an uproar that night that Jen had to sleep in the children's room, to calm them.

Most troubling of all were a series of supernatural incidents connected with a case I was involved in a few years ago. The first was quite minor. One night I received a call from a woman whose daughter was dabbling in the occult—as a member of a Santeria cult—and who feared the girl had become possessed. Santeria is an Afro-Caribbean religion that arose during the era of slavery. Since the slave owners didn't approve of what they considered pagan practices, they forced their slaves to convert to Christianity. In order to preserve their own religion, these men and women connected their deities—the seven African powers—to seven Catholic saints. Santeria is mainly used for "white magic," but it also can have a dark side. If it's used to influence someone to go against the free will God gave us, then it becomes "black magic," since that violates the divine plan.

Through patrolling public housing projects where Caribbean immigrants live and my reading on the occult, I've become very familiar with Santeria. Its priests, or *santeros*, are well versed in herbal lore, which they draw on in conjuring up spells to cure illness and misfortune, create good luck talismans, or curse one's enemies. Should practitioners of this religion become victims of *bilongos*, as curses are called, they can go to their own *santero* to have the curse lifted with an *ebbo*, or ritual cleansing. What it all comes down to is a battle of *santeros*, as the curses and counter-curses are hurled back and forth until the most powerful Santeria priest wins.

I remember once responding to a 911 call for a domestic dispute. When I got to the location, I noticed an "altar," with a statue of St. Barbara, the Catholic saint that represents the Orisha "Chango," one of the seven African powers. I've seen these shrines in many tenement apartments: They're typically surrounded by objects like railroad spikes, coins, or bread, all of which are offered to appease the gods. I said to the woman who answered the door, "Santeria?" She spoke very little English but shook her head violently and said, "No, no Santeria!" with a heavy Spanish accent. I told my partner not to touch the things on the altar while we got the argument under control. After everyone had cooled off, the woman walked us to the hall. Just as she was about to close her door, she gave me a mischievous grin and said, "You know Santeria?" I smiled back and nodded. She looked surprised and must have been asking herself, "What could an Italian cop know about Santeria?"

Well, this Italian cop knew enough to suspect that the daughter of the woman who called me wasn't practicing Santeria at all but something much more sinister. From what this woman described, it sounded like the girl was actually involved with Palo Mayombe. I felt frightened for the woman's daughter, who was only about twenty, but had already fallen under the sway of the black arts. Since her mother lived in the area where I patrol, I arranged to stop by and do a formal interview the following week.

After talking to this woman on the phone for about an hour, I went to my office to write up my notes about her case before my midnight shift. After I was done, I went into the living room and found my wife and Christina very shaken up. They both told me they'd heard a male voice—not mine—calling Jen's name. I told them it might be connected to this case, but didn't sound too serious. I hated to leave them in this agitated state, so I used blessed salt and ordered the spirit to leave, in the name of Jesus Christ. I left Jen with a bottle of holy water by her side and told her to call me at work if there was any further trouble. I didn't realize it at the time, but this was just the opening move of this particular demon.

The following Wednesday, after stopping off for the two crucial nutrients cops need for a long night on patrol—coffee and doughnuts—my police partner and I went to the woman's home, in uniform, so I could do a quick interview. She lived in a typical ghetto apartment, dark, dirty, and extremely cluttered. It looked like the perfect dwelling place for evil, but when I checked for signs of Santeria or Palo Mayombe worship, I found none. Despite her forbidding residence, the woman was very pleasant and sincere.

In a low, pained voice, she told us that her daughter had been committed to Bellevue the previous day. As a cop, I've been at that well-known New York hospital hundreds of times with suspects who need psychiatric evaluation or medical treatment. I was there with a deranged perp the night Hedda Nussbaum was brought in and got the fright of my life when I saw her face so horribly beaten up and scarred. It was around Halloween and I couldn't imagine a worse mask than the one she was already wearing. Two female cops told me that Hedda and her boyfriend had beaten their adopted six-year-old daughter, Lisa, to death, an atrocity that made headlines all over the country the next morning. At Central Booking, where I dropped my suspect off, I saw the child's father and killer, Joel Steinberg, sitting on the floor of his cell. I told him I hoped he rotted in Hell, because if there was ever someone who truly deserved the most hideous torments of the damned, it was he. I don't like to pass judgment on people, but it was a good thing Steinberg was behind bars, because I wanted to choke the life out of that depraved monster.

With a touch of embarrassment, as if she felt I'd be disappointed, the woman then explained that she'd decided to take her daughter to a Catholic priest after the girl was released from the psych ward. She apologized profusely for having taken up my time and for having decided to go to the priest. I assured her I wasn't the least bit upset and wished her the best. I was *glad* a priest wanted to get involved—that was his job. I've always felt that if more priests were open to this work and were staunchly against the Devil, instead of taking the wishy-washy tone some of them do on the pulpit these days, there would be no need for me to do this Work. It's not that I don't want to do it, but I'd much rather have the Church and clergy handle these matters. Feeling that this woman was in good hands, I left.

Although I thought this was the end of this case, it wasn't. A few months later, rather late in the evening, the phone rang. My wife was pregnant with Daniella and was having some problems with bleeding. The doctor had done all sorts of tests but couldn't find the cause. Jen was lying on the sofa resting, terrified that she might miscarry. To protect her and the fragile, unbaptized child in her womb, I'd decided to take a break from the Work. Thinking the call might be about a case, I let the machine answer it.

It was the same woman who had called before: The priest hadn't resolved the problem, and her daughter was still possessed. I stood there, listening to her say that she wanted me to investigate, but didn't pick up the receiver. I was in a quandary: I knew I must protect Jen and our unborn child, but as the night wore on, I kept thinking about it. The woman's pleading voice was tugging at my heart, but I also felt I should go with my gut and leave the case alone. I went into the bathroom to shave and get ready for work, thinking maybe I should give the bishop a call and drop the whole thing in his lap.

Just as I finished this thought, I heard something hit my dog, Max, out in the living room. He started barking and growling like crazy. I ran into the room and saw Jen staring at the dog. Every hair on his back was standing up as he stared into the dining room, growling louder than he'd ever growled before.

"What the hell happened?" I asked.

"I don't know," Jen said. "He was walking into the dining room and it looked like he suddenly ran into a brick wall. I could see his whole body knocked to the side, and then he started that awful growling." I calmed the dog and checked him all over, but he wasn't hurt, just shaken up. That was the answer to my question—I should stay far away from this case. It was one of the hardest things I've ever had to do: I'm not one to run from helping people, but if I can't give it 100 per-cent, I won't take a case. I never heard from that woman again, but I pray she got the help she needed.

Max was never quite the same after that. He wasn't the best-behaved dog to begin with, but after being terrorized and knocked around by a diabolical force, he grew wilder and wilder. He became increasingly destructive and once leapt through our sunroom window in a berserk frenzy. There was blood and glass everywhere, that's how wild and uncontrollable he'd become. Despite all the trouble he caused, I loved that dog, and immediately took him to the vet to be stitched up.

His barking became almost incessant—except for one peculiar occasion where, like the dog in the Sherlock Holmes mystery, Max did nothing in the night. It was around three o'clock in the morning, and I'd long since kissed my wife and daughter good-bye as they slept, as I always did before going to work, never knowing if I would ever see them again. Jen woke up to the sound of the kitchen door rattling, as if someone were trying to break in. Thinking it might be the dog, scratching to go out and do his business, she got up and saw Max asleep on Christina's bed.

The noise got louder, and she peeked into the kitchen to see what was the matter. Fear poured through her when she saw the door shaking violently. As fast as a heavily pregnant woman can run, she ran to the cordless phone. Just then the kitchen light dimmed—and she realized that whatever was battering on the door wasn't a human. Holding the phone receiver like a talisman, she ran back to the bedroom and was about to call me when the pounding abruptly stopped. What struck me about this story was Max's behavior—this animal usually barked like mad if so much as a leaf dropped in the yard, and suddenly he can't summon the energy to get up and give even one woof? He must have remembered what happened the last time he was visited by the demonic!

When I reached Frank and JoAnn's building, I saw Keith approaching it with a confident cop swagger. I knew he was a brave man, but had I really done enough to prepare him for dealing with beings so evil that they think nothing of beating up your dog or terrorizing your pregnant wife, just to get even with you? I hoped he'd followed my instructions about getting into a state of grace.

The condo was on the twentieth floor of a beautiful building that looked out at the Verrazano Narrows Bridge. The view was spectacular on this clear winter night, with the lights on the bridge sparkling in the distance. I was struck by the contrast between this lovely setting and the dark, purposeful evil that had brought us here. I told Keith we were about to meet a man who in his lucid moments hated Catholics and while under the sway of the demonic hated humanity.

"Remember that we could be dealing with a very powerful spirit that doesn't want anyone around who give its victim hope," I said. "Hope is a very dangerous thing to the demonic."

"Will we know if Frank is possessed?" Keith wondered.

"At this point, consider him a suspect," I explained. "Although it's hard to tell at first if you're speaking to the person or the demon, eventually the true nature of the beast will show through, if he's possessed."

We rode the elevator up to the condo. As JoAnn had warned me, it *was* a mess. Although the rooms were generously sized, this was clearly a couple who never threw anything out. The living room was extremely cluttered: Piles of books, old newspapers, and papers were everywhere. Judging by the number of take-out cartons and dirty plates lying around, Frank and JoAnn lived mainly on Chinese food and didn't spend much time doing the dishes. Seeing the poor state of hygiene in this home—and several cockroaches—we both declined JoAnn's offer of coffee.

Among the vast array of objects that filled the living room were numerous photographs of Frank. Even though he wasn't a particularly handsome man, variations of his toothy grin could be seen on just about every wall, with an occasional shot of JoAnn, a thin blonde of about thirty, with bags under her eyes, rumpled clothing, and a sloppy ponytail. Her husband was rather overweight but very elegantly dressed in a cashmere sports jacket and navy blue pants that probably cost ten times as much as my entire outfit. As he shook my hand, I noticed his fingernails were not only neatly manicured but had a coat of clear polish on them.

The dapper dry cleaner, who was a bit *too* dapper for the tastes of working-class cops like Keith and me, was in his midthirties and had no kids. Soon after high school he'd joined the Jehovah's Witnesses, a group that puts an enormous emphasis on Bible study. Soon he could recite biblical passages all night long. The trouble started about eight years ago, when Frank was reading one of the numerous publications this group puts out and distributes door-to-door in the hope of finding converts. "All of a sudden," he said, "I heard a voice inside my head saying that I was 'a chosen one.'"

I could see his delight at being so honored. In a slightly patronizing tone, he explained that one of his religion's beliefs is that certain people are selected by God to become leaders and teachers. Frank was convinced that this message came from God and offered a biblical passage to prove it. "As the Good Book says in John 16:13, 'When he comes, however, being the spirit of truth he will guide you to all truth. He will not speak on his own, but will speak what he hears, and will announce to you the things to come.'"

I, however, felt this voice was anything but holy. Frank described it as a deep male baritone, not unlike his own voice, and said it began forecasting events that later came true. For example, it told him that a friend of his was pregnant. "The voice even predicted that she'd have a boy," the dry cleaner added. "And that was before she'd even told anybody she was expecting!"

After that, Frank found that when he'd meditate on the Bible, his mind seemed to open up and he could understand its passages perfectly. This filled him with pride rather than a reverence for God—definitely a sign that he was under the influence of a demon. By feeding his ego, the fiend was gradually luring him away from righteousness and into the sin of pride.

Over time, Frank began to trust the voice more and more, eventually reaching a point where he'd do nothing without its approval. This went on for several years, until his life abruptly took an upsetting twist. It seemed that the other people in his group didn't share his view that he was a "chosen one," turned against him, and actually kicked him out of their group. In a bitter tone, Frank quoted another biblical passage: " 'Yet for all this they sinned still more and believed not in his wonders . . . though their hearts were not steadfast towards him, nor were they faithful to his covenant. Yet he, being merciful, destroyed them not; often he turned back his anger and let none of his wrath be roused. He remembered that they were flesh, a passing breath that returns not.' "

I took his ouster from the Jehovah's Witnesses as further evidence of diabolical influence, since I've seen time and time again how the demonic lead people down a path of isolation, to make them more vulnerable to possession. The evil spirit's goal was clear: to separate Frank from his support system so it could more effectively break down his will.

That's when he noticed that he wasn't just hearing the voice in his mind: It now spoke out loud, as if somebody nearby were talking to him. Frank refused to see that he was heading further and further in the wrong direction: Even during the interview, he quoted the Bible constantly, making it difficult for us to get the information we needed to help him. When Keith asked what kind of religious upbringing Frank had, the dry cleaner's answer, if you want to call it one, was this passage from Ecclesiastes: " 'Remember your Creator in the days of your youth, before the evil days to come and the years approach of which you will say, I have no pleasure in them before the sun is darkened.' " Understandably, Keith didn't pursue this line of questioning.

Later in the interview, I saw Frank swell with pride at what he thought were clever interpretations of certain passages. He even went so far as to tell me how the demonic work according to the Scriptures, yet he refused to see how twisted this was. Instead, he arrogantly informed me that he had such "respect" for God and His authority that he refused to listen to anybody else. Never once, however, did he speak of "love" for God.

After being expelled from the Jehovah's Witnesses, he began putting on weight rapidly, even though he wasn't eating any more than usual. Being exceedingly vain about his appearance, he promptly consulted a doctor, only to learn that he was in excellent physical health, other than being about forty pounds overweight. He grew fatter and fatter, so rapidly that his clothes no longer fit him, even ones he'd just bought. More disturbing still, he'd find brand-new shirts and pants he'd never worn split at the seams, or ripped and tattered. JoAnn offered to show us some of this clothing, but I declined.

Hearing about the damaged clothing set off an immediate alarm bell for me, since I've seen this happen in many cases I've handled. People who are possessed will often find their clothes, bedding, or draperies mysteriously torn up. It's one of the Devil's many terror tactics. Frank's story got even worse: He started seeing horrifying visions of things that the voice said would come to pass, and he began to lose control over his bodily movement, as if something else were controlling him—another hallmark of possession. Finding his life harder and harder to deal with, the dry cleaner found himself filled with rage and pain about being thrown out of the religious group he loved, even though this had happened long ago.

Finally the voice that now ruled his life suddenly turned cruel, telling him that he was a miserable excuse for a man—too stupid and incompetent to handle anything at all without its "help." That's when Frank turned to the psychiatrist in fear and despondency, terrified that he was going crazy, only to find that Prozac had no power to heal him. It was then that he finally opened his mind to the possibility that he was possessed and agreed to meet with me.

I spent about two hours probing every detail of this disturbing story, with an occasional question from Keith, and found Frank and JoAnn to be intelligent people who were clearly telling the truth. Not only was there no doubt in my mind that the dry cleaner was possessed by a demonic spirit, but after my investigation, I felt strongly that he was the victim of a curse by someone who wished him ill and used black magic to send evil his way. This, of course, is impossible to prove, since in most cases the victim is unaware that he or she has been cursed and probably doesn't even know it's possible. Most people don't believe in hexes—but you don't have to believe to be affected by someone else's malignant intent. As to who cursed him, I suspect that a member of his former religious group felt Frank had somehow done him—or her—wrong.

I wasn't at all surprised when Frank hotly disputed my theory about what brought the dark force into his life. It's typical for someone who is under the sway of a demon to resist having any light of understanding thrown on his problems, since these evil spirits can thrive only in darkness. I felt that while a curse may have made him a tempting target to the demonic, it was Frank's own pride and vanity that ultimately gave the evil spirit a foothold into his soul. Basically, this demon attacked through his weaknesses and preyed on his desires.

To put it another way, it was almost as if Frank were a drug addict: The longer he listened to the voice, the harder it got for him to give it up, even when its words hurt him. Now he'd become totally dependent on it. Yet to a degree, he was still resisting the spirit that had possessed him and had agreed to an exorcism. The question was, could he summon up the will to free himself?

It was a beautiful day for an exorcism, almost absurdly warm for December in New York. I carefully blessed my car with holy water inside and out, even the tires. Although I consider myself a good driver—as a police officer, I spend forty hours a week behind the wheel of a patrol car—I can't tell you how many close calls I've had driving my own car to exorcisms. Thinking of all the times I barely escaped collisions, sometimes during blinding snowstorms or on roads that had turned to sheets of ice, other times on lovely, sunny days like this, I sprinkled a little extra holy water around, to be on the safe side.

Now I was ready to pick up Joe, who'd volunteered to help—despite his sabbatical from the Work—when I told him that Keith was busy that day. The Warrens' nephew, John Z., would be joining us at Our Lady of the Rosary Chapel. As my partner and I pulled into the Bridgeport, Connecticut, train station, where the bishop had sent us to pick up Frank and JoAnn and bring them to his church for the exorcism, we said a brief prayer that the ritual would be successful. I always hate having a possessed person in my car, since the satanic spirit inside him might spring a surprise attack at any moment, forcing me to be hypervigilant for any diabolical drama.

At an exorcism a few years ago, I was sitting with the possessed woman and her husband in a pew, getting ready for the ritual, when the woman suddenly lunged at her husband, grabbed him around the neck, and started choking him. I slammed both my knees into the pew as I hastily leapt up to rescue him, while the other assistants showered the three of us with holy water. Just as I've often done on the street with deranged, drugged up, or violent criminals, I quickly subdued her. We stopped the murderous assault, immediately put her in arm and leg restraints, and began the exorcism.

To make matters worse, the ritual proved so long and exhausting that the bishop decided to finish it the next day, at the woman's home. As soon as he walked in, she sprang from the sofa at a dead run, clearly determined to strangle him. You'd think it was Superbowl Sunday, the way three of us tackled her right there on her living room rug. That stopped the demon's physical attack, and the exorcism proceeded as planned.

My body went on red alert when I saw Frank and JoAnn get off the train. Frank didn't look too dangerous, however: He was even more impeccably dressed than before—except that his designer sweater was definitely a size or two larger than the clothes I'd seen him in then. His wife was wearing a rumpled green sweatsuit with a stain on the sleeve. Both wore anxious, serious expressions and had little to say.

Leaving the parking lot, my Ford Thunderbird was suddenly jolted violently. I looked back and saw that another car had hit us, but miraculously, no one was hurt. Was it the supernatural—or just an incompetent suburban driver? Since neither car was damaged, we continued on our way to the church. I hoped that the ritual would be successful and not violent. Since each exorcism is different, I couldn't help but feel apprehensive, not knowing how this particular demon might attack. The one constant in our Work is that battling the Devil is extremely taxing to the mind, body, and spirit—and puts you at risk of all sorts of dangers.

Although I was now driving extracautiously, as we entered the driveway of Our Lady of the Rosary Chapel, where Frank's ritual was to be held, apparently I wasn't being careful enough and narrowly missed having a head-on collision with the Mother Superior. Seeing her in her traditional black habit, staring at me in astonishment through her car window, I couldn't help thinking *Boy, would I have gotten the ruler for that one, as I did so many times as a boy in parochial school! I can't believe I almost hit a nun!*

Once we were safely inside the church, I finally felt calm and at peace, despite the battle that lay ahead. JoAnn remarked on the beauty of the church. Although I'd seen it hundreds of times before, my spirit was still refreshed by the sight of this peaceful chapel and the room-sized rosary that surrounds the chapel's pews, attaching to the figure of Christ on the cross that hangs behind the altar.

Frank was clearly nervous. Like most possessed people at exorcisms, he had no idea what to expect. None of us did, really, since each exorcism is different. I told them why we would be strapping him into a chair but didn't go into any details about the ceremony. It's not important for the exorcee to know anything about the prayers: They are for the evil spirit hiding inside, which is well aware of what will be taking place shortly.

"How long is this going to take?" Frank asked.

"As long as Bishop McKenna feels it should."

Joe and I began to set up for the exorcism, while the bishop spoke privately with Frank. We placed a sturdy wooden chair in front of the altar and readied the restraints. JoAnn sat in a side pew, looking extremely pale and distraught. I went over and talked to her but could give no guarantees about the outcome. "It's up to the bishop and ultimately, to God now," I told her. "But Frank also has a hand in it, because if he continues to view the demon as part of his life, forcing it to leave will be very hard."

She squeezed my hand and thanked me for everything I'd done. "If it weren't for you, my husband wouldn't be here at this church right now," she said.

Joe and I secured Frank firmly to a chair, using wrist restraints and a nylon strap around his chest to keep him from injuring himself—or others—should the exorcism turn violent. Wearing his black cassock, white surplice, and purple stole, the bishop glided silently into the chapel. After being in places that are so oppressive with evil, I appreciated this house of God more each time I came here.

But battle was imminent, and we began to prepare, stocking up on our supplies: having the bishop bless salt, incense, and saints' medals; filling five-gallon jugs with holy water; and saying prayers for our families, who waited for us at home, that the good Lord would protect them during this exorcism. Then we said more prayers to keep us strong for what was to come and for the ritual to succeed.

Finally it was time for the exorcism.

In Latin, the bishop recited the Litany of the Saints; calling upon each and every one of them to help free this man from the evil spirit. I sat next to Frank, watching his face intently.

For the first half hour, there was no reaction at all. The pretense was very strong in this exorcism. Sometimes a demon shows itself quickly, and other times it hides for quite a while.

Either way, as an assistant, my job was to be ready for any sign of its presence, whether a strange movement from Frank or an indication that he was in pain. During exorcisms, certain areas of the body are most likely to be affected—usually the head or stomach, but occasionally the back. These major chakra, or power, points, often serve as portals of entry for the demonic. Sometimes the person will be shivering as if it's below zero in the church, even in summer; other people go into a seemingly comatose state or just sit there as if they are watching a movie.

Alert for any clue that the demon was being forced to come forward, I monitored Frank's breathing, facial expressions, and movements, aware of even the slightest quiver in his skin. I was intent on all the sounds of the church and watching all the assistants for signs they were being affected, just as they were watching me. I was also keeping an eye on JoAnn, imagining how hard it must be to sit to the side and see a loved one going through this when she was powerless to help him. If possible, I don't let family members assist in an exorcism, because I don't know if they are in a state of grace. If they are not, they might become possessed themselves, either briefly or long enough to need an exorcism of their own. They are also extremely emotionally involved in the case and can be targeted for that reason, since the demonic are drawn by negative emotions.

As the ritual progressed, the bishop asked Frank how he was feeling. "I'm okay," the dry cleaner replied, "but I feel that the voice inside me is scared. It is talking to me and saying all kinds of things."

The bishop continued the exorcism. "Demon, I command you in the name of Jesus Christ to come forth!"

Suddenly I saw Frank's breathing change from slow and rhythmic to rapid and shallow. I could tell at once that the demon was present. Even in this holy place, there was an unmistakable, overpowering sense of evil. The dry cleaner's face tensed up and he began to blink very rapidly, as I felt a subtle drop in the temperature of the church. His eyes widened as if he were seeing some threat that was invisible to me and darted from side to side, looking for an escape. His face took on an expression of hatred and fear, loathing and terror.

Frank reminded me of the criminally insane that I've taken off the street as a cop: all wrapped up in restraints and powerless to do anything as we load them into the bus (cop slang for an ambulance) for a trip to the psych ward. This demon didn't want to be here, but through the providence of God, it had no choice. I've seen facial expressions as strange and frightening as Frank's before, but not what he did next: His entire body began to shudder in stiff, jerky, decidedly unnatural motions.

He opened his mouth and spoke in a voice that sounded much like his own, except deeper and full of scorn. "I don't want to be here. Who do you people think you are?" The question was obviously rhetorical, and we didn't dignify it with a reply. We all knew that the demon had been forced to come forward and was now here for the battle. Breakpoint was here.

"Evil spirit, tell me your name, in the name of our Lord, Jesus Christ!" thundered the bishop, touching Frank with a relic of the True Cross.

The mocking laughter that issued from Frank's lips wasn't the least bit convincing. Even though it was sneering, the satanic power was suffering agonies worse than the fires of Hell. It didn't want to leave; it had to be compelled and commanded to depart in Jesus' name. This battle was taking place in a little church in Connecticut but also was being fought on another plane of existence, a spiritual plane older than man; this battle has been raging since before the creation of humanity. This mental, physical, and spiritual struggle was a battle that we humans are caught up in whether we believe or not.

I had a hunch about this demon because of the manner in which it had gotten hold of Frank. Since it snared him through his intellect and spirituality, I suspected that was how it would respond during the exorcism, rather than with physical brutality.

The bishop's dark eyes narrowed into a piercing stare. "Demon, what brought you into this man?"

The voice deepened. "I'm not talking to *you*. I hate you people!"

As if drawing a gun, Bishop McKenna held up a cross. "Demon, begone!"

Now speaking in a low, almost inaudible tone, the evil spirit retorted, "I don't want to be here anymore. I'm sick of you! Stop talking!"

Touching Frank with a holy relic, the bishop asked, "Am I bothering you, demon?" A veteran of over one hundred exorcisms, Bishop McKenna knew better than to fall into the trap of quarreling with evil spirits, since giving them any sort of recognition can be dangerous. The goal isn't to beat these demons in a battle of wits, which could tempt even the most devout exorcist into the very sins of pride and vanity that had led to Frank's possession. Instead, the priest must maintain a humble attitude, remembering that his only power to defeat the Devil comes from serving God's will, not his own charismatic gifts.

The reply sounded like a petulant three-year-old. "You're stupid and everything about this place is stupid! Stupid, stupid, stupid! I'm not telling you anything!" Here again I felt the demon was simply making malicious mischief, by encouraging us to think, in our conceit, that we must be a lot smarter than such a seemingly childish entity—a very dangerous thought to entertain.

"We can't believe you anyway, demon," the holy man snapped back, draping a black rosary around Frank's neck and dousing him with holy water.

The evil spirit let out a taunting laugh. "You people don't make sense. Why are you here?"

"Because we believe in God!" retorted John, the Warrens' nephew, provoked past control.

The bishop ignored the interruption and continued his fierce interrogation: "Don't *you* believe in God, Devil? Where did you come from?"

"If I tell you the truth, you wouldn't believe me. I came because I wanted to. You can't find me because I'm not here."

Touching Frank again, first with a holy relic, then replacing the black rosary with a white one, the bishop never broke eye contact as he steadily intoned the Roman Ritual of Exorcism.

"Stop! Stop! Stop talking!" the demon shrieked. Frank's head and shoulder jerked in a more intense robotic tic, as if the evil spirit were trying to shrug off the torture it must be suffering. The exorcism was proceeding just as I anticipated—a lot of head games, but no rough stuff so far, thank God.

"What keeps you in this man? Answer me in the name of Jesus Christ! Who cursed him?"

That evoked a defiant outburst. "I won't tell you. What you're doing is not working," the diabolical force repeated over and over. The torrent of words stopped for a moment, then Frank's eyes began blinking much more rapidly, and his lips moved again. "I cursed him because he was too good, so very good. I had to have him make a wrong decision."

Bishop McKenna had heard enough of this nonsense. It was Frank's vanity—not his virtue—that had allowed the demon to possess him. The priest held up a crucifix and made the sign of the cross over Frank's body. "With the help of God, I'm commanding you to go out of him, Devil!"

The demon's remarks became increasingly incoherent: "What are you? If I stay here, it's because I want to! Stop talking. . . . I won't do it. . . . Stupid people. . . . I won't do anything. . . ." The words became quieter and quieter until I found myself straining to hear them. This can be a distraction technique satanic forces use to break an exorcist's concentration. If so, it didn't work, since the bishop never wavered in his recitation of the ritual. Acknowledging defeat, the deep, contemptuous voice finally sputtered to a halt.

The priest's voice remained firm and steady as he finished the ritual, touching Frank repeatedly with relics, making the sign of the cross over and over, and giving many sprinkles of holy water. I could see Frank's breathing slowly return to normal, and the shuddering stopped.

Although the demon had been banished for the moment, all of us sensed that the war wasn't won yet: Frank wasn't free. When I spoke to him afterward, I could see that he was still confused about the true nature of the demonic spirit possessing him and still didn't grasp how warped his religious experiences really were. The demon was causing so much pain in his life but, at the same time, was giving him what he believed to be special insight into God. In his own mind Frank became more important than God. His aim was to know the divine plan, but he had no reverence for God. That's what this demon gave Frank: not a sense of hope and love that true religious experience brings, but a twisted sense of cold "understanding" that had no real meaning.

"Where do we go from here?" JoAnn asked.

"Frank needs another exorcism, whenever he feels he's ready to try again. This isn't like going for surgery, where the doctor opens you up and removes the poison from your body. This is spiritual and has a lot to do with the spirituality of the person. When a demon attacks through the intellect, as it did with your husband, it's harder for the possessed person to see his situation clearly. Sometimes this happens soon after the exorcism. In other cases it takes longer for someone to find his free will and help us force the demon out."

Frank was very somber after his exorcism and was completely silent when I drove him and JoAnn back to the train station. The only words of encouragement I could offer Frank were that we would continue for as long as he was willing to accept our help. The bishop, however, wasn't discouraged. He's found that fewer than half of his exorcisms succeed on the first try, and even repeated attempts may fail if the person isn't willing to let God back into his soul.

"By no means is this over," he assured me when I returned to the church to pick up Joe. "Heaven only knows why this man refuses to give up the demon that is such a cross of suffering to him, but if he's determined to punish himself, we must pray that the Lord in His providence will allow Frank's soul to be saved." Bowing our heads, we each lit a candle for the dry cleaner and his wife and stood in silence, watching the brave, hopeful flames shed their glow on the little church in Connecticut.

14

POSSESSED OVER THE PHONE

Like serial killers and sexual predators, whose crimes often have a distinctive pattern or "signature," the demonic have their own M.O. While the goal is always the same—to destroy humanity—some evil spirits act like street punks, announcing their presence with lurid acts of vandalism and senseless destruction; others attack physically, clawing and scratching their victims in maniacal rage.

Donna was a thirty-year-old divorcée who lived in Pennsylvania with her eight-year-old son. She had a peculiar problem with her phone. While she was chatting with her boyfriend, Mike, one night, their conversation was repeatedly interrupted by bursts of static on the line. When Mike joked that it must be a poltergeist, the call was abruptly disconnected. Puzzled, he immediately called Donna back and asked if she'd hung up on him. She said she hadn't, so Mike repeated his joke, "It must be a polter—" Before he could finish the word, the phone went dead again.

When Mike called me, my first question was, *why* did he say that word? He said he didn't know—it just popped into his head from nowhere. *Not from nowhere,* I thought. *Definitely not from nowhere!* Now, you may say, "Hey, come on, how could you be sure that anything was really happening? Someone just happens to mention a poltergeist—and then they have one?" But that's not what I thought at all, because I knew this was no poltergeist. These supposedly childlike, noisy little spirits that like to stir up mischief are pure folklore, but are sometimes confused with human spirits (ghosts of departed people that remain earthbound) or inhuman spirits (demons that are pure evil, and never walked Earth in human form). In this case, I saw the demonic at work, concealing its intent by sending Mike a misleading telepathic message. The bait was taken, and now he and Donna were primed to believe they were dealing with a harmless "poltergeist."

I kept these thoughts to myself, however, and scheduled a face-to-face interview with the couple the next day, at Mike's Pennsylvania home. His block was a maze of dreary low-rise brick buildings, set off at angles to the street. His two-bedroom apartment had a tidy but neglected appearance. Other than a few sickly-looking plants next to an old but comfortable sofa, he'd made no effort to decorate. Apparently, he preferred to spend his spare cash on toys, since the living room was dominated by a huge TV, a very elaborate stereo system, and one of the largest collections of CDs I'd ever seen. I also noticed a tape recorder attached to his phone and a pile of neatly labeled cassettes next to it.

After setting up my video and audio equipment, I began by explaining that I'm not a parapsychologist or ghost hunter. "I'm a Catholic and approach cases from a religious point of view," I told the couple. "I don't charge any money and make no guarantee of success, but I will do my best to help you. If you ignore my advice, however, or aren't completely honest with me, my involvement ends. I'll walk away and not come back. If that's OK with you, please confirm for the tape that you asked me to investigate the problems you're having."

Both of them immediately agreed to these terms. I approached the interview the same way I would any crime report: I try to stay neutral and let the people explain what's been going on, *then* ask questions, using the police formula of who, what, when, where, how, and why. There are times, of course, in both the Work and on the Job, that we never find out the why. In this case, I felt there might be a combination of factors. While Mike didn't strike me as a gullible guy, he had a rather limited knowledge of spirits, which can be a dangerous thing. Although I can't say for sure what attracted a demon to them, my chief suspect was a man they both knew. Not only was he a reputed drug dealer, but he was also a practicing Satanist.

As the couple began telling their story, I could tell they were good people—and I could also see, in a single glance, exactly who Mike was: a fellow police officer. He didn't have to tell me his profession; it was written all over him. There are basically two types of cops: Those who consider police work just a job and the buffs, who have blue running through their veins. Mike was obviously a superbuff, what we call a "four-by-four," a guy who works the 4:00 P.M.-to-midnight shift, then goes to a cop bar with his partner and drinks until 4:00 A.M.

I knew the type well—I used to be one of them myself. He had all the hallmarks of a buff: a large muscular build, with the distinctive doughnut gut we cops get teased about; a macho swagger; eyes that constantly scanned his surroundings for signs of trouble; and, of course, that stereotypical cop mustache: bushy, black, and trimmed with military precision. Like Donna, he'd been married before, and was the father of two young children.

Donna was as feminine as her boyfriend was masculine. She favored pretty prints, tight pants, and high heels. Despite her devout Catholicism, she had a strong earthy streak and often used language you definitely wouldn't hear in church. Her son, Bruce, didn't seem embarrassed by his mother's loud voice and raunchy speech. He was a fat little kid with dark olive skin, remarkably white teeth, and a sulky expression. Throughout the interview, he chewed gum and played with an action figure he was holding.

The day after the poltergeist incident, Donna's cordless phone seemed to develop a mind of its own. "It was driving me crazy with its beeping, so Mike came over to fix it," she explained, speaking with a strong Italian accent. "He tried new batteries and moved it different places around my house, but nothing worked. Then he suggested we talk to the phone. I told him he was out of his fucking mind—and that's when the phone stopped beeping, like it was listening to us."

That convinced the cop that his hunch was right: The phone must be haunted. With cop-like persistence, Mike started to interrogate the poltergeist—not realizing he'd fallen right into the evil spirit's trap by giving it recognition. Instead of communicating telepathically, as inhuman entities often do when they speak to humans, this one replied with beeps, but only if Mike and Donna were both on the line.

"Donna got very scared," Mike added. "She said she didn't like doing this—and didn't believe in poltergeists. Without her knowing it, I started taping the calls. I set up a very simple format so I could communicate with whatever was on the phone—one beep for 'yes' and two beeps for 'no.' Through my questioning, I found out the spirit—or soul—on the phone was a little girl." His questions eventually elicited an extremely touching tale from the spirit, who claimed that she and her brother had died as children, victims of an unspeakable crime.

Mike soon amassed hours and hours of recordings of his questions and answers, with an occasional comment from Donna. Listening to the tapes, which I transcribed, I heard Mike ask a question that got no response. "She went away," he says in a disappointed tone, then asks Donna accusingly, "Or was that you beeping? I want you to swear on your son that you weren't doing that!" Even though she instantly did, I also had to wonder if one of them was making the beeps.

During the interview, I questioned each of them separately, as I would crime suspects at the police station, and asked Mike to write down the details of the case, which I carefully compared to the tapes. I also listened to their voices and reactions to what they were hearing and experiencing. Unless they were the world's greatest actors, I knew what I was hearing wasn't staged. Here's an excerpt from one of the tapes in which Mike asked the questions:

Are you a little girl? YES
Are you dead? YES
Did you die in an accident? NO
Were you killed by a fire? NO
Did someone kill you? SERIES OF LONG BEEPS YES
Was it your parents? NO
Were you stabbed? NO
Shot with a gun? SERIES OF LONG BEEPS FOR YES
Did you die a long time ago? YES
Was it before the house was built? YES
Did they find your body after you died? NO
Did they find the killer? NO
Do you want us to help you? YES

On the other tapes, the story unfolds in bits and pieces, through Mike's questions, which sometimes drew immediate beeps for yes or no, and sometimes received no reply at all. About fifty years ago, according to the spirit, she and her brother were kidnapped by two men and brought to the swamp behind Donna's house. There they were both raped and shot in the head. Their bodies were then buried in the muck and never found. This story was enough to break your heart—and that's exactly what it did. I could hear Mike and Donna getting more and more upset and more and more emotionally involved with the spirit. At first, they refer to it as "little girl"; later Mike calls it "honey" and "cutie." Sometimes he even chides the spirit in a loving, fatherly way for being naughty when it made the phone go into outbursts of random beeps.

Fascinated and shocked by this ghastly tale, Mike wanted to know more. To find out the pathetic poltergeist's name, he began with the letter "A" and worked through the alphabet. "I got a yes beep when I said the letter 'I,'" he told me. "Then I went through a list of girls' names beginning with that letter and kept getting two beeps for no until I said the name 'Isabel.' The phone went crazy with 'yes, yes, yes!' so I knew I had the right name." He laboriously repeated the process for the brother's name, until he was finally rewarded with a yes beep for "Louis."

On the tape, I heard Mike pressing for details: "How old were you when you died, Isabel?" The phone beeped six times. "Oh, God!" His voice shook with emotion: That was exactly the age of his own son!

"And how old was your brother?" When the reply was eight forlorn beeps—the age of Donna's son—the macho cop actually broke down in tears, as did his girlfriend.

While the couple considered this just a horrible coincidence, I shuddered at how evil this spirit was, to prey on these two parents' sympathies with these touching details.

What a cruel scam, I thought. *Such a tear-jerking story that would break the heart of any mother or father, but it's all bullshit. The demonic are truly masterful, dangerous and extremely cunning! It reminded me of the Halloween horror: Although both cases happened years apart—to families in different cities who didn't know each other—there were striking similarities in the demonic M.O. Not only did both spirits use old-fashioned female aliases and concoct sob stories about being murdered, but each cunningly included a second victim in their tale, who, not at all coincidentally, had some trait sure to tug at the heartstrings of someone else in the household. Just as the Westchester "ghost" claimed to have a fiancé who had committed suicide, thereby gaining the sympathy of the groom's mother, this spirit pretended that she and her dead brother were the same age as Mike and Donna's children.*

Through sobs, Mike told Donna, "Babe, these kids need us! We've got to free them up—help them move on!" He then started a new line of questioning, and again the demon knew just what buttons to press. "Can you ever leave the property?" he asked, and got two muted beeps for no. "Do you want us to find your little bodies?" A series of awful wailing tones made the spirit's longing plain. "If we find your bones and move them, can you leave?" The answer was a long beep for yes. Strangely, however, the spirit insisted that only Donna could locate its remains.

While Mike, true to his cop nature, wanted to charge into action, Donna was dubious. "I said, 'What are we going to do—ask the police to dig up the swamp because of beeps on the fucking phone?' They'd think we were crazy! Hell, I was starting to think we were crazy! The beeps went wild when I said that, then I remembered something really strange."

Looking at her little boy—who suddenly stopped chewing his gum and began listening intently, as if he knew what she was about to say—Donna told me, "A couple of months ago, I heard Bruce talking when he was all by himself. I asked what he was doing, and he said he was talking to two kids who lived in the house. I figured it was some bullshit game—you know, just a kid's imagination. After all that phone stuff started, I thought, 'Oh my God, he was talking to those murdered kids!'"

Bruce refused to meet her eye. "I don't want to talk about that," he whined. "Don't make me!"

"Come on—tell Mr. Sarchie about 'the big one,'" his mother cajoled.

"He's . . . he's very bad!" The boy's lips began quivering as if he was going to cry. His mom gave his chubby shoulder a comforting squeeze.

"My son said some kind of creepy thing lived upstairs. I thought he'd been watching scary shows on TV and didn't pay much attention," she explained.

On the tape, I heard her saying "Mike, I'm scared, really scared." To reassure her, the cop asked the poltergeist if it meant any harm to Donna or her son. No, no, no, it beeped emphatically. And *was* there a "big one" upstairs? Yes, it replied. Was Donna in any danger from that spirit? A furious, frightening series of yeses shrilled from the phone, followed by dead silence. Was Mike in danger too? Yes. More than Donna? A long beep yes.

Listening to this had an oddly familiar ring. Suddenly I realized I was hearing a variation of the well-known "good cop/bad cop" routine, where one police officer intimidates the perp with harsh questions, threats, and a bullying manner, then leaves the room. The other cop then brings the suspect coffee, sympathizes with him, and implores him to confess before the mean cop comes back for round two. Here the game was good spirit/bad spirit, except that both spirits were actually the demon. The spirit ingratiated itself with Donna and Mike in the guise of a pitiful murdered child, then insinuated itself further into their lives by warning that a malevolent force meant them harm. Naturally this made them feel more dependent on the so-called good spirit to protect them from the bad one.

Despite being a cop himself, Mike didn't recognize this ploy. Instead, he was drawn even deeper into the demon's world of lies, even though Donna begged him to stop talking to the phone. On the tape you can hear her crying that she's frightened, then shouting at Mike when he persists with his investigation. Fear, anger, and discord are the negative emotions that the demonic feed on and use to gain strength for new assaults. Things were beginning to heat up.

In another call, Mike asked a question that was totally out of the norm: "Does Donna love me?" A melodic chime proclaimed that she did. For once the demon wasn't lying: These spirits will tell the truth when it advances their cause. "I'm going to take her out of her house," Mike announced, only to be dissuaded by a double beep for no. The demon wanted Donna right where she was, so it could insidiously break down her will, opening the way for possession. Donna then suggested that they call in psychic researchers, receiving another dismissive double beep.

"Are you afraid of them?" she asked, and heard a brief, timid beep. Damned right, "Isabel" was afraid of us—if we came to that house, the spirit would be exposed for what it really was. Here was another parallel with the Westchester case, where the demon insisted that "holy ones must not come!"

Not seeing the incredible illogic of a spirit who claimed to need help yet objected to getting it, the couple became consumed and enthralled by the events the "poltergeist" described. Communicating with it became such an obsession that Mike actually took a vacation from work so he'd have even more time to pursue his investigation of the spirit's claims. The mystery fueled his cop's curiosity. He and Donna began combing through phone books, trying to identify what town the two dead kids might have come from. The spirit beeped no to each possibility but remained strangely silent when towns that ended with the word "brook" were brought up.

The couple's confusion only added to the creature's credibility. Using this clue, Mike combed old newspapers at the library, looking for stories about missing children from a town whose name ended in "brook." Of course, he found nothing, but being a cop, this only intrigued him even more. He began keeping case notes of what he'd discovered so far. One entry he showed me read:

Isabel, age 6. Comes from Brook? Broadbrook? Foster-brook? Potterbrook? Blue car; two males. Remains: located in swamp. Sexually molested, then killed. Deceased, 50 years. States that she had blond hair and green eyes. She also states that her brother has blond hair. It is my opinion that due to the age at which she was killed, she has a very limited vocabulary. We are dealing with the mentality of a 6-year-old. We have to speak in words she understands.

Intensely curious about the spirit, Mike invited it to reveal more of its powers. "Isabel, can you move things?" After an agreeable beep was heard, Donna shouted in astonishment. A cloth heart she kept on her kitchen wall had just tumbled to the ground on its own! She picked it up and put it on the kitchen table, but when she turned around, the heart was back on the wall in its usual spot. "Isabel, did *you* put the heart back?" she asked in bewilderment, and the phone chimed affirmatively.

On the other end of the line, Mike had more suggestions. "Can you turn the water on?" Nothing happened. "She can't do it," he said sadly. A kitchen faucet gushed in response.

"The hell she can't," Donna gasped.

To me, this was further proof that the culprit in this case was a demon: Ghosts are much weaker spirits and don't have the ability to move anything but the lightest objects, so they couldn't possibly turn a faucet handle. It's also debatable whether a human spirit could make a phone beep: I've never heard of a case where this happened, but if several ghosts were in the house, they might be able to pool their spirit energy to accomplish this feat.

"Isabel, can you touch Donna's arm?" Mike asked twice, but got no response—until he heard a blood-curdling shriek from Donna.

"Never do that again!" she cried, sobbing so hard she was choking.

"What happened?"

Unable to find words for the indescribably icy terror of that touch, she just sobbed. "Oh, shit! Never, ever do that again." Angry and afraid, she finally caught her breath and railed at her lover for putting her through such heart-stopping horror. "What the fuck are you trying to do to me?"

Mike reminded her that the spirit wasn't out to hurt her and had helpfully warned them about the "big one" in her house. His remarks were punctuated by soothing single beeps of agreement, which calmed Donna considerably.

Her kitchen was suddenly filled with brilliant flashes of light. Each of them appeared at the very edge of her peripheral vision, so she stood there, turning her head from side to side in astonishment. Although she didn't know it, she was seeing what we call "ghost lights," bursts of energy from either human or inhuman spirits. Hardly daring to ask, she whispered into the phone, "Isabel, was that you?" A long, triumphant tone echoed through the phone, and Donna hung up, too upset to talk further. The spirit, however, had something else to say; it gave Mike a quick beep of farewell.

Once encouraged to get physical, Isabel intensified the attack. First, she started intruding into Mike and Donna's phone conversations uninvited. In one call, Donna wondered what they should do. Should they contact psychic investigators about the strange events in her home? "I don't even believe in this stuff," she grumbled. Mike got mad. "How much more proof do you need? We know you have the spirit of a little girl who was six and a little boy who was eight. We know they came from a 'brook' somewhere, and were murdered. And we know their remains are in your damned swamp! Did we make all this up?"

"Maybe the little girl did," replied Donna, closer to the truth than she realized. Beep, beep, denied the spirit, then went into a frenzy of tones up and down the scales.

"Don't worry, little girl," Mike said. "We believe you."

That wasn't the only time the spirit sparked a lovers' quarrel. In subsequent tapes, it showed a real talent for stirring up trouble. No strategy was too petty, if it helped drive a wedge between Donna and Mike. In one call, Mike, who was extremely health-conscious, innocently asked his girlfriend if she'd taken her vitamin pill that day. Yes, she lied, only to have the ghost tattle on her with two beeps. "She's giving you up, babe." Mike laughed; he thought the whole thing was pretty funny. Donna didn't—and they got into a heated argument about it, much to the delight of the spirit. Divide and conquer—that's the favorite M.O. of the demonic.

Soon, however, they both started to suspect that the allegedly friendly ghost had a dark side. When Donna mentioned contacting the Warrens, the spirit revealed a creepy new power: The woman was immediately hit with a blinding headache. Within days she was a virtual hostage in her own home, since every time she tried to go out, she'd suddenly feel extremely tired and get an excruciating headache that sent her straight to bed. These killer headaches, marked by a powerful feeling of pressure on her temples, never let up, and her whole body ached right down to her bones. Donna began sleeping more and more, as the demon drained her of energy.

The next time she called Mike, there was a lot of static on the line but no beeps, until she said she'd like to go over to his house. That provoked a frenzy of shrill tones—clearly Isabel wasn't pleased with this idea. "I think she has a mean streak," Mike remarked, while Donna complained that her heart was pounding. "Is that your doing, Isabel?" With a firm beep, the spirit said yes.

"I really want to leave here, and come to your house," Donna pleaded. Before Mike could say a word, two more beeps followed: Donna wasn't going anywhere if the spirit could help it.

Mike, however, still didn't want to blame the little girl he called "cutie" for this. "Is the big one around today?" he asked. Three long tones followed, implying that the evil force had made three appearances so far. That number was yet another clue to the spirit's true nature, since, the demonic love to do things in threes, to mock the Christian trinity of Father, Son, and Holy Ghost.

Isabel was quick to offer an alibi, a little later in the tape. Again, Mike asked the questions.

Do you love Donna? YES
Then why are you hurting her? N/R (NO RESPONSE)
You don't hurt people you love. N/R
Will you make Donna's headache go away? N/R
Is there a reason why you want her to stay home? YES
Do you feel you are protecting her? YES
I can protect her. NO
Is somebody in the family in danger? YES
Is there going to be an accident? YES
Will somebody die? YES
Is it going to be Donna's brother? N/R
Donna's father? N/R
Her mother? N/R
Is it going to be Donna or me? N/R
Do you know who? YES
If I guess, will you tell me? NO
If Donna stays in the house, will she be okay? YES

When Mike begged it to please cure his girlfriend of her horrible headaches, within seconds the pain vanished. He began bargaining with the so-called little girl: Would the spirit stop giving Donna headaches if she'd agree to stay home? Okay, it beeped. And how about lifting the relentless fatigue she was afflicted with? Absolutely not, Isabel replied. It was essential to keep Donna tired, for her own good, and that meant her body would keep on hurting. This was obviously another demonic tactic to isolate the young mother, by keeping her apart from her friends and lover.

Nor could Mike come to her house, as Donna's parents, who lived upstairs, had taken a mysterious dislike to him and invariably started an argument with him whenever he dropped by. Clearly, the evil spirit was doing its utmost to separate Donna from her support system, all the better to break down her will.

So the young mother became a prisoner. One morning she tried to escape, calling Mike to say that she felt better than usual, was getting dressed, and would be over to visit him soon. Two furious beeps interrupted her. Putting down the phone, Donna headed out to her car, only to find that the battery was dead. A kindly neighbor came out in the pouring rain and tried to jump-start her car, with no success. Soaking wet, she trudged back to her house in defeat—and was struck by the worst headache ever. "Mike," she said, weeping into the phone, "Isabel has killed my car." A long, gloating beep echoed over the line, followed by a dial tone.

Mike quickly called back and began hinting around that he'd be by with his car. He was afraid to actually come out and say this, for fear he'd be disconnected again. Can you imagine a grown man and woman, each with children of their own, unable to see each other and too intimidated to talk plainly on their own phones? While the demon was finally showing its true colors, amazingly, this couple *still* thought they were dealing with the spirit of a six-year-old girl! Donna was reduced to asking Isabel's permission to speak to her boyfriend in privacy. No, beeped the spirit, you can't. "But I miss Mike," she whined. "And I lo—" It seemed that the spirit could read her mind, since a soft tone signaled

that it too "loved" Mike. "I need to be with him," Donna
pleaded. Two much louder beeps signaled that no trysts were
allowed.

"That's it," shouted Mike. "I'm coming right over!"

The phone went berserk, letting out a mad cacophony of
deafening tones, then disconnected. He tried to call back, di-
aling her number over and over, but got a busy signal each
time. Just then *his* phone rang. Hesitantly he lifted the
receiver—and was blasted by a long, furious tone that seemed
to stretch on forever. "Okay, okay, I'm *not* coming!" he shouted.
The wail immediately ceased. Again Isabel put a benevolent
spin on things, telling Mike that if he came over, the "big one"
would hurt him. Being only a little girl, the spirit contended it
wasn't powerful enough to protect both of them.

The last tape Mike made was the most disturbing of all. A
series of up-and-down beeps that sounded like mechanical
laughter answer his call, then Donna picked up. "Guess who
just greeted me." Mike chuckled.

"I'm not talking to *her*," his girlfriend insisted. "I'm sore
all over, feel sick to my stomach, and don't want to talk on the
phone anymore."

Mike was so in awe of Isabel's powers that he couldn't resist going into a long question-and-answer session with the
spirit anyway. "Am I going crazy?" he wondered. Two beeps
assured him he was not. "You're real?" That elicited louder
beeps, as Donna's breathing became slow and steady, as if she
were in a trance. What an amazing power, he thought. She
can make Donna go to sleep just like that! I wish I was over
there, Isabel. I want to meet you, see your miraculous powers,
feel your touch.

A moment later, at his request, the spirit woke up the
young mother. "What's happening?" she asked groggily. When

Mike told her that she'd been fast asleep a moment before, she refused to believe it. "No way!" she argued.

As the tape played, Mike encouraged the spirit to show off its tricks. "Turn on the water," he said, and the water went on. "See, if she can do that, Donna, she can put you to sleep."

Sounding like she was about ninety years old and weary beyond imagining, his girlfriend implored him not to do this. She'd barely finished the sentence when Isabel thought of a new game. The spirit threw open a kitchen cupboard and made a box of saltines float over to her. Although Donna protested that she wasn't hungry, the next sound Mike heard was his girlfriend obediently opening the cracker box and munching away.

It was as if Mike had been hypnotized himself; only now did he wake up to the full horror of the situation. The little girl or whatever was lurking in the phone was moving the woman he loved around like a marionette, opening and closing her eyes, forcing her to eat on command. Could Donna be possessed?

"What are you doing? Let her go!"

Three thunderous crashes resonated through the phone—and Mike found himself screaming at a dial tone. Engulfed with fear, he called Ed Warren, nationally renowned due to frequent newspaper and TV coverage of his cases. After hearing about "Isabel's" terrifying powers, Ed instantly agreed to take the case.

Later that day Mike's phone rang. "I just looked at it," he told me. "Fear was building inside me. It was Donna"—or was it? "It didn't sound like her at all—the change in her voice was incredible. I told her everything Ed had told me: This is no little girl—it's a devil. No human spirit had the power to do these things. This creature has been keeping you prisoner so it can feed off your energy—that's why you're so tired!"

Donna laughed at this. "I feel fine," she insisted in her strange new voice. "And my car is working perfectly. I think I'll take my son to the beach."

"Are you nuts? Get out of that house while you still can," Mike yelled, then realized what was happening. His girlfriend had dreamed up a ruse to escape Isabel. He called the Warrens, who arrived at his office shortly before Donna and her son pulled up in their car. How did she escape? The demon had achieved its goal—possession—and no longer found it necessary to keep the woman trapped in her house. The sudden, chilling change in her personality was conclusive proof that the evil spirit had entered her, after using its terrifying powers to break down her will.

Other than looking exhausted, the mother seemed fine when she arrived, but she went into a trance during the meeting and said nothing. Finally Lorraine suggested that Mike take Donna to a motel for the night, while she and Ed reviewed the tapes he'd made, but Donna refused.

"She gave me a very evil look," Mike recalls, a haunted glare of overpowering hatred. No longer under the sway of "Isabel," he was finally starting to wake up to the truth. "I knew I wasn't looking at Donna, and whatever was inside her knew that I knew. After about fifteen minutes, the real Donna came back—happy and full of energy, and I thought everything was okay. Boy, was I wrong!"

That night Mike's doorbell rang. "When I saw Donna at the door, the caution flags went up immediately, because she had that scary look again. 'Hi, baby,' she said flirtatiously. 'Glad to see me?' I said I was glad to see *Donna*, but we both knew that only her body was there. 'Why the dirty looks, baby?' she asked. 'You don't love me anymore?'"

Mike just stared, too appalled to say anything, as Donna entered his home, sashayed right by him, and plopped down in his favorite recliner. Not wanting to be in the same room with her, he retreated to the kitchen, shouting "Go to hell, Isabel!"

"Why don't *you* go to hell?" Contempt dripped from her voice. Just as she spoke, a thunderbolt of staggering pain hit Mike in the head, and he clung to the kitchen sink so he wouldn't fall to the ground.

At that very instant, Donna laughed harshly from the next room. Although she was sitting in a recliner facing away from the kitchen and couldn't possibly see Mike reeling with pain, he shouted to her—or whoever was inhabiting her body, "You know what you just did, don't you?" Donna only laughed harder, as Mike staggered into the room and looked right into a pair of eyes that didn't look like his girlfriend's at all. "You're trying to take me over, aren't you?" he accused.

With that, Donna cackled more maniacally than ever. "Have a little headache, Mike?" the woman he'd loved for the past two years taunted in her strange new voice. "Fuck you!"

Since the Warrens were about to leave for England, Ed asked me to handle the case for them. After hearing the whole story, I was amazed by the demon's power and cunning. In just two weeks it had managed to break down Donna's resistance and enter her. While successfully keeping Mike away, it had also gotten him so thoroughly on its side that he only grasped that he'd been conned after his girlfriend was already possessed! This was a crucial element of the evil spirit's strategy, because it needed to separate Donna from her source of strength: the tough cop you couldn't push around without getting a face full of fist. While we don't know all the factors that made possession possible at this time, it's clear that Donna had no power to resist without Mike at her side.

Luckily, a light had finally gone on in Mike's head while Donna was still in the earliest stage of possession. Had he called the Warrens sooner, she might have escaped invasion entirely. But at least the demon hadn't had time to really dig in. That made it important to hold an exorcism for the young mother as soon as possible, before the evil spirit could gain complete control.

My priority now was to prepare her for the upcoming ritual. Being a Catholic, that meant she had to make a full confession of her sins and get into a state of grace. (For people of other religions, I tell them to do whatever their faith prescribes to get them into a righteous relationship with God.) Prayer is extremely important, but some possessed people, including Donna, can't pray, because the demon won't allow it. Whenever she attempted to pray, she became violently ill.

Donna strenuously resisted my first instruction. Since she and Mike weren't married to each other—and in the eyes of the Church were still joined in holy matrimony to their previous spouses—I warned her that both of them had to resist romantic temptation. That drew a mocking look from Donna, who pretended she didn't know what I was talking about. "No messing around," I said. "Is that clear enough for you?"

"No sex?" Her tone was taunting. "Not even sometimes?"

What does she expect me to say? I thought. *It's okay to have sex on Wednesdays, but not on Sundays? Sin is sin, any day of the week.* "No, none, and that's final!"

* * *

The night before Donna's exorcism, a peculiar thing happened at the station house where I work. Since it was a slow night for crime, the other cop on duty and I didn't have much to do, so I decided to finish transcribing Mike's tapes. A cop friend of mine, Frank, came in the room and we started talking about the case. It was just after 3:00 A.M. when a phone nearby rang three times. Because this was an inside line, which can only be used by people in the station house, Frank and I were very puzzled. There were only two other people there that night—and I could see that neither of them were using the phone. *How could anybody else call this particular number? It simply wasn't possible.* When I picked up the receiver, I got only silence.

A few minutes later the phone rang again. I picked it up. Again no one spoke. Within a minute or two it was shrilling away. I just sat there, and Frank didn't budge either. "Ralph, I'm getting spooked," he finally admitted. And this was a guy who'd previously worked at the morgue, reconstructing the faces of decaying, unidentified corpses! I told him to check if anyone was on the phone now. He looked around and said no. Not wanting to make a lot of drama about it, I silently commanded whatever was on the other end to depart peacefully. The phone stayed silent for the rest of the night. I had the feeling the demon I was dealing with was trying to scare me off from the exorcism.

If so, it didn't work. Joe and I got to Our Lady of the Rosary Chapel in Monroe, Connecticut, where Bishop McKenna was holding the exorcism, early. The other assistants began to arrive around 9:00 A.M. We gathered our equipment: a video camera, tape recorder, and still cameras. I use these videos as training tools for student investigators and, most important of all, for the legal protection. It's not impossible—or even unheard of—for a victim of demonic possession to die during an exorcism. In fact, it happened to a young girl named Analise Michele during an exorcism many years ago in Germany. I don't put any savagery past the demonic. Many exorcists' lives have been destroyed by false accusations of physical abuse or other wrongdoing.

Once we were ready, we walked in the church as if we owned it. Inside, two elderly women were praying the rosary. One jumped up and asked me in a stern whisper if I knew where I was. I was in no mood to explain myself—I'd been working all night and was now here to do battle with the demonic. I just said, "Yeah, I know where I am." Just then Bishop McKenna came out and removed the Most Holy Eucharist, then ushered the two old ladies into the sacristy. I had to laugh when I returned to the church a few weeks later, when the same woman who had scolded me now asked sweetly if we were having an exorcism that day. The bishop must have explained it all.

Anyway, the church was buzzing with activity when Donna finally arrived, nearly half an hour late. Mike took me aside and told me his car had a full tank of gas when he and Donna left their house, but after he'd driven just twenty miles, he looked at the gauge, which now read empty. When he remarked on this, his girlfriend gave the same horrible laugh she had when he was hit with racking pain in his kitchen.

"Did anything else happen?" I asked. He said that Donna had been complaining of an agonizing headache. It's not uncommon for a possessed person to suffer physical torments on the way to an exorcism. We wasted no time getting ready for what we feared would be an extremely violent ritual.

Being a cop to the core, Mike brought handcuffs to the church and suggested we use them on his girlfriend, but I couldn't allow it. At least he'd left his gun home, as I'd instructed. No metal restraints are ever used during exorcisms, because they can easily become weapons. And as a policeman myself, I knew how easy it is for someone whose hands are improperly cuffed in front of them to swing his or her arms up and injure bystanders or the arresting officer. Even with her hands cuffed in the correct way—behind her back— Donna would be at risk of injuring herself, which is why the bishop later started using soft fabric restraints like those the New York City police force uses to secure mentally disturbed individuals.

Unfortunately, at this time we didn't have those restraints, so Donna was left unbound on her chair as the Roman Ritual began. She flinched from the bishop's first words as if from a blow, then slumped forward, her hair spilling over her face. Four of us grabbed her so she wouldn't collapse on the church floor and held her firmly throughout the exorcism. We saw that it was no longer Donna sitting in that chair—the demon had made its presence palpable.

Her body went into a fit that took the strength of all the assistants to subdue, as first her hands, then her entire body began to quiver uncontrollably, like someone in the throes of a raging fever. The bishop sprinkled holy water on her, and the demon moaned in inhuman anguish. Outside, the bishop's dog began to bay, almost as if it wanted to help its master, and its long, drawn-out howls echoed through the church. Donna's face was now masked in murderous fury—and we were the enemy!

As the prayers continued, her chest heaved, and she started retching. Thinking she might vomit, as possessed people often do during exorcisms, Joe put a bowl in her lap, and she bent over it until all we could see was her wildly tangled hair.

When the bishop reached the part of the ceremony where he must make the sign of the cross on the exorcee, Donna let out a low growl and suddenly sprang forward, slapping his hand away. Being a true warrior of God, the bishop moved forward and made the holy sign over her head and chest. That provoked rhythmic panting and groaning that made her sound like a woman in childbirth, except that what we hoped she'd expel was the demon.

The groans gave way to horrible growls, and she rocked from side to side, baring her teeth like an animal. Although she looked as if she might snap or bite us at any second, we maintained our firm grip on her arms. With amazingly supernatural strength, she fought against our grasp and lunged at the bishop with bestial fury every time he touched her with a cross. The battle had lasted only a few minutes so far, and we were already exhausted. During the next few hours, holy water was sprinkled on Donna over and over, which caused even more frenzied struggling, and dreadful screams filled the church. At one point, her eyes rolled back in her head, and she appeared unconscious. The demon was in torment—the agony of the damned.

The bishop put a blessed crucifix on her, and her body went limp. But he wasn't fooled by this apparent retreat. "I know you're in there, demon!" the exorcist said. Donna lurched wildly, desperately trying to break free of the crucifix.

"I command you to speak, in the name of Jesus Christ," the bishop thundered. The demon was silent. The struggle continued for another half hour before the devil was finally defeated.

In a weak voice, Donna whispered, "It's gone." Naturally, the bishop continued the ritual, in case the demon was screwing with us to make the exorcism stop.

But we could see a dramatic difference in Donna. Her features had softened and that murderous look was gone. The sense of oppressive evil that had filled the church had also lifted. Sun streamed through the stained-glass windows, and I felt relaxed and peaceful again. Donna, on the other hand, was sore as hell from all her struggles and could barely get out of her chair. She was in such pain that Mike had to help her walk. Yet her face was radiant—you could feel her joy and immense relief. She bowed her head as we said prayers of thanksgiving to our Lord for freeing her from the creature that seeks the ruin of souls.

Before we left the church, I asked the couple to swear they'd *never* attempt to contact the demon again. They both promised and we left the church together. Outside, I told Mike to call in a few days and let me know how Donna was feeling. A week later he did. "She's doing great," he said. "She's attending mass and praying a lot." That was the best possible sign, since she'd been unable to worship God during her possession.

"Any more trouble with the phone?"

"Not one beep," he assured me. I knew the case was closed.

AFTERWORD

I thank God for calling me to a vocation where I can rejoice in the triumph of ultimate good over ultimate evil. My journey of discovery is far from over: Even after ten years, I continue to learn with each new investigation. There are no experts in this Work, and anyone who tells you differently is full of it. Demonology isn't something you can study in a classroom: You have to go out on cases and get your hands dirty. Over the years, Joe and I have had many trials and made many errors, but the methods we use have been effective in more than half of our cases. A combination of faith, common sense, experience, and contact with very learned people are what we use to reach our goal of helping people. We don't do this for money or reputation, or to satisfy our egos. Instead, our only mission is the greater glory of God.

I found my faith again because of the Work, but it's not because of the Work that I have faith. Faith doesn't just happen: It comes to those who seek it and are willing to let it into their lives. Sometimes you reach a higher spiritual level quickly, and sometimes you stagnate until more is revealed to you. For people in religious life, like Bishop McKenna, everything is centered on faith. For people in secular life, who may be married and have jobs, it's harder to keep your eyes only on God. I can understand that: I definitely don't have *my* eyes on God when I'm wrestling some violent perp to the ground, but He's never far away. Once you accept God into your life, it's very hard to live without Him. My faith goes through cycles, however. Sometimes God is at the forefront of my mind, and other times I have dry spells where I don't go to church or pray that much. Even then, however, a part of me is always conscious of Him. I know it's wrong to ever let prayer take a backseat, but that's what can happen when there are many aspects of life competing for your attention.

The key, I feel, is to set time aside for spirituality. When I was a kid, I remember seeing my grandmother sitting in a chair and praying the rosary. She did this every day, at the same time. At Queen of Peace School, they didn't push the rosary, so I didn't understand how important this prayer was. It was only after Sister Philomena at Our Lady of the Rosary Chapel opened my eyes to its virtues that I began to make this devotion part of my life. One of St. Alphonsus di Liguouri's teachings is that God appointed Jesus Christ the King of Justice and made Him the judge of the whole world. But at the same time, He gave us the Virgin Mary and made her the Mother of Mercy. That's why I have such a devotion to her. I've inherited my grandmother's rosary beads and now use them for my own prayers. I've also taught my children about the rosary. Recently my daughter Christina and I shared a special moment on Christmas Eve, when I came home from the Four-Six around 4:00 A.M. and found her awake. We prayed the rosary together. It was a beautiful way to begin Christmas.

Joe and I feel that one of the ways God works is by putting people in your path who influence you to develop a better re-

lationship with Him. That's certainly been true for me. Father
Martin and Bishop McKenna have helped my faith grow. As
my spirituality evolved, I came to see things differently. I was
raised a Roman Catholic, but became a Traditionalist Catholic
in July of 1999, around the time when Father Martin died. It
took me a long time to realize that I wasn't comfortable with
the modernization of Catholic liturgy that resulted from Vatican II. Once I started going to Traditionalist masses, I immediately felt at home with the old way of worship. Traditionalist
priests aren't afraid to talk about the Devil during their sermons and don't shy away from the Church's teachings on satanic evil. This fits my own belief that once the enemy is
exposed, people will be better able to protect themselves from
the demonic. It's like having a serial rapist running around
preying on unsuspecting people: Once the word is out, the
public will be watchful and alert to avoid becoming victims.

Whether you believe in God or not is strictly up to you. I
don't force my faith on anyone. Toward the end of writing
this book, I got a new editor, Joe Cleemann. One of his concerns was that skeptics and agnostics who read my story
would not be convinced by assertions based on religious belief. I agree with him 100 percent. No matter what I say, these
people won't believe anyway. I've encountered enough of
these skeptics to know that. But it's my hope that sharing my
experiences will help people of faith—and investigators of
the paranormal—to recognize demonic activity, should they
have the misfortune to encounter it, or at least to consider the
possibility that pure evil could touch their lives. Once you believe in the Devil, you also have to believe in God who sent
His son, Jesus Christ, to defeat Satan and secure everlasting
life for us.

I recently saw the powerful impact this knowledge can

have. A cop I know, Vinnie, was promoted to sergeant at the same time I was. I happened to run into him at the New York City police force's Career Advancement Review Board, where we—and other officers up for promotion—were dressed to the nines in our Class A uniforms, waiting to meet with the board. A captain came out and decided to get humorous about the Work. "Hey, Ralph," he said, "why don't you exorcise some of these assholes?"

"Give me a break, Captain," I said. "I'm trying to get promoted here." Seeing my serious look, he didn't push the joke any further.

After the review, Vinnie came up to me. "There's something I've been wondering," he said. "What is this exorcism stuff the captain was talking about?" When I gave him a quick rundown, he was amazed. "You're kidding! Tell me more." I did, and he was so interested that he's phoned me several times since to talk about exorcisms—and God. During these talks, he told me that our chance conversation had sparked an intense spiritual hunger in him. Although he was already a Catholic, from that moment on he became more religious. God can enter your life just as suddenly as the demonic can. Once God was foremost in his mind, Vinnie realized that up to that point, his life had been dismal and dead. Rediscovering his faith gave him renewed hope, helping him cope with some personal problems he was having at that time.

I take no credit for Vinnie's return to faith, just as Joe and I take no credit for the successes we've had in the Work. We know better than to swell up with pride, because these victories have nothing to do with us. All credit belongs to God, who works through people for His greater glory. Our payment—our glory—is serving His will. Two of the most important commandments are to love God and to love your neighbor. There are many ways of showing this love. Some people visit the sick and read to them. Some people donate their time to soup kitchens to feed the hungry. Some go into prisons to spread the word about God. My act of Christian charity is to help people who fall under the sway of the Devil. It's just one charity in a sea of charities offered up to God.

It troubles me when I see the Web sites of some paranormal investigators. You'll see boasts like "We're number one. We're the famous ghost hunters." I know how these people work. They'll go out on a case and it's circus time. Some of them exploit people's pain and fear for financial gain, by charging for their services. Others want to be paid in publicity and walk in with news cameras and reporters to further their own fame. Instead of trying to help people who are snared in a living hell, they're too busy taking infrared photos and exclaiming "Wow, look at this! The temperature dropped!" Then they'll say "Good-bye and thanks for all the good stuff," while the frightened family is saying "Please don't go! We're being thrown out of bed at night. We're getting beaten up and terrorized by something we can't even see." But the ghost hunters don't want to hear it. "It's just spirit and that won't hurt you," they'll say. Or maybe they'll brush it off as electromagnetic energy—or tell the people to consult a shrink.

That's a travesty of everything Joe and I believe in. We're not in this for the hoopla. Our only concern is to help people solve their problem, if we possibly can, then leave—leaving the family with the name of Jesus on their lips. We're not out to sell T-shirts, as some of these people do, or enrich ourselves. Like everyone who goes up against ultimate evil, we've paid a price. When I look back on my very first case, I had no idea that I was crossing a dangerous line when I decided to battle the Devil. As to my wife and daughters, they had no say in the matter and were dragged along with me. Being involved in the Work has caused problems in my marriage and my home life, but I will not blame it all on the demonic. Even with all the adversity we've had to deal with, Jen has given me her support in many ways that have enabled me to continue the Work.

As a husband and father, I don't like my family to experience these things, but the graces from God outweigh the negatives. So I continue in the Work, and look forward to helping more people who are caught up in the very dangerous and terrifying world of the demonic—a world where nightmares become real. People often ask, "Why does God allow this to happen?" That's one of the toughest questions to answer, since God allows things to happen for His own reasons. I'm a firm believer that evil does not go unchecked. Whenever something bad happens in someone's life, something good comes out of it. Jesus asks us to follow Him and pick up our cross. Some of us suffer so others can benefit. How can they deny the existence of God when they are victims of the demonic?

As I close the door on the cases in this book and anticipate new battles I may embark on in God's name, I think of my favorite quotation from Archbishop Fulton Sheen: "There are 10,000 times 10,000 roads down which we may travel. It makes no difference which, but at the end of those roads, you're going to see one of two faces, either the beatific face of Jesus or the miserific face of Satan. One or the other, there's no escape."

LETTER TO THE READER

I hope you've enjoyed my book. If you have any comments, or want to contact me, you can reach me by writing to me care of my publisher, St. Martin's Press, 175 Fifth Avenue, New York, NY 10010. Since I continue to work full-time on the New York City police force and remain involved in the Work, my free time is extremely limited, but I'll try to respond as quickly as I can.

May God bless you and keep you,
Ralph Sarchie
Bethpage, New York

APPENDIX I:
PRAYERS OF EXORCISM

The following prayers are excerpted with permission from the third edition of the *Catholic Laypersons' Exorcism Prayer Manuel,** by Joseph Forrester. These are the prayers we actually recite in our cases. They've been reviewed by Father Malachi Martin, who thought so highly of them that he recommended them to other Catholic clergy. We invite you to use them yourself, if you wish. The symbol "†" indicates that the sign of the cross should be made at this point in the prayer.

Prayer when preparing to repulse the attacks of powers of darkness or their human agents, and when arriving at a site of demonic infestation.

†

Eternal God, Our Father, let not the enemy prevail against us, nor let the son of iniquity have the power to harm us. For our faith is in you our God who made heaven and earth, not just in our religious beliefs or the power of our prayers. Rather, it is in you our God who can do all things if You choose. So Father have mercy on us, grant us the grace of perfect contrition

---

*Note: "Manuel" is the Middle English spelling for "manual."

that we may be cleansed from all sin, attachment to sin, plans to sin, and fond memories of sin. Free us from any false prideful belief that we deserve to be punished for our lives.

Forgive us O Lord so that in right relationship to Jesus—we as members of His mystical body, may claim His authority over all spirits not in worship to Your Holy Trinity. Send us the holy Paraclete to purify our hearts so we may truly forgive all who have wronged us, and let the Holy Spirit illumine our minds and wills—so we may proclaim Your Son who told us: "Go into the whole world and preach the gospel to all creation . . . and these signs shall attend those who believe . . . in My name they shall cast out devils . . . they shall lay hands upon the sick and they shall be healed." (Mark 16: 15–18)

†

"I will go to the altar of God—the God of my joy and my youth."

"Put on the whole armor of God that you may be able to stand against the wiles of the devil . . . take up the whole armor of God that you may be able to withstand in the evil day, and having done all to stand. Stand therefore having girded your waist with truth, having put on the breastplate of righteousness, and shod your feet with the preparation of the gospel of peace. Above all taking the shield of faith with which you will be able to quench all the fiery darts of the wicked one; and accept salvation as a helmet, and the word of God as the sword which the spirit gives you. Do all this asking for God's help." (Paul to Ephesians)

†

In the name of Jesus Christ, by the power of His precious blood shed on the cross at Calvary, we as members of his mystical body and fully imbued with the Holy Spirit, bind all

spirits not in worship to the Trinity not to interfere with, im-
pede or evade our holy work. We adjure you in Jesus' name
not to hurt or molest any living creatures of God nor bother in
any way ourselves, our loved ones, our families, our friends,
our neighbors or acquaintances, even our pets or homes and
personal property now and in the future.

We beg God send his angels to block all psychic powers
sent against us. And we plead the blood of Jesus over every
living creature in our lives, in this building on this land and
in this place or neighborhood. And in Jesus' name we take
authority over all spirits of any kind not in worship to the
Trinity from the North—South—East—West, in the air and
below the ground, in fire, water and nature. By the power of
the precious blood we bind these forces in Jesus' name.

Heavenly Father, mark not our sins but the faith of Your
church and send Your warrior angels to rebuke all forces of
evil that are presently among us; let them clear a path before
us and link arms around this building and property to prevent all communication between the enemy here and else-
where.

We ask this in Jesus' name not for our own ego, reputation
or to impress any being—rather knowing our sinfulness we
offer this work for the glory of Thy name. Amen.

"Not by might, nor by power but by My spirit say the Lord of
Hosts. You will succeed because of My spirit though you are
few and weak." (Zechariah 4:6)

*This is a modified version of the Pope Leo XIII exorcism prayer,
which the Holy Pontiff gave express permission to all Catholics to
say in their own name to repulse the attacks of evil. Such permission,
once given by the Vicar of Christ, may not be revoked by anyone at*

any time. This version has been modified by addition only; no dele-
tions were made from the original form, which received the impri-
matur from Manuel, Bishop of Barcelona, December 19, 1931, and
again from Francis Cardinal Spellman, Archbishop of New York,
February 24, 1961.

✝

In the name of the Father and the Son and the Holy Ghost.
Amen.

Prayer to Saint Michael the Archangel

Glorious prince of the Heavenly Host, St. Michael the Archangel, defend us in the conflicts which we have to sustain
"against principalities and powers, against the rulers of the
world of this darkness, against the spirits of wickedness in
high places." (Ephes. 6:12) Come to the rescue of men, whom
God has created to His image and likeness, and whom He has
redeemed at a great price from the tyranny of the devil.

It is Thou whom Holy Church venerates as her guardian
and protector, Thou whom the Lord has charged to conduct
redeemed souls into Heaven. Pray, therefore, the God of Peace
to subdue Satan beneath our feet, that he may no longer re-
tain men captive nor do injury to the Church.

Present our prayers to the Most High, that without delay
they may draw His mercy down upon us. Seize "the dragon,
the old serpent, which is the devil and Satan," bind him and
cast him into the bottomless pit ". . . that he may no more se-
duce the nations." (Apoc. 20:2–3)

Exorcism

In the Name of Jesus Christ, our Lord and Savior, by the
power of His Precious Blood, and strengthened through the
intercession of the Immaculate Virgin Mary, Mother of God,

of St. Joseph, patron of the universal Church, of St. Michael, St. Rafael, St. Gabriel, and all the Heavenly Host, of the Holy Apostles Peter and Paul and all the Saints; we, in union with the mystical body of Christ, baptized and sealed with the gifts of the Holy Spirit, and given authority over all evil spirits by our Lord Jesus Himself, now confidently undertake to repulse the attacks and deceits of the devil.

Let God arise, and let His enemies be scattered; and let them that hate Him flee before His face. "As smoke vanisheth, so let them vanish away; as wax melteth before the fire, so let the wicked perish at the presence of God." (Psalm 68:2)

V. Behold the cross of the Lord! Flee bands of enemies.

E. The lion of the tribe of Juda, the offspring of David, hath conquered!

V. May Thy mercy descend upon us.

R. As great as our hope in Thee.

We drive you from us whoever you may be, unclean spirits, satanic powers, infernal invaders, wicked legions, assemblies and sects, all malfeasant workings or creations and all spirits not in worship to the Trinity. In the Name and by the virtue of our Lord Jesus Christ (†), may you be snatched away and driven from the Church of God and from the souls redeemed by the Precious Blood of the Divine Lamb (†).

Cease by your audacity, cunning serpent, to delude the human race, to persecute the Church, to torment God's elect, and to sift them as wheat (†). This is the command made to you by the Most High God (†) with whom in your haughty insolence you still pretend to be equal (†), the God "who will have all men to be saved, and come to the knowledge of the truth." (1 Tim. 2:4)

†

Binding

In the Name of Jesus Christ Crucified, we plead His Precious Blood against all inhuman and human spirits not in worship to the Holy Trinity and all evil—attacking and desecrating (this child of God), (these children of God), (this creature of God), and infesting (this home) (this place) (this land) (this thing).

Furthermore in Jesus' Name, we bind you evil spirits by His Precious Blood that you may not transfer into any living or dead person or creature nor take refuge within or in any inanimate object; that you will remain silent; that you will not harm any person, creature, place or thing while you remain, depart or at any future time in any way, nor will you cause any such harm now or at any future time.

V. The Blood of Christ binds Thee!
R. O Father in Heaven—in Jesus' name so be it!

†

In the Name of the Father—depart!
In the Name of the Son—depart!
In the Name of the Holy Ghost—depart!
In the Name of the Holy Trinity—depart!
In the Name of Mary, the Immaculate Conception—depart!
In the Name of St. Joseph, Protector of Jesus and Mary—depart!
In the Name of St. Michael—depart!
In the Name of St. Gabriel—depart!
In the Name of St. Rafael—depart!
In the Name of all Choirs of Angels—depart!
In the Name of all guardian angels—depart!
In the Name of the Angel of Gethsemane—depart!

†

In the Name of Abraham—depart!

In the Name of Moses—depart!

In the Name of Elijah—depart!

In the Name of the prophets—depart!

In the Name of Joachim and Ann—depart!

In the Name of Elizabeth and Zachary—depart!

In the Name of the Holy Innocents—depart!

In the Name of John the Baptist—depart!

†

In the Name of the Holy Apostles: Peter, John, James, Andrew, Phillip, Thomas, Bartholomew, Matthew, James, Simon, Jude, Matthias and Paul—depart!

In the Name of Mary Magdalen—depart!

In the Name of the Holy Disciples—depart!

In the Name of Sts. Stephen, James, Cecelia, Pancras, Felicity, Perpetua, Polycarp, the Nagasaki and all martyrs—depart!

In the Name of Sts. Martin, Patrick, Benedict, Maur, Placidus, Gregory the Great, Scholastica, Augustine—depart!

In the Name of Sts. Basil, Bede, Bernard, Meinrad, Cyril, Methodius, Elizabeth, Catherine, Margaret—depart!

In the Name of Sts. Francis of Assisi, Clare of Assisi, Anthony of Padua, Dominic Guzman, Thomas Aquinas—depart!

In the Name of Sts. Thomas Becket, Catherine of Siena, John of the Cross, Theresa of Avila, Rose of Lima, Thomas More, John Fisher, Martin of Porres—depart!

In the Name of Sts. Ignatius Loyola, Francis Xavier, Isaac Jogues and John Debrebeuf—depart!

In the Name of Sts. John Vianney, Bernadette Soubirous, Therese Lisieux, Peter Julian Eymard, and Pius X—depart!

In the Name of Blessed: Don Diego, Kateri Tekawitha, Andre Bessette, Miguel Pro, and Mother Teresa—depart!

In the Name of Pierre Toussaint, Leo XIII, Paul of Moll, Solanus Casey, Padre Pio, and all Marian visionaries—depart!

In the Name of Sts. Joan of Arc, Maximillian Kolbe, Sister Benedicta (Edith Stein), and all victims of war, holocaust, racism, pestilence, slavery, persecution, and injustice—depart!

In the Name of all exorcists in Heaven—depart!

In the Name of all the Saints in Heaven and on earth—depart!

V. May God rebuke thee Satan!

R. In the Name of Dominus depart!

V. The Lord be with you.

R. And also with you.

Let Us Pray

"God by Your Name save me, and by Your might defend my cause . . . for haughty men have risen up against me, and fierce men seek my life . . ." (Psalm 53) "Yet they . . . that dwellest beneath the shelter of the Most High . . . fear neither the terrors of night nor the arrow that flies by day; neither the plague that prowls in the darkness nor the attack of the devil at noonday." (Psalm 90)

Shield us O Lord with Your loving light from all evil sent against us by our brothers and sisters who do the work of the evil one by intent or through ignorance. Grant us the grace to refuse all their evil and the grace to forgive them. Hear our prayer, strengthen our faith, so like St. Peter who defeated Simon Magus and whose intercession we now implore, we too may triumph over all evil knowledge in Your Name.

Let their evil plans be clouded by confusion and their actions come to naught. Send Your holy angels to block all their psychic powers and let your angels touch us and remove any evil that has attached itself to us or penetrated us. Let this evil turn upon itself; and let evil seek out evil on the spirit plane, harming no one on the earthly plane. For You O God do not desire the death of sinners, rather that they would repent and come to knowledge of the truth.

V. In Jesus' Name we refuse and rebuke this evil sent against us, and for Jesus' sake we forgive those who sent it.
R. O Father in Heaven in Jesus' Name so be it.

We plead the Blood of Christ against you evil spirits (†). We root you out with the Light of Christ (†). We command you depart in the name of the Sacred Heart of Jesus (†), and the Immaculate Heart of Mary (†). God your Creator knows your name, your number—His mark is upon you. God beckons you depart (†). God your Creator knows how and when you entered here; depart lest He rebuke you (†). Christ's love compels you to depart. Leave now harmlessly, silently, swiftly in Jesus' Name.

In the Name of Jesus, by the power of His Precious Blood, we permanently negate and loosen any bindings or any form of magic, sorcery, curses, wishes, incantations, boluses, spells, pentagrams, pacts, dedications or maleficium holding any inhuman or human spirits not in worship to the Holy Trinity to: (this person or persons), (this animal or creature), or (this home, apartment, place, land, waters or thing). We bind you spirits by the Blood of Jesus never again to obey those who sent you!

O Father in Heaven in Jesus' Name so be it!

God the Father commands you (†), God the Son commands you (†), God the Holy Spirit commands you (†), Christ Himself commands you, the eternal word of God made flesh; He who to save our race outdone through your malice, "humbled Himself, becoming obedient unto death." (Phil. 2:8) He who has built his Church on the firm rock and declared that the gates of hell shall not prevail against her, because He dwells with her: "All days even to the consummation of the world." (Matt. 28:20) The hidden virtue of the Cross requires it of you as does the power of the mysteries of the Christian faith (†). The glorious Mother of God, the Virgin Mary commands you (†). She who by her humility and from the first moment of her Immaculate Conception crushed your proud head. St. Joseph, Foster Father of Jesus commands you (†), he who is known as the terror of demons. Loyal St. Michael and the entire Heavenly Host command you (†). The faith of the Apostles Peter, John, Paul and the other Apostles command you (†). The blood of the martyrs and the pious intercession of all saints command you (†).

Thus cursed dragon, and you wicked legions, we adjure you by the Living God (†), by the True God (†), by the Holy God, by the God Who "so loved the world, as to give his only begotten Son, that whosoever believeth in Him, may not perish, but may have life everlasting." (Jn. 3:16)

We take authority over this place and land in Jesus' Name; we sign all four corners with the sign of the Cross, just as the Apostles, St. Martin of Tours, St. Benedict, St. Maur and St. Patrick did to consecrate pagan temples to the worship of the One True God and whose intercession we now implore (†). We seal all spirit entry points, wells or portals with the Blood of Jesus Christ, the Paschal Lamb, and deny entry to all and any spirits not in worship to the Trinity until the end of time (✝).

O Father in Heaven in Jesus' Name so be it!

Let Us Pray

"In the beginning was the Word and the Word was with God, and the Word was God. He was in the beginning with God. All things were made through Him, and without Him nothing was made that was made. In Him was life, and the life was the light of man. And the light shines on in the darkness and the darkness did not overcome it." (John 1: 1–5)

V. May the Lord be with thee.

R. And with thy spirit.

✝

In the Name of Jesus Christ by the power of His Precious Blood shed on the Cross at Calvary for all creation, and with the intercession of the Blessed Mother, St. Joseph, St. Michael and the entire Heavenly Host with Sts. Peter, John, Paul, Jude, Thomas and the other Apostles, St. Martin and Gregory of Tours, St. Benedict, St. Maur, St. Patrick, St. Norbert, Sts. Francis and Clare of Assisi, St. Anthony of Padua, St. Thomas Aquinas, Holy Curé D'Ars, St. Therese Lisieux, St. Bernadette, Blessed Brother Andre, Padre Pio and all the holy martyrs and Saints:

We (✝) adjure, block, break, bring together, cast off/out, cut, cut out, detach, eliminate all fear, impediments, constraints, barriers or self-punishment, expel, forgive, heal, loosen, make normal, make visible and known all evil/evildoers, negate, neutralize, peel, push away, purify, rebuke, refuse, remove, repel, rescind, restore, reverse, sever, unbind, unblock, unknot, untie, unwind, uncover—in Jesus' Name (✝) now and forever—any, all forms of maleficium that affect or effect free will, emotions, thoughts, decisions, actions, health or desires. All/ any: astral attachments, familiar or familial spirits, all inhuman or human spirits not in worship to the Holy Trinity; and in particular any and all: apports, astral creations, chantings, contact objects, curses, death rituals or spells, demonic pacts or dedications, evil bindings, evil eye sendings, illnesses of body-mind or spirit, incubus attacks, magic in all forms: (ceremonial, contagious, sympathetic, religious, ritual, root, herbal, satanic, sexual, erotic, word, imitative, spells, incantations, music, thought, wishes, writings, movements, vibrations, evocative, invocatory) plus all parasitic attachments either external or internal, written pentagrams, psychic attacks or molestations, spells, sorcery, succubus attacks, tulpas, wishes, witchboards, witchcraft, all thoughts, words, deeds, plans contrary to faith, hope and charity—either evoked or invoked in secret invisibility (†).

We exorcise any and all of these abominations in Jesus' Name; and by the power of His Precious Blood, we encapsulate them in His light; and return them through whence they came to Satan, father of lies and enemy of mankind. Let this evil harmlessly disperse on the spirit plane, injuring no one on this earthly plane. We bind all spirits not in worship to the Trinity never again to obey those who sent this evil, in Jesus' Name. And by the power of the Blood of Christ Crucified, we bind and surround the senders with the Lumen Christi that all their evil efforts will immediately come to naught and cause no harm now and in the future; and may the evil they create harmlessly remain in their presence until they repent and come to the knowledge of the truth. In Jesus' Name so be it!

God the Father commands it. (†)

God the Son commands it. (†)

God the Holy Ghost commands it. (†)

The Blessed Virgin Mary commands it. (†)

St. Joseph commands it. (†)

St. Michael, St. Rafael, St Gabriel command it. (†)

The Angel of Gethsemane and all guardian angels command it. (†)

All the choirs of the Heavenly Host command it. (†)

St. Peter and the other Apostles command it. (†)

The holy martyrs and all the Saints command it. (†)

May the fiery love of the Holy Spirit burn away any remaining remnants of this evil. Amen.

Let Us Pray for Those Who Sent This Evil

"May the light of Christ Risen in Glory scatter the darkness of their heart and mind and contain their evil. Light of Christ deliver them from evil." (†)

V. O Lord hear my prayer.

R. And let my cry come unto Thee.

O God strengthen our wills to resist the lies and temptings of the evil one; have mercy on us and send your holy angels to drive all evil from this place; and let your angels of peace come in and gently guide any confused earthbound human souls to Your loving light; let them not be afraid but move towards the light. May their souls and all the souls of the departed rest in peace. Amen.

Final Adjuration

In the Name of Jesus Christ of Nazareth (†), by the power of His Precious Blood, we cast you out evil spirits (†). We shine the Light of Christ upon you, flee (†). We burn you with the fiery darts of God's love (†). We rebuke you with the glory of Mary the Immaculate Conception (†). We rebuke you with the mystery of Christ's Incarnation: "For the Word was made flesh and dwelt among us . . . (genuflect) . . . and we saw His glory." (John 1:14) (†) We rebuke you with His victory on the Cross (†). We rebuke you with His Resurrection (†). We rebuke you with His Second Coming and His final judgment.

We plead the Blood of Christ against you evil spirits (†). In the Name of Jesus and by His authority, we command you to harmlessly depart and go where the Lord send you. We bind you by the Precious Blood never to return, even though given recognition, invitation, or command. And we bind you by the Blood of Jesus never again to harm or cause to be harmed any creature of God. O Father in Heaven in Jesus' Name so be it.

†

Now we echo the words of Michael the Archangel.
V. May God rebuke thee Satan! (†)
R. In the Name of Dominus depart! (†)

Cease deceiving human creatures and pouring out to them the poison of eternal perdition; cease harming the Church and hindering her liberty. Retreat, Satan, inventor and master of all deceit, enemy of man's salvation. Cede the place to Christ in Whom you have found none of your works. Cede the place to the One, Holy, Catholic and Apostolic Church, acquired by Christ by the price of His Blood. Stoop beneath the all powerful hand of God. Tremble and flee at the evocation of the Holy and Terrible Name of Jesus. This Name which causes hell to tremble; this Name to which the angels, archangels, virtues, powers, principalities and dominations of Heaven are humbly submissive; this Name which the cherubim, seraphim, and thrones praise unceasingly—repeating: Holy, holy, holy is the Lord, the God of Hosts.

V. O Lord, hear my prayer.
R. And let my cry come unto Thee.
V. May the Lord be with thee.
R. And with thy spirit.

Let Us Pray the Magnificat in Thanksgiving

My soul doth magnify the Lord, and my spirit hath rejoiced in God my Savior, because He hath regarded the lowliest of His handmaids; for behold from henceforth all generations shall call me blessed. For He that is mighty hath done great things to me, and holy is His Name. His mercy is from generations unto generations to them that fear him; He hath showed might with His arm; He hath scattered the proud in the conceit of their heart. He hath put down the mighty from their seat and exalted the humble. He hath filled the hungry with good things and the rich He has sent away empty. He hath received Israel his servant, being mindful of His mercy, as He spoke to our fathers, to Abraham and to His seed forever. Amen.

God of Heaven, God of Earth, God of Angels, God of Archangels, God of Patriarchs, God of Prophets, God of Apostles, God of Martyrs, God of Confessors, God of Virgins, God Who hast the power to give life after death and rest after work, because there is no other God than Thee and there can be no other, for Thou art the Creator of all things visible and invisible, of Whose reign there shall be no end, we humbly prostrate ourselves before Thy glorious majesty and we supplicate Thee to deliver us from all the tyranny of the infernal spirits, from their snares and their furious wickedness. Deign O Lord to protect us by Thy power and to preserve us safe and sound. We beseech Thee through Jesus Christ Our Lord. Amen.

From the snares of the devil deliver us O Lord, that Thy Church may serve Thee in peace and liberty, we beseech Thee to hear us. That Thou wouldst crush down all spiritual enemies of Thy Church, we beseech, Thee to hear us.

Father in Heaven, thank You for all Your blessings seen and unseen, for Your mercy and love. Fill us with Your peace and let us go forth day by day to sow love where love does not thrive. Amen.

(The ritual is now ended. Sprinkle holy water in the place.)

Deliverance Prayer

(This is a shorter deliverance prayer to be said room by room, after the modified Leo XIII ritual of exorcism has been read at the site of demonic activity. It is also effective when read over oneself or another or in one's home to drive away the effects of witchcraft, psychic attack or demonic activity.)

Defend us O Lord with Your Holy Name from all the powers of darkness; protect us with Your holy angels from the attacks of the evil one; and from the malevolent wishes, wicked knowledge and psychic attacks of our brothers and sisters who do his work either intentionally or through ignorance; help us to refuse and rebuke all evil in Your Name.

In the Name and by the authority of Jesus Christ of Nazareth, by the power of His Precious Blood, strengthened by the intercession of the Blessed Virgin Mary, of St. Joseph, of the Archangels Michael, Gabriel and Rafael, of the Angel of Gethsemane, of all the choirs of angels, of the holy Apostles Peter, Paul, John, Jude, and the other Apostles, of St. Benedict, St.

Maur, and all the Saints: We adjure (†) and bind (†) all spirits not in worship to the Holy Trinity that they may no longer exercise dominion (over myself) (over *person's name*) (over this place or land and all the people and creatures who dwell in this place or land) (†).

We plead the Blood of Christ against you evil spirits, and by its power seal all spirit entry points or portals (†). In Jesus' Name we command you and all spirits of any kind not in worship to the Trinity to harmlessly depart now, lest God rebuke you; in the name of Dominus depart (†). We bind you by the Precious Blood never again to obey those who sent you, never again to hurt or cause to be hurt any of God's creatures nor ever to return even through recognition, invitation or command. In Jesus' Name we negate and harmlessly disperse all evil sent by the human servants of darkness (†). May the Holy Spirit extinguish all the evil and illness they've sent to: (myself) (this person *name*) or (the people or creatures living here).

May the angels of peace come in to protect us, and to propel any earthbound human spirits to God's loving light.

O Father in Heaven—in Jesus' Name so be it.

After a home has been cleared from all evil, then it is wise to establish an invisible spiritually protective fence around the property; approximate a rectangle on the land.

A   B

D   C

Starting at point "A," bury a blessed religious medal at least six inches in the ground and recite the following prayer composed by Pope Leo XIII and formerly said after the traditional Latin mass:

"Saint Michael, defend us in battle; be our defense against the wickedness and snares of the devil. May God rebuke him we humbly pray; and do thou, O prince of the Heavenly Host, by the power of God, thrust into hell Satan and other evil spirits, who prowl about the world for the ruin of souls. Amen."

Then walk from point "A" to point "B" saying this prayer as you walk. When you reach point "B," again bury a blessed medal in the ground. Then say the prayer again at this spot and as you move to the next point. After you have buried a medal at point "D," walk from "D" to "A" before closing the fence. In an urban setting, use holy water in place of medals and the four corners of a block as your points.

Before leaving the home of a family that has suffered through a negative supernatural experience, you may choose to use one of the following blessings, before the final blessing of St. Maur is given over the family.

For a person:
(Bless him/her with holy oil or water and touch the person with a relic while saying):
We heal this child of God in body-mind-spirit in Jesus' Name, and surround him/her with the Light of Christ Risen in Glory.

For an animal:
(Bless it with holy oil or water and touch it with a relic while saying):
In the Name of Jesus, we heal this creature of God in body and spirit, and restore it to the authority of God.

For a place:
(Sprinkle holy water and blessed salt)
In the Name of Jesus, we bless and restore this place to the authority of God.

For an object:
(Touch with holy oil or holy water)
In the Name of Jesus, we bless and restore this object to the authority of God.

Prayer of Renunciation

This is used when a person has renounced his/her baptism and made a pact with the Devil or one of his fallen spirits; this is said prior to the blessing of St. Maur.
I *(person's name)* renounce Satan, all his works, all bargains, oaths or agreements made with him, and all wicked practices and beliefs; and I revoke and recall all evil wishes, words, thoughts or deeds with which I have sinned against God and injured my brothers and sisters. I say this without any mental reservations or deception.

(If a satanic pact was made, the person must renounce it word for word, or as close as possible, three times. Then he or she should say the following prayer):
Jesus mercy, I invite you into my life and offer you my mind, body, soul, will; teach me to pray and fill me with the Holy Spirit so I may love you and my neighbor as myself. Amen.

"All praise to God the Father Be, and to His Son eternally with equal glory as is meet to God, the Holy Paraclete. Amen."
(Benedictine Hymn)

Blessing of St. Maur

Blessing of St. Maur over the sick with a relic of the True Cross or a properly blessed medal of St. Benedict is an ancient prayer. In the early Church it was used for healing and also as a form of exorcism.

The blessing requires two beeswax candles to be lighted, unless, of course, open flames are prohibited, such as in a hospital. The person reading the blessing holds the relic of the Sacred Cross or medal of St. Benedict in his/her right hand and begins by praying three Our Fathers, Hail Marys, and Glory Be's. Then the ritual begins:

V. Benediction, and glory, and wisdom, and thanksgiving, honor, and power and strength to our God forever and ever.
R. Amen.
V. My foot has stood in the direct way.
R. In the churches I will bless you O Lord.

Through the invocation of the Most Holy Name of the Lord may that faith, in which St. Maur by employing the words that follow, healed the sick and which I though an unworthy sinner, utter the selfsame words, restore your health as you desire.

In the name of the Most Holy and Undivided Trinity, and supported by the merits of the Most Holy Father St. Benedict, I bid you (*name of person or group of people*) to rise, stand upon your feet and be cured in the name of the Father, and of the Son and the Holy Spirit (†). Amen.

Antiphon: Surely He has borne our infirmities and carried our sorrows, by his bruises we are healed.
V. He that forgives the iniquities of men.
R. May he heal your infirmities.

V. O Lord, hear my prayer.
R. And let my cry come unto you.
V. The Lord be with you.
R. And with your spirit.

Let Us Pray

O God the Creator of all things, who willed that Your only Son should take flesh of the Virgin Mary, by the power of the Holy Spirit for the restoration of mankind and didst deign to heal the wounds and infirmities of our souls by the redemption accomplished upon the sacred and glorious wood of the life-giving Cross; do then also vouchsafe through this powerful sign to restore health to this Your servant (*name*) or servants. Through the same Christ our Lord. Amen.

Let Us Pray

Lord Jesus Christ, who conferred upon my teacher, Blessed Benedict, the privilege of obtaining from You whatsoever he might ask in Your Name; vouchsafe, through his intercession to heal all the infirmities of this your servant, in order that being restored to health (he or she) may give thanks to Your Holy Name, who livest and reignest with the Father and the Holy Ghost, forever and ever. Amen.

Blessing

Through the invocation of the Immaculate Mother of God and ever Virgin Mary, and the intercession of Saints Joseph, Benedict and Maur: May the power (†) of God the Father, the wisdom (†) of God the Son, and the strength (†) of the Holy Ghost free thee from thy infirmities. Amen. May God's holy will be done, and may it be done unto you as you wish and pray, for the praise and honor of the Most Holy Cross of our Lord Jesus Christ.

(The sick person is now blessed with the relic of the Cross or medal of St. Benedict, while the following words are said):

Blessing

May the blessing of Almighty God, of the Father and of the Son (†) and of the Holy Ghost descend upon thee and abide with thee forever. Amen.

(The person or persons then individually kiss the relic or medal. The blessing of St. Maur is now completed.)

Prayer of Thanksgiving Litany of St. Joseph

Lord, have mercy on us; Christ have mercy on us; Lord have mercy on us; Christ, hear us; Christ, graciously hear us.

God, the Father of Heaven, have mercy on us; God the Son, redeemer of the world, have mercy on us. God, the Holy Ghost, have mercy on us. Holy Trinity, one God, have mercy on us.

Holy Mary, pray for us.

St. Joseph, pray for us.

Illustrious Son of David, pray for us.

Light of the Patriarchs, pray for us.

Spouse of the Mother of God, pray for us.

Chaste Guardian of the Virgin, pray for us.

Foster father of the Son of God, pray for us.

Watchful defender of God, pray for us.

Head of the Holy Family, pray for us.

Joseph Most Just, pray for us.

Joseph Most Chaste, pray for us.

Joseph Most Prudent, pray for us.

Joseph Most Valiant, pray for us.

Joseph Most Obedient, pray for us.

Joseph Most Faithful, pray for us.

Mirror of Patience, pray for us.

Lover of Poverty, pray for us.

Model of Workmen, pray for us.

Glory of Domestic Life, pray for us.

Guardian of Virgins, pray for us.

Pillar of Families, pray for us.

Solace of the Afflicted, pray for us.

Hope of the Sick, pray for us.

Patron of the Dying, pray for us.

Terror of Demons, pray for us.

Protector of Holy Church, pray for us.

Lamb of God, who takes away the sins of the world, spare us, O Lord. Lamb of God, who takes away the sins of the world, graciously hear us, O Lord. Lamb of God, who takes away the sins of the world, have mercy on us.

V. He made him the lord of his house.
R. And the rule of all his possessions.

O God who in your unspeakable providence did choose Blessed Joseph to be the spouse of your Most Holy Mother, grant that as we venerate him as our protector on earth, we may deserve to have him as our intercessor in Heaven, who live and reign forever and ever. Amen.

(The prayer of thanksgiving litany of St. Joseph is now completed.)

APPENDIX II:
THE ROSARY

The rosary is a devotional prayer to the Virgin Mary, who is the mother of Jesus Christ. Many people neglect to honor her, but Jesus wishes for us to seek His mother. She deserves our devotion for this reason. She gave birth to Jesus, raised Him, and then watched at the foot of the cross when He died. Jesus gave His mother to us while He was suffering on that cross.

For this prayer, you need a rosary, which is a string of beads with a crucifix. A short string of five beads is attached to the crucifix, which is joined to a circular string of beads consisting of five sets of one large bead and ten smaller beads, known as "decades." Each decade is recited in honor of a mystery of the life of our Lord and His Blessed Mother, beginning with the Annunciation of the Incarnation and ending with Mary's triumphal Coronation in heaven. There are three sets of mysteries: the five Joyful Mysteries, the five Sorrowful Mysteries, and the five Glorious Mysteries. Although the entire rosary consists of fifteen decades, it's customary to recite five decades at a time, while meditating on one set of mysteries.

To say the rosary, make the sign of the cross. Take the crucifix of the rosary and pray the Apostles' Creed (the prayers appear later in this section). Move to the first large bead and pray the Our Father. For the three small beads, say one Hail Mary per bead, followed by the Glory Be and the prayer that Our Lady of Fatima asked the Fatima children to add after each decade: the Decade Prayer. For the next large bead, pray the Our Father.

After these prayers, move to the circular section of the rosary. For the first large bead, announce and meditate on the first mystery, then say the Our Father. A Hail Mary is said for each of the ten small beads, followed by the Glory Be and the Fatima Decade prayer. This completes one decade of the rosary. Proceed to the next mystery and repeat the process until five decades of the rosary have been said. Conclude with the Hail, Holy Queen prayer. (After completing the rosary, I also like to say the St. Michael prayer.)

How to Pray the Rosary

✝

In the name of the Father, and to the Son and the Holy Ghost. Amen.

Apostles' Creed

I believe in God the Father Almighty, Creator of heaven and earth; and in Jesus Christ, his only Son, Our Lord, who was conceived by the Holy Ghost, born of the Virgin Mary, suffered under Pontius Pilate, was crucified, died, and was buried. He descended into hell; the third day He arose again from the dead. He ascended into heaven, is seated at the right hand of God, the Father Almighty; from thence He shall come to judge the living and the dead. I believe in the Holy Ghost, the Holy Catholic Church, the communion of saints, the forgiveness of sins, the resurrection of the body and life everlasting. Amen.

Our Father

Our Father, who art in heaven, hallowed be Thy name; Thy kingdom come, Thy will be done on earth as it is in heaven. Give us this day our daily bread; and forgive us our trespasses as we forgive those who trespass against us; and lead us not into temptation, but deliver us from evil. Amen.

Hail Mary

Hail Mary, full of grace! The Lord is with thee; blessed art thou among women, and blessed is the fruit of thy womb, Jesus. Holy Mary, Mother of God, pray for us sinners, now and at the hour of our death. Amen.

Glory Be to the Father

Glory be to the Father, and to the Son, and to the Holy Ghost. As it was in the beginning, is now, and ever shall be, world without end. Amen.

Fatima Decade Prayer

O my Jesus, forgive us our sins; save us from the fires of hell. Lead all souls to heaven, especially those most in need of thy mercy.

The Five Joyful Mysteries

(These are said on Mondays and Thursdays, as well as Sundays from the beginning of Advent until Lent.)

The Annunciation

And when the angel had come to her, he said, "Hail full of grace, the Lord is with thee. Blessed art thou among women." (Lk. 1:28)

Our Father, Ten Hail Marys, Glory Be to the Father and the Fatima Decade Prayer

The Visitation
And Elizabeth was filled with the Holy Ghost, and cried out with a loud voice, saying, "Blessed art thou among women and blessed is the fruit of thy womb!" (Lk. 1:41–42)

Our Father, Ten Hail Marys, Glory Be to the Father and the Fatima Decade Prayer

The Birth of Jesus
And she brought forth her firstborn Son, and wrapped Him in swaddling clothes, laid Him in a manger, because there was no room for them in the inn. (Lk. 2:7)

Our Father, Ten Hail Marys, Glory Be to the Father and the Fatima Decade Prayer

The Presentation
And when the days of her purification were fulfilled according to the Law of Moses, they took Him up to Jerusalem to present Him to the Lord. (Lk. 2:22)

Our Father, Ten Hail Marys, Glory Be to the Father and the Fatima Decade Prayer

Finding Jesus in the Temple
And it came to pass after three days, that they found Him in the temple, sitting in the midst of the teachers, both listening to them and asking questions. (Lk. 2:46)

Our Father, Ten Hail Marys, Glory Be to the Father and the Fatima Decade Prayer

The Five Glorious Mysteries
(These are said on Wednesdays and Saturdays, as well as Sundays from Easter until Advent.)

The Resurrection
"He has risen. He is not here. Behold the place where they laid Him." (Mk. 16:6)

Our Father, Ten Hail Marys, Glory Be to the Father and the Fatima Decade Prayer

The Ascension
So then the Lord, after He had spoken to them, was taken up into heaven, to sit at the right hand of God. (Mk. 16:19)

Our Father, Ten Hail Marys, Glory Be to the Father and the Fatima Decade Prayer

The Descent of the Holy Ghost
And suddenly there came a sound from heaven, as of a mighty wind coming, and it filled the whole house where they were sitting. (Acts 2:2)

Our Father, Ten Hail Marys, Glory Be to the Father and the Fatima Decade Prayer

The Assumption
And a great sign appeared in heaven: a women clothed with the sun, and the moon was under her feet, and upon her head a crown of twelve stars. (Rev. 12:1)

Our Father, Ten Hail Marys, Glory Be to the Father and the
Fatima Decade Prayer

The Coronation
Thou art the glory of Jerusalem . . . the honor of our people . . .
the hand of the Lord hath strengthened thee, and therefore
thou shalt be blessed forever . . . (Jdt. 15:10–11)

Our Father, Ten Hail Marys, Glory Be to the Father and the
Fatima Decade Prayer

The Five Sorrowful Mysteries
(These are said on Tuesdays and Fridays, as well as Sundays during Lent.)

The Agony in the Garden
And his sweat became as drops of blood running down upon
the ground. And rising from prayer he came to the disciples,
and found them sleeping for sorrow. (Lk. 22:44–45)

Our Father, Ten Hail Marys, Glory Be to the Father and the
Fatima Decade Prayer

The Scourging at the Pillar
Pilate then took Jesus and had Him scourged. (Jn. 19:1)

Our Father, Ten Hail Marys, Glory Be to the Father and the
Fatima Prayer

The Crowning with Thorns
And they stripped Him and put on Him a scarlet cloak; and
plaiting a crown of thorns, they put it on His head, and a reed
into His right hand . . . (Mt. 27:28–29)

Our Father, Ten Hail Marys, Glory Be to the Father and the Fatima Decade Prayer

Carrying of the Cross
And bearing the cross for himself, he went forth to the place called the skull, in Hebrew, Golgotha. (Jn. 19:17)

Our Father, Ten Hail Marys, Glory Be to the Father and the Fatima Decade Prayer

The Crucifixion
And Jesus cried out with a loud voice and said, "Father, into thy hands I commend my spirit." And having said this, He expired. (Lk. 23:46)

Our Father, Ten Hail Marys, Glory Be to the Father and the Fatima Decade Prayer

With the Fatima Decade Prayer after the last decade, the rosary is concluded. The Sign of the Cross may then be made to close the devotion. Catholics, however, customarily add the Hail, Holy Queen to close the devotion:

Hail, holy Queen, Mother of mercy, our life, our sweetness, and our hope. To thee do we cry, poor banished children of Eve; to thee do we send up our sighs, mourning and weeping in this valley of tears.

Turn then, most gracious Advocate, thine eyes of mercy towards us; and after this our exile, show unto us the blessed fruit of thy womb, Jesus, O clement, O loving, O sweet Virgin Mary!

Pray for us, O holy Mother of God, that we may be made worthy of the promises of Christ.

Let Us Pray: O God, whose only-begotten Son, by his life, death, resurrection, has purchased for us the rewards of eternal life: grant, we beseech Thee, that meditating on these mysteries of the most holy Rosary of the Blessed Virgin Mary, we may imitate what they contain and obtain what they promise. Through the same Christ Our Lord. Amen.

APPENDIX III:
ACT OF CONSECRATION TO THE VIRGIN MARY

I, an unworthy Christian, renew and ratify today in thy hands, O Immaculate Virgin Mary, the vows of my baptism; I renounce forever Satan and all his works; I give myself entirely to Jesus Christ, the Incarnate Wisdom, that I may carry my cross after Him all the days of my life and be more faithful to Him than I have ever been before. In the presence of all the Heavenly Court I choose thee this day for my Mother and Mistress. As thy slave I deliver and consecrate to thee my body and my soul, all that I have of interior and exterior goods including all the value of my good actions, past, present and future; giving to thee the entire and full right of disposing of me and all that belongs to me, without exception according to thy will, for the greater honor and glory of God in time and in eternity. Amen.